AMERICA REBELS

ALSO BY RICHARD M. DORSON

*America in Legend: Folklore from the Colonial Period
to the Present*

British Folklorists: A History

Buying the Wind: Regional Folklore in the United States

Folk Legends of Japan

American Folklore

AMERICA REBELS

☆ ☆ ☆ ☆ ☆

*Personal Narratives
of the American Revolution*

EDITED, WITH AN INTRODUCTION, BY
Richard M. Dorson

PANTHEON BOOKS

New York

ACKNOWLEDGMENTS

The All-College Research Fund of Michigan State College has provided assistance for secretarial help. Mr. Jackson Towne, librarian of the College, generously cooperated in the acquisition of Revolutionary materials. The staff of the William L. Clements Library at Ann Arbor made working in their splendid collection a pleasure. I am particularly grateful to Mr. Colton Storm for suggestions in the selecting of illustrations. My colleague, John A. Garraty, and my publishers, Mr. and Mrs. Kurt Wolff, gave useful suggestions.

CONTENTS

LIST OF ILLUSTRATIONS

viii

LIST OF ILLUSTRATIONS

NARRATIVES OF THE PATRIOTS

EUROPEANS explored and tested a new continent in the seventeenth century, and upon it Americans fought a new nation into life in the eighteenth. These contrasting facts read coldly in our history books, but they take on reality in the living narratives of the colonists. For a hundred and fifty years their chronicles concern chiefly the nature of the wilderness, its alligators and rattlesnakes, the bounty of the land and the ways of the savages, as continuous novelties to Old World eyes. But from the year of independence the accent shifts. Travel and description dwindle, and a new type of writing emerges, generated by a momentous action, crude and homespun, the work often of men of the plow and the lathe, yet bearing an authentic American voice. These personal histories come from the pens—and, when their authors are illiterate, from the lips—of buckskin patriots devoid of literary ambitions, apologizing in their forewords for their unpolished prose, but nonetheless impelled to record their part in the drama of Revolution. The War of Independence produced literary as well as political freedom, and has left us as one of its by-products a proud, ragged literature from the ordinary folk who helped change colonial subjects into a sovereign people.

The sheer bulk of this personal history, apart from its quality, should evoke our tribute to the farmers and sailors who wrestled with syntax more painfully than ever they shouldered a musket or grappling-iron. Over two hundred entries in the Library of Congress catalogue testify to the wealth of Revolutionary narratives, and with these belong many scores of manuscript diaries and journals printed in historical magazines, every surviving scrap indeed of comment and reference descriptive of those heroic times.

This body of writings ranges widely in time and substance. It originates with the formation of the United States, and includes vigorous tracts written at the time of battle, but it swells to a climax long after, following still another war with Britain, when septuagenarian patriots began to write or dictate their Revolutionary adventures. It issues from rebels and Loyalists, soldiers

1

and civilians, ministers and doctors, maidens and housewives, celebrated officers and obscure privates, all alike caught in the birth-struggle of defiant Yankees. It takes the form of memoir, diary, and narrative, sometimes written in private notebooks with no thought of publication, and again set down with a national audience in view. Much is lifeless and clumsily written, but some of these neglected records are touched with the genius to re-create mood and scene and tell a gripping story, and they bring the Revolution stark before our eyes. We cannot completely reconstruct the Revolutionary battles from these accounts, as we can for the Civil War; they are piecemeal, haphazard productions of a country primitive in publishing facilities and college-trained writers. But we find an ample mirror of Americans at war, for the first time under their own flag.

A good portion of the Revolutionary narratives come from reminiscent veterans four decades and more after the end of the fighting. Between 1820 and 1840 revealing titles straggle into print: *Memoirs of Andrew Sherburne, a Pensioner of the Navy of the Revolution, Written by Himself; The Adventures of Ebenezer Fox in the Revolutionary War; Life and Remarkable Adventures of Israel R. Potter, a Native of Cranston, Rhode-Island, Who was a Soldier in the American Revolution; Narrative of the surprize and capture of Major-General Richard Prescott, of the British army, in his head-quarters . . . by a party of American Soldiers under Major-General William Barton, July 9, 1777, detailed from facts furnished by Gen. Barton himself, and never before published.* What explains this long-delayed cycle of wartime experiences by the unknown and forgotten soldiers of the Revolution, printed in such unlikely places as Utica, New York, Paris, Maine, and Windsor, Vermont?

Behind the motives that brought forth this spate of tales lies one substantial fact, the hallowed and romantic veil which time and the successful course of American history had cast about the War of Independence. The nation had survived its Confederation bickering, its perilous diplomacy with France and England, its second struggle with British might, and in the peaceful, westward-

looking years that followed 1815, the American eagle began to
flap its wings, croak shrilly on the Fourth of July, and think back
to its fledgling days with self-conscious pride. Then the old
men who had humbly and dutifully stood watch at Bunker Hill
and Valley Forge found themselves invested with an historic
glamour.

They began to tell stories to their grandchildren. Storytelling
had flourished among the American settlers from the first land-
ings; in place of European fairy tales sprang up New World
traditions, of inland travels, Indian barbarisms, white and red
witchcraft, the legends of a wilderness world. Into this repertoire
of personal adventures and experiences the Revolutionary sagas
readily fitted, and thrilled story-hungry children, who gaped to
see the intrepid actors right before their eyes. That youngsters
clambered onto grandpa's knee begging for his patriot memories
we know for a fact; Ebenezer Fox, for example, tells us so.

> "Grandfather," said my eldest grandchild, last Thanksgiving
> eve, "I wish you would relate to us all your Revolutionary
> stories. You have told us a great many stories, but we wish
> very much to hear the whole at once."
>
> In this request the second joined, who was soon followed
> by the third, while the fourth caught me by the hand, saying,
> "Do, grandpa, tell us something about the war." "O yes, do
> grandpa," said the fifth: while the next, a little boy of three,
> jumped up on my knee, and lisped out his request that I
> would tell a story; and the baby, making her way into the
> circle, added to the clamor with the most articulate sounds
> she could utter; and then all seven joined in one grand
> chorus, though not in unison, and the burden of the song
> was, "Do tell us your Revolutionary adventures."

But seventy-five-year-old Ebenezer Fox had a racking cough, so
he sat down and wrote out his adventures, for the eldest child to
read to the others, and a book was born. In much the same way
John Joseph Henry set forth his dismal march to Quebec in
Benedict Arnold's ill-fated army. A Virginia judge, Francis T.
Brooke, titled his pamphlet of war reminiscences "A Narrative of
my Life for my Family" and dictated much of it to his daughter.
Christopher Hawkins composed a manuscript in his old age
for his "children, grandchildren, and their descendants, with the
hope that they will duly appreciate not only my own sufferings,

but those of my contemporaries in the arduous struggle of my country for independence." Not only the children but historically-minded adults urged the veterans to speak and write. Josiah Priest gathered some bloodcurdling *Stories of the Revolution* from survivors of the Wyoming and Cherry Valley massacres; Benson Lossing inserted into his *Pictorial Field-Book of the Revolution* oral reminiscences from old people he interviewed; a zealous antiquarian, Charles I. Bushnell, in the middle of the nineteenth century printed rare Revolutionary narratives, written and verbal, at his own expense. Thus the aged warriors were prompted to relate their experiences for entertainment and for the historical record.

Another less innocent motive inspired much of this autobiography—plain cash. The patriots paraded their past hardships and present distresses without qualm or blush, as eminent reason for expediting the sale of their books. They had fought and suffered for their country; the federal government had failed to grant them proper pensions for their penniless old age; perhaps their countrymen would feel charitably disposed to give them honest coin in buying their histories, and avoid the disgrace of seeing the old soldiers become public charges. And besides, the patriots had their families to think of. Andrew Sherburne, speaking of his children, declared he was "not ashamed to confess that the avails which may arise from the sale of this humble performance must be almost their only inheritance." Major-General Barton even appended to the recital of his daring capture of General Prescott the details of an unjust lawsuit and jail sentence that had impoverished him.

In writing their memoirs for a rising market, the patriots were catering to the new nationalism that spread throughout the land following the War of 1812. American character types had begun to emerge in newspapers, almanacs, farces, and public-house stories, the frontier boaster and the cunning Yankee, and the Revolutionary chronicles amplified these homespun heroes, giving them actual dimensions and proven triumphs. Ethan Allen synthesized the two figures, in the role he cast for himself in the most celebrated captivity saga. In one scene he looms as a braggadocio giant, who astounds his British captors by chewing an iron tenpenny nail; in another he "comes Yankee" over them with a protesting letter to the American authorities slyly slanted toward the British officials, into whose hands he knows it will fall. So the Green Mountain Boy topped his enemies by both force and guile, in the two native comic traditions, and set the model for later recitals. A quarter of a century after, Nathaniel Fanning, who sailed with John Paul Jones, related Yankee tricks and frontier conquests on an heroic scale. As a prisoner in the hold of a British frigate, he and his fellow-captives punched a hole into the ship's storeroom and helped themselves to delicacies and the Captain's wine throughout the voyage, arriving in such plump condition that the amazed Captain exclaimed, "D—n them, there is nothing but thunder and lightning will kill them!" As commander of his own ship he sailed through the entire British home fleet, pretending with supreme Yankee sass to be an English corvette. In his description of the *Bonhomme Richard's* death-struggle with the *Serapis*, John Paul Jones becomes an avenging demigod, of the Salt River breed, who crumples the skull of a poltroon carpenter whining for quarter. The twin heroes show again in George Rogers Clark, as he disarms the lukewarm French with a supple tongue, and conquers the unsuspecting English with seven-league strides over river and forest. Patriots writing in the 20's and 30's projected themselves into these images; even doddering old Israel Potter, abused by the London Overseer for the Poor as a "d—d Yankee vagabond," boasted that in his prime he would have thrashed the villain with proper Yankee spleen, right under the King's nose. Young America relished this vainglory, and read in the deeds of the Sons of Liberty a newly created, native mythology, of farmer-heroes who outwitted and outfought the decadent power of Old World dandies, redcoats, and hirelings.

In 1828 Andy Jackson, who had himself licked the British at New Orleans, and carried a boyhood scar for defying a British officer, entered the White House from the backwoods, to signify the political completion of the Revolution. The age of the common man had formally commenced, and common men felt encouraged to write about their war—Israel Potter, Ebenezer Fox, Andrew Sherburne, Rufus Avery, Nathaniel Segar, John Blatchford, Ebenezer Fletcher, the ragged rank and file of the Continental Army and Navy, unknown to history, or even to their own generation. Some were mere boys when they entered the war: Blatchford and Sherburne shipped to sea at fifteen. They shared in no publicized victories, and performed no conspicuous deeds; they served as cabin-boys, were captured, rotted in prison, escaped, fought again, endured shipwreck, were captured once more—and in the ordinary course of events would have gone to their graves with their stories unwritten. The leaven of the democratic ideal, honoring the foot-soldier along with the general (a tradition continued in our time by Ernie Pyle and Bill Mauldin), helped evoke these personal histories, and bequeathed us a democratic literature, crude, forthright, and often powerful in its simplicity.

This kind of writing had already existed in the colonies, principally in the form of the Indian captivity, and the patriots found it so much the easier to satisfy their narrative urge. The Indian captivity had specialized in sensational atrocities of a barbarous foe, with the suspense of enslavement and the relief of escape or release to furnish a ready-made and exciting plot.* Throughout the two colonial centuries captivity booklets steadily issued from local presses, often, as in the gruesome tales of Mary Rowlandson and Peter Williamson, running through a score of editions. The form had by 1776 become firmly set in the minds of authors and readers, and many Revolutionary narratives merely followed the mold. The savage redskins give way to the venomous redcoats, the tribal village yields to the anchored prison ship, the threat of the stake is replaced by that of the gallows, while the starvation and brutality remain unchanged.

Like the Indian captives, the Revolutionary prisoners came to feel they had undergone a literary adventure which must be related. In some cases the two types of captivity merge. Frontier fighters were captured by Indian allies of the English during the War of Independence, and wrote of their sufferings, just as they had done in the earlier French and Indian Wars and border raids. The stories of Dr. Knight and John Slover, luridly titled "Indian Atrocities," belong in time to the Revolution but in form to the earlier Western shockers, while the *Brief Narrative of the*

* A selection of seventeenth-century Indian captivities can be found in my *America Begins* (Pantheon Books, 1950), Chapter 4.

*Captivity & Sufferings of Lt. Nathan'l Segar, who was taken
prisoner by the Indians and carried to Canada during the
Revolutionary War,* shows the extra touches of a patriot's pen,
and concludes with an eloquent plea for the old soldier.

From the earlier captivities the literary veterans plucked as
their prime motif the torture episode, and spared no disgusting
detail for an audience conditioned to horror. Sometimes the incidents of vengeful sadism run parallel. Levi Hanford witnessed a British atrocity very like the Indian practice of making
prisoners run the gantlet. A good-natured English sentryman,
guilty of harmless fraternizing with the rebels, was sentenced to
pass through a double line of his fellow-soldiers, who each lashed
his bare back, breast, head, and legs with a rawhide, while an
officer behind the soldiers stood poised to clout them with the
flat of his sword should they show leniency. Under the rain of
lashes the offender, who at first walked firmly and erect, soon
drooped and writhed, while his wounds streamed blood, and so
he was literally beaten to death, in full view of the American
prisoners. Charles Herbert saw a Yankee in the Plymouth prison,
caught stealing, treated in the same fashion. In *A Narrative of
Joshua Davis, an American Citizen who was pressed and served
on board six Ships of the British Navy,* the author supplies an
appendix illustrating the various punishments of flogging, hanging, and running the gantlet meted out to English sailors and
those Americans unlucky enough to be impressed on British ships.
In the latter case, he writes, "It is in vain for you to cry, scream,
jump, roll, for you must *grin and bear it,* as none will pity you.
Finally, you look like a piece of raw beef from your neck to the
waist of your trousers." Davis lingers over specific barbarities. A
sailor who blacked the eyes of his lieutenant was sentenced to
receive eight hundred lashes, but expired before the quota was
complete; nevertheless the remaining lashes were laid on his
bloody bones until each ship in the fleet had witnessed the execution of British discipline. David Perry, in his *Recollections of
an Old Soldier,* reports a similar punishment as "a specimen of
British cruelty without a parallel." A doctor stood beside three
men being whipped, and revived them with smelling salts when
they fainted, long after all the flesh had fallen from their

shoulders. Since this occurred in the French and Indian War (Perry wrote as a veteran of two wars), clearly the English had a long tradition of sadism behind them.

The high-water mark in prison atrocities was reached in *The Life and Surprising Adventures of Captain Talbot*. According to the unnamed author, these descriptions came straight from the lips of the doughty seaman who, after serving with distinction in the Continental Navy, fell into British hands in the summer of 1780. First placed on board the *Jersey,* he was after transferred to the New York City jail, where prisoners were welcomed by the commanding officer with these words: "Was not your brother in the rebel army? Aye, I thought as much; the d—d yankee was hung as a spy a few days since. Yes, I know your family well; your mother has been my whore many a good time." This gallant commander proved charming alongside Captain Ludwige of the *Yarmouth,* where Talbot and seventy-one other American officers were confined in November to be shipped to England. The Americans were closeted in a small, airless compartment deep in the hold, so suffocating they were obliged to strip off all their clothes, and so small they must lie on top of each other. In these quarters they relieved themselves. The abominable stench, lack of water, and oppressive heat soon rendered the air foul and infectious, and men became delirious and died. To protests Captain Ludwige replied, "We don't consider your companions as prisoners of war, but as rebels and traitors to your King and country!" His subaltern officers urinated on the uncalked orlop deck above the prisoners, while singing "Yankee Doodle." When some of the sentries, and a lieutenant sent into the dungeon to plug a leak, caught the fever and died, the prisoners were finally removed to have the hold disinfected, and placed in the wintry air half naked above the hogpens. The survivors reached Plymouth hairless from fever and crawling with vermin. Talbot tried four times to escape, and was at length exchanged.

Massacres of the wounded and helpless vied with prison atrocities in the angry recollections of the patriots. In 1840 a booklet of three eyewitness accounts triply reviewed the infamy of traitor Benedict Arnold in burning and looting New London fifty-nine years before, and murdering the garrison of Groton Fort and its captain after their surrender. Although the original words would have conveyed emotion enough, they received editorial additions to heighten the reader's outrage. The curious narrative of John Shaw, the well digger and "water witch" of Lexington, Kentucky, who fought for both sides, paints "a most inhuman massacre" that occurred near Tappan in New York, when an English regiment fell on a small company of Virginia light horse, and put all to the sword, although "the shrieks and screams of the hapless victims whom our savage fellow-soldiers were butchering, were sufficient to have melted into compassion the heart of a Turk or a Tartar. . . . Some were seen having their arms cut off, and others with their bowels hanging out crying for mercy."

Prisoners of the British, like captives of the Indians, sought continually to escape, and the same dreadful game of hide-and-seek keeps the reader at tension until the fugitive reaches shelter. Young Ebenezer Fletcher, left for dead on the battlefield at Hubbardston and picked up by the British, seized an opportunity to make off through the woods, and then faced the dangers of wolves, Indians, the enemy, Tories, starvation, cold, and infection from his wound before gaining his way to friends. Fleeing rebel prisoners had always the added hazard of running into Tories who would give them away, and Thomas Andros and Christopher Hawkins, both of whom miraculously escaped from the old *Jersey,* found their troubles only beginning when they reached the Tory-infested Long Island and New Jersey shores. Hawkins had the further disadvantage of landing stark-naked, after a two-and-a-half-mile swim, and in this state inadvertently encountered an unsuspecting maiden in a potato field, whereupon both high-tailed it in opposite directions. John Blatchford had a similar experience in reverse; he met a nude female aborigine in the woods of Sumatra. Before arriving in that situation, Blatchford had been captured and sent to England, exhibited to ladies in a Portsmouth drawing room who had never seen a real live Yankee, placed on an East Indiaman and sentenced to five years of soldiering in Sumatra, forced to work in the pepper gardens under an equatorial sun, attempted an escape with two companions, been captured by sepoys and flogged eight hundred lashes, escaped again, seen his companion die from eating poisonous fruit, and brushed past a lioness and a monstrous tiger. It is pleasant to record that his new acquaintance befriended him and made possible his return to civilization. Blatchford's experiences no doubt surpassed those of the average war prisoner, and some captives, of course, like Henry Laurens and Ethan Allen, waited out their time until exchange or peace brought them freedom. But surprisingly many of the Revolutionary authors could relate hair-raising escapes to armchair readers.

As white men in their turn scalped Indians, so too did rebels maltreat redcoats and Tories. The Simsbury mines in Connecticut, where captured Tories were deposited, rivaled the old *Jersey* in dank horror, yet relatively few Loyalist narratives issued from the scattered and broken adherents of George III in America. Nova Scotia fishermen would find little interest in Tory reminiscences. Some Loyalists published their histories in London, to aid their cause in securing compensation from the Crown, and this motive produced one spine-tingling tract worthy to rank with the patriot thrillers, the narrative of Lieutenant James Moody, an Ethan Allen in reverse. Moody's swaggering tale shows rebel Americans abusing helpless prisoners, and Loyalist Americans performing feats of derring-do.

A further curious parallel unites the Indian and Revolutionary thrillers, for in both cases the lurid factual tales inspired fictional imitations that deceived readers. The *Journal kept by John Howe, while he was employed as a British Spy, during the Revolutionary War,* printed at Concord, New Hampshire in 1827, contains thrills galore. Howe scouted central Massachusetts for the English, viewed the excitement of Lexington and Concord, but finally cast in his lot with the Yankees, and had adventures in the War of 1812 as well. Written in the early nineteenth-century comic idiom, the daredevil yarn intrigued scholars, who reprinted it in 1927 in the Magazine of History, in 1939 in the Photostat Americana series, and talked of issuing it in book form under the imprint of a major historical society. None perceived that the alleged journal simply alters the words written by Ensign De Berniere when spying for General Gage, and published at Boston in 1779 as a *Curious Narrative of Occurrences during their Mission, wrote by the Ensign.*

While using many devices of the Indian captivity relations, the Revolutionary authors strove for one new effect, patriotic pride in the steadfastness of American prisoners. Promised life and freedom by their captors if they took up arms for the British, when to refuse often meant agonizing and anonymous death, the patriots rejected all bribes with derision. Ethan Allen had to force one dying Yankee, whose brother had just perished in the filth of the British prison pen in New York, to turn coat that he might live to desert and fight for his country another day. After detailing the hideous conditions aboard the Long Island prison ships, Alexander Coffin added proudly that the prisoners all mocked the frequent English offers of liberation to deserters, and "hooted and abused" till his boat was out of earshot the one weak wretch of all their number who capitulated. Coffin concluded with a ringing peroration, by a patriot for the patriots: "And if there be no monument raised with hands to commemorate the virtue of these men, it is stamped in capitals on the heart of every American acquainted with their merit and sufferings, and will there remain so long as the blood flows from the fountain."

So the veterans set down their memories, for posterity, for money, for the awe and inspiration of their countrymen. Compared with the slick volumes written or ghostwritten by our military men today, in superidiomatic journalistic prose, these fugitive pamphlets and scribbled journals make a sorry show. But they pulse with the homely speech of simple settlers who fought for independence and freedom, and some of them qualify as noteworthy documents in our literary heritage.

From the available abundance of Revolutionary narratives, memoirs, and journals, a handful of selections are here presented, as high spots in the literature.

Our fourteen authors present a decided variety. In age they range from a bent old man of seventy-nine to a sprightly young miss of sixteen. In importance they vary from national heroes known to every schoolboy, to ordinary farmers and seamen whose names never enter the history books. In education they run the gamut from a Harvard graduate to a complete illiterate. They come from the farms of New England, the drawing rooms of Philadelphia, and the dark and bloody ground of the Ohio frontier. We may well wonder how this disparate group finds any common meeting point, yet each has lived through the storm of Revolution and left us a vivid memorial.

One negative fact stands out clearly enough: that none of our group rank as professional writers. Only Jonas Clark possesses a university degree. Even the two doctors simply apprenticed out to older physicians, following the colonial custom. Sally Wister attended the fashionable finishing school of Anthony Benezet in Philadelphia, and the Baroness von Riedesel enjoyed the private education accorded a Continental noblewoman, but neither became a *femme de lettres*. Ethan Allen missed his chance when his father died, and instead of going to Harvard he must tend the farm, and read haphazardly on his own. Andros taught himself, to qualify for the ministry. George Rogers Clark ended his schooling at eleven, after a few months' effort to learn the classics from his Scotch grandfather, and slipped home to his hunting, trapping, and, eventually, surveying. Nathaniel Fanning tells us that he had "nothing but the barest common education." John Slover could not read or write.

In fact, some of these narratives represent collaborative rather than individual authorship. Israel Potter's story, while told in the first person, is copyrighted by Henry Trumbull, of whom no doubt he requested literary aid. The manuscript left by Thomas Dring required editorial care at the hands of Albert G. Greene to sort it into chapters and form a connected account, and in our own time the historian Milo Quaife has wrestled with George Rogers Clark's memoir, to supply some grammatical essentials. The novelist Hugh Henry Brackenridge returned from Princeton to the Pennsylvania backwoods just in time to hear and record John Slover's tale of Indian barbarities. As with most diaries, those of Waldo and Cresswell and Sally Wister need paragraphing and other mechanics to satisfy modern printing style. In sum, six of our manuscripts were posthumously published, and two were dictated to copyists who undertook their publication. Half of our authors produced but this one solitary work. Thacher and Andros, it is true, and even Ethan Allen can point to a respectable list of publications, but their productions take the forms of compilations, sermons, manuals, and treatises rather than belles-lettres.

Oddly enough, the generals and the statesmen from whom we would expect gripping memoirs completely fail us. Generals Charles and Henry Lee, James Wilkinson, and William Heath wrote their personal histories in flat military prose interspersed with dry documents. Heath has some readable moments, in describing the siege of Boston. Washington penned his diaries and correspondence in impersonal if dignified vein. Franklin composed a few superb hoaxes, Jefferson wrote official papers, and Hamilton stiff military letters. John Adams alone left a memorable diary, taking us, if not out to the battlefield, behind the scenes of army politics and Parisian diplomacy. The founding fathers preferred essays, epistles, facetiae, and meditative journals to action-filled narratives. Similarly, among the English, French, and German memoirs that belong to the Revolutionary literature, curt military writing predominates, although one finds dramatic scenes in the journals of Georg Pausch, the Chevalier de Pontgibaud, and Andrew Serle. The outstanding chronicle by a non-American belongs, however, to a lady, the Baroness von Riedesel, whose candid record of her Revolutionary tribulations conveys a shock and immediacy missing from the stodgy memorials of the professional warriors.

In their very artlessness no doubt lies the secret of our successful compositions. They come direct from the minds, from the lips almost, of their authors, with a minimum of literary affectations and refinements. Their prose, shaped by plain speech and sharpened by powerful emotion, fits perfectly its matter; it tells a stark story swiftly. The effects, such as they are, come from oral rather than literary expression. Two men, Slover and Potter, actually told their adventures to an amanuensis. Jonas Clark simply transferred his pulpit oratory to the printed page. Allen, Fanning, and Moody, we are told, enjoyed bombasting listeners with recitals of their exploits. At sixteen Sally Wister wrote an unaffected journal for a girl friend, before literary models steered her into the genteel verses she composed in later life. Our narratives may frequently need editorial trimming; but straighten out their paragraphs, prune their repetitions, ungarble their sentences, and literature emerges.* We can see, when this service is done for Clark's memoir and Dring's notes, how a

* This has been the practice in the present volume.

crude manuscript suddenly leaps to life. Compare Herman Melville's fine tale of *Israel Potter* with the humble account which it rewrites, and notice how closely the artist follows the veteran's story line. Melville recognized an honest, dramatic, and peculiarly American record in the odd little book hawked through the country by Yankee peddlers. These Revolutionary chronicles form a true people's literature, rude and sturdy, marking the departure of American from English prose, as too they mark the founding of the republic in blood and fire.

Enough of preamble, then; let the patriots speak.

RICHARD M. DORSON

AMERICA REBELS

THE OPENING SHOTS

On the nineteenth of April, 1775, English rule over Americans snapped. Probably the most influential day in American history, and a vital one in world history, it signalized a new direction in the energies of the transatlantic settlers, and marked the climax of one hundred and sixty-eight years of English plantation. Where the first great challenge to New World colonists had come from the wilderness, from a novel climate and marauding savages, the second came from their own kin, from the might of established Empire. They had conquered harsh winters and forbidding forests; now they must deal with the armies and navies of the foremost world power.

The shots fired at Lexington and Concord by militia farmers on British regulars represented an open act of rebellion. This was no mob lawlessness or fringe defiance, as in the Boston Massacre five years before, but a concerted, fully calculated action, proceeding from the substantial farmers who composed the main stock of the Bay Colony. Their training companies were drilling regularily against such a crisis. The archpatriot Sam Adams had organized committees of correspondence to keep the towns informed of British moves. And in the atmosphere of tension that had existed since the home government quartered the King's troops in Boston, and cracked down on Massachusetts with a series of stringent regulatory acts, in 1774, any jarring incident could lead to war.

Behind the exchange of shots on Lexington Common lay twelve years of mounting tension. The sweeping of the French from North America by the combined efforts of English and American troops in 1763 had removed their common enemy, and opened the way for imperialist legislation that drove colony and mother country ever further apart. Parliamentary taxes, to defray the cost of the Seven Years' War, met with mass meetings of outrage, colonial boycotts on English goods, and thunderous pamphlets on the rights of self-governing colonists. The issue sharpened with each successive attempt at taxation, from the Stamp Act of 1765 to the Tea Act of 1773, until Lord North and his

17

Tory party felt the very base of Parliamentary authority attacked. When Massachusetts men dressed as Indians dumped the offensive tea into Boston Harbor (and never again would Americans indulge in the English passion for tea) Parliament closed the Port of Boston to commercial shipping and sent General Thomas Gage, with six regiments, to govern Massachusetts.

These troops lived and moved in the midst of hostility. Boston, the intellectual capital of the colonies, was being singled out for special punishment, because Boston was politically the most subversive American city. Her rabble had broken into and wrecked the mansion of Governor Hutchinson in the Stamp Act riot of 1765; they had provoked the King's troops beyond endurance in the so-called Boston Massacre of 1770, an action in which John Adams and Josiah Quincy had successfully defended the accused captain and his soldiers; they, alone among all the seaport cities, had done violence to the cargoes of tea shipped over in 1773. When Gage arrived, patriots drilled openly on the commons, organized a Provincial Congress, harangued in town meeting, coerced the magistrates, threatened the Loyalists, insulted the King's men, and gathered military supplies.

The new military governor bore all this patiently for a while, in hopes of conciliating the irate colonists. Squeezed between the pressure of the home government and the defiance of the patriots, he faced an impossible task. Lord Dartmouth wrote to Gage in January, 1775, that a small force acting now against the "rude rabble" who had collected arms would prove more effective than a larger force meeting a more determined resistance later. In March Franklin sailed home from London, giving up his diplomatic battle for peace after the Commons had voted funds for six thousand more troops for Boston. In April Gage decided, or agreed, that the time had come for a show of force, to restore the dignity of Crown and Parliament. His spies reported a concentration of stores in Concord. The night of the eighteenth, boatloads of redcoats slipped secretly across the Charles River, and began their early morning march eighteen miles inland. The efficient patriot intelligence service spied their movements and forewarned the minutemen along the route. When Colonel Smith and Major Pitcairn reached Lexington with their seven hundred troops, some seventy militiamen stood on the green. Someone *fired a shot—and a stormy debate would ensue as to which side fired first, and committed the overt act of war—and a general exchange followed. Through the rest of that shattering day, Yankee farmers fired at the King's soldiers.*

Both sides rushed their version of the affair to London. The American ship outraced the English, and won a propaganda victory with a document of atrocity tales more lurid than General Gage's sober account of insurrection. Participants and historians have since greatly swollen the testimony. Among the available accounts, that set down by Jonas Clark, minister of Lexington, on the first anniversary of the fateful day, best reveals the intensity of patriot emotion.

Jonas Clark

Jonas Clark (1730/1-1805) was born in Newton, Massachusetts, of old Puritan stock, graduated from Harvard College in 1752, and from 1755 until his death half a century later occupied the First Parish Church of Lexington. Puritanism in the late seventeenth century had crystallized into orthodoxy and lost much of its theological vigor, and Jonas Clark preached more as a sturdy farmer and staunch patriot than as a Calvinist reformer. The titles of his published sermons reveal his thinking: "The Importance of Military Skill, Measures for Defense, and a Martial Spirit in a Time of Peace" (1768); "The Fate of Blood Thirsty Oppressors and God's Tender Care of His Distressed People" (1776). To this latter was appended the factual narrative here reprinted, describing the events of the first day of war. Clark possessed a commanding voice and energetic presence, and in moments of excitement his resounding tones startled the cows in nearby pastures. He reached his full heights of rhetoric in the 1776 sermon denouncing the British invader:

> . . . more like *murderers* and *cutthroats* than the troops of a *Christian king*, without provocation, without warning, when no war was proclaimed, they draw the *sword of violence* upon the inhabitants of this town, and with a *cruelty* and *barbarity* which would have made the most innocent savage blush, they *shed* INNOCENT BLOOD!—But, O *my* God!—! How shall I speak!—or how describe the distress, the *horror* of that *awful morn*, that *gloomy day!—Yonder* [representation of a hand pointing] *field* can witness the *innocent blood* of our *brethren slain!* And from thence does *their blood* cry unto God for vengeance from the ground!

Eight of Clark's parishioners had died on the commons to which he pointed.

Oddly enough, the husky farmer and Puritan parson paid considerable attention to dress, and appeared in the pulpit in gown, cassock, and bands crowned by a great white wig. Clark enjoyed important connections; John Hancock and Sam Adams were close friends and stayed with him on the eve of battle; one son-in-law became president of Columbia College and another the Hollis Professor of Divinity at Harvard. The latter, William Ware, wrote a useful sketch of Clark in W. B. Sprague, *Annals of the American Pulpit* (New York, 1857), I, 514-519.

The present text is edited from the original edition: *A Sermon, Preached at Lexington, April 19, 1776; To commemorate the MURDER, BLOOD-SHED and Commencement of Hostilities, between Great-Britain and America, in that Town, by a Brigade of Troops of George III, under*

Command of Lieutenant-Colonel SMITH, *on the Nineteenth of April, 1775. To which is added, A Brief* NARRATIVE *of the principal Transactions of that Day*. By Jonas Clark, A.M. Pastor of the Church in Lexington. (Massachusetts-State: Boston. Printed by Powars and Willis. 1776.) The narrative is paged 1-7 following the sermon on pp. 1-32. It was reprinted separately, with four plates from the contemporary engravings of Amos Doolittle, in a large folio edition, Boston, James R. Osgood & Co., 1875, under the title, *Opening of the War of the Revolution, 19th of April, 1775.*

ON THE EVENING of the eighteenth of April, 1775, we received two messages; the first verbal, the other by express, in writing, from the committee of safety, who were then sitting in the westerly part of Cambridge, directed to the Honorable John Hancock, Esq. (who, with the Honorable Samuel Adams, Esq., was then providentially with us), informing, "that eight or nine officers of the King's troops were seen, just before night, passing the road towards Lexington, in a musing, contemplative posture; and it was suspected they were out upon some evil design."

Both these gentlemen had been frequently and even publicly threatened by the enemies of this people, both in England and America, with the vengeance of the British administration. And as Mr. Hancock in particular had been, more than once, personally insulted by some officers of the troops in Boston, it was not without some just grounds supposed that under cover of the darkness sudden arrest, if not assassination, might be attempted by these instruments of tyranny!

To prevent anything of this kind, ten or twelve men were immediately collected, in arms, to guard my house through the night.

In the meantime, said officers passed through this town on the road towards Concord. It was therefore thought expedient to watch their motions, and if possible make some discovery of their intentions. Accordingly, about ten o'clock in the evening, three men on horses were dispatched for this purpose. As they were peaceably passing the road towards Concord, in the borders of Lincoln, they were suddenly stopped by said officers, who rode up to them, and putting pistols to their breasts and seizing their horses' bridles, swore, if they stirred another step, they should be all dead men! The officers detained them several hours as prisoners, examined, searched, abused, and insulted them; and in their hasty return (supposing themselves discovered) they left them in Lexington. Said officers also took into custody, abused, and threatened with their lives several other persons some of whom they met peaceably passing on the road, others even at the doors of their dwellings, without the least provocation on the part of the inhabitants, or so much as a question asked by them.

Between the hours of twelve and one, on the morning of the nineteenth of April, we received intelligence, by express, from the Honorable Joseph Warren, Esq., at Boston, that a large body of the King's troops (supposed to be a brigade of about twelve or fifteen hundred) were embarked in boats from Boston, and gone over to land on Lechmere's Point (so called) in Cambridge. It was shrewdly suspected that they were ordered to seize and destroy the stores belonging to the colony, then deposited at Concord (in consequence of General Gage's unjustifiable seizure of the provincial magazine of powder at Medford), and other colony stores in several other places.

Upon this intelligence the militia of this town were alarmed and ordered to meet on the usual place of parade. This was not with any design of commencing hostilities upon the King's troops, but to consult what might be done for our own and the people's safety; and also to be ready for whatever service Providence might call us out to upon this alarming occasion, in case overt acts of violence or open hostilities should be committed by this mercenary band of armed and bloodthirsty oppressors.

About the same time two persons were sent express to Cambridge, if possible to gain intelligence of the motions of the troops, and what route they took.

The militia met according to order, and waited the return of the messengers, that they might order their measures as occasion should require. Between three and four o'clock one of the expresses returned, informing that there was no appearance of the troops on the roads, either from Cambridge or Charlestown, and that it was supposed that the movements in the army the evening before were only a feint to alarm the people. Upon this, therefore, the militia company were dismissed for the present, but with orders to be within call of the drum, waiting the return of the other messenger, who was expected in about an hour, or sooner if any discovery should be made of the motions of the troops. But he was prevented by their silent and sudden arrival at the place where he was waiting for intelligence. So that, after all this precaution, we had no notice of their approach till the brigade was actually in the town, and upon a quick march within about a mile and a quarter of the meetinghouse and place of parade. However, the commanding officer thought best to call the company together—not with any design of opposing so superior a force, much less of commencing hostilities, but only with a view to determine what to do, when and where to meet, and to dismiss and disperse.

Accordingly, about half an hour after four o'clock, alarm guns were fired, and the drums beat to arms, and the militia were collecting together. Some, to the number of about fifty or sixty or possibly more, were on the parade, others were coming towards it. In the meantime the troops, having thus stolen a march upon us, to prevent any intelligence of their approach seized and held prisoners several persons whom they met unarmed upon the road. They seemed to come determined for murder and bloodshed, and that whether provoked to it or not! When within about half a quarter of a mile of the meetinghouse they halted, and the command was given to prime and load; which being done, they marched on till they came up to the east end of said meetinghouse, in sight of our militia (collecting as aforesaid), who were about twelve or thirteen rods distant. Immediately upon their appearing so suddenly, and so nigh, Captain Parker, who commanded the militia company, ordered the men to disperse, and take care of themselves, and not to fire.

Upon this our men dispersed—but many of them not so speedily as they might have done, not having the most distant idea of such brutal barbarity and more than savage cruelty, from the troops of a British King, as they immediately experienced! For, no sooner did they come in sight of our company but one of them, supposed to be an officer of rank, was heard to say to the troops, "Damn them, we will have them!" Upon which the troops shouted aloud, huzza'd, and rushed furiously towards our men. About the same time, three officers (supposed to be Colonel Smith, Major Pitcairn, and another officer) advanced on horseback to the front of the body, and coming within five or six rods of the militia, one of them cried out, "Ye villains, ye rebels, disperse! Damn you, disperse!"—or words to this effect.

One of them (whether the same or not, is not easily determined) said, "Lay down your arms! Damn you, why don't you lay down your arms!"

The second of these officers about this time fired a pistol towards the militia as they were dispersing. The foremost, who was within a few yards of our men, brandishing his sword and then pointing towards them, with a loud voice said to the troops, "Fire! By God, fire!"—which was instantly followed by a discharge of arms from the said troops, succeeded by a very heavy and close fire upon our dispersing party, so long as any of them were within reach. Eight were left dead upon the ground! Ten were wounded. The rest of the company, through divine goodness, were (to a miracle) preserved unhurt in this murderous action!

Having thus vanquished the party in Lexington, the troops marched on for Concord, to execute their orders in destroying the stores belonging to the colony deposited there. They met with no interruption in their march to Concord. But by some means or other the people of Concord had notice of their approach and designs, and were alarmed about break of day; and collecting as soon and as many as possible, improved the time they had before the troops came upon them to the best advantage, both for concealing and securing as many of the public stores as they could, and in preparing for defense. By the stop of the troops at Lexington, many thousands were saved to the colony, and they were, in a great measure, frustrated in their design.

When the troops made their approach to the easterly part of the town, the provincials of Concord and some neighboring towns were collected and collecting in an advantageous post on a hill, a little distance from the meetinghouse north of the road, to the number of about one hundred and fifty or two hundred. But finding the troops to be more than three times as many, they wisely retreated, first to a hill about eighty rods further north, and then over the North Bridge (so called) about a mile from the town; and there they waited the coming of the militia of the towns adjacent to their assistance.

In the meantime the British detachment marched into the cen-

1. THE BATTLE OF LEXINGTON, 19 APRIL 1775.
THE FIRING ON THE COMMON

A. A Yankee Version.   B. A French Version.

ter of the town. A party of about two hundred was ordered to take possession of said bridge. Other parties were dispatched to various parts of the town in search of public stores, while the remainder were employed in seizing and destroying whatever they could find in the townhouse and other places where stores had been lodged. But before they had accomplished their design they were interrupted by a discharge of arms, at said bridge.

The provincials, who were in sight of the bridge, observing the troops attempting to take up the planks of said bridge, thought it necessary to dislodge them. They accordingly marched, but with express orders not to fire, unless first fired upon by the King's troops. Upon their approach towards the bridge, Captain Lawrie's party fired upon them, killed Captain Davis and another man dead upon the spot, and wounded several others. Upon this our militia rushed on, with a spirit becoming free-born Americans, returned the fire upon the enemy, killed two, wounded several, and drove them from the bridge, and pursued them towards the town till they were covered by a reinforcement from the main body. The provincials then took post on a hill at some distance north of the town; and as their numbers were continually increasing, they were preparing to give the troops a proper discharge, on their departure from the town.

In the meantime, the King's troops collected; and having dressed their wounded, destroyed what stores they could find, and insulted and plundered a number of the inhabitants, prepared for a retreat.

The troops began a hasty retreat about the middle of the day, and were no sooner out of the town but they began to meet the effects of the just resentments of this injured people. The provincials fired upon them from various quarters, and pursued them (though without any military order) with a firmness and intrepidity beyond what could have been expected on the first onset, and in such a day of confusion and distress! The fire was returned for a time with great fury by the troops as they retreated, though (through divine goodness) with but little execution. This scene continued with but little intermission till they returned to Lexington,. when it was evident that, having lost numbers in killed, wounded, and prisoners that fell into our hands, they began to be not only fatigued but greatly disheartened. And

2. THE BATTLE OF CONCORD, 19 APRIL 1775

A. The Engagement at Concord Bridge
B. Minutemen Shooting at the Retreating Redcoats

it is supposed that they must have soon surrendered at discretion, had they not been reinforced. But Lord Percy's arrival with another brigade of about a thousand men and two fieldpieces, about half a mile from Lexington Meetinghouse, towards Cambridge, gave them a seasonable respite.

The coming of the reinforcement, with the cannon (which our people were not so well acquainted with then, as they have been since), put the provincials also to a pause, for a time. But no sooner were the King's troops in motion but our men renewed the pursuit with equal and even greater ardor and intrepidity than before. The firing on both sides continued with but little intermission to the close of the day, when the troops entered Charlestown, where the provincials could not follow them without exposing the worthy inhabitants of that truly patriotic town to their rage and revenge. That night and the next day they were conveyed in boats over Charles River to Boston, glad to secure themselves under the cover of the shipping, and by strengthening and perfecting the fortifications at every part against the further attacks of a justly incensed people, who, upon intelligence of the murderous transactions of this fatal day, were collecting in arms around the town, in great numbers and from every quarter.

In the retreat of the King's troops from Concord to Lexington, they ravaged and plundered, as they had opportunity, more or less, in most of the houses that were upon the road. But after they were joined by Percy's brigade, in Lexington, it seemed as if all the little remains of humanity had left them, and rage and revenge had taken the reins, and knew no bounds! Clothing, furniture, provisions, goods, plundered, broken, carried off, or destroyed! Buildings (especially dwelling houses) abused, defaced, battered, shattered, and almost ruined! And as if this had not been enough, numbers of them doomed to the flames!—Three dwelling houses, two shops, and a barn were laid in ashes, in Lexington! Many others were set on fire, in this town, in Cambridge, etc., and must have shared the same fate, had not the close pursuit of the provincials prevented, and the flames been seasonably quenched! Add to all this: the unarmed, the aged and infirm, who were unable to flee, are inhumanly stabbed and murdered in their habitations! Yes, even women in childbed, with their helpless babes in their arms, do not escape the horrid alternative of being either cruelly murdered in their beds, burnt in their habitations, or turned into the streets to perish with cold, nakedness, and distress! But I forbear—words are too insignificant to express the horrid barbarities of that distressing day!

Our loss, in several actions of that day, was forty-nine killed, thirty-four wounded, and five missing, who were taken prisoners, and have since been exchanged. The enemy's loss, according to the best accounts, in killed, wounded, and missing, about three hundred.

PRISONERS OF WAR

Two weeks after the shooting in the Massachusetts countryside, an independent band of Vermont backwoodsmen stormed the English fort commanding Lake Champlain and the gateway to Canada. Daredevil Ethan Allen and his pack of Green Mountain Boys had decided to take the war into their own hands. They seized Fort Ticonderoga and presented it to an astonished Continental Congress, which was still dallying with the question of declaring war. Later in the year Allen joined the impulsive invasion of Canada that ended disastrously with the defeat of Arnold's men at Quebec, and Allen himself was taken prisoner early in the campaign in a misguided sortie outside Montreal. For three years he fumed inside English prisons and aboard English ships, and when he came to write up his war experiences, they took the form of a captivity narrative.

Allen's story is characteristic of much Revolutionary personal history. For many Americans the war meant languishing in confinement rather than participating in campaigns, and if we would get the true picture of their lives in wartime we cannot follow the continuous chronology of conventional military history. As John C. Miller has recently shown us, by painting in the protracted interim periods between campaigns, and describing the ebb and flow of patriotism, the eight years of Revolution contained a good deal besides fighting. Farmers who enlisted for short terms returned to their chores when their contracts expired, or even before if pay were not forthcoming and domestic duties were pressing. Spurts of enthusiasm and sudden threats from British invasions rallied minutemen and militia around Boston to hem in Gage, or along the route to Saratoga when Burgoyne struck for New York, or down in South Carolina during Cornwallis's forays into the Southern interior. But with the urgency over and a victory won, the armies melted away once more. When Americans gave ground or lost ships, large bodies of men disappeared into British prison pens.

A complete soldier's chronicle, therefore, might contain a few military scenes interspersed among chapters of civilian life and *morbid stretches of imprisonment. The wartime career of Thomas Andros illustrates this pattern. He dropped his farm tools to enlist in the Continental Army in the war fever of 1775; returned to farming after his enlistment expired; served in the Connecticut militia when the British threatened his state; worked and idled again; and finally succumbed to the privateering mania and embarked for trophies on a New London ship in 1781, when he was captured and thrust into the* Jersey. *His recollections concern chiefly his captivity and escape through Tory-infested Long Island. Many other Revolutionary narratives deal largely or in part with prison life.*

The American prisoner in the eighteenth century entered a system of confinement and release now largely obsolete. Three types of detention awaited him: the dread hulks of prison ships, in which the captives languished below decks; prisons ashore in England, chiefly Mill Prison in Plymouth and Forton Prison in Portsmouth, or makeshift churches and jails in New York; and parole, the restricted liberty in village or city given an officer on his word as a gentleman that he would not attempt to escape. A distinguished captive like Henry Laurens, the former President of the Continental Congress, who was captured while sailing to Holland as American Ambassador, received special treatment, and Laurens rested in the Tower of London, until exchanged for Cornwallis. The machinery of exchange and its welcome symbol, the unarmed cartel that came to carry prisoners away, dominated the thoughts of the imprisoned and affected the policies of the military and naval commanders. Washington desperately needed British prisoners in order to ameliorate the conditions of Americans captured at the Battle of Long Island and aboard privateers. With the large bag he secured after Saratoga he could threaten reprisals and offer exchanges. Because American privateers had difficulty in keeping prisoners—John Paul Jones had to release over five hundred, since France would not open her prisons to British seamen until she entered the war—sailors fared worse than soldiers in British hands.

For the whole course of the war the problem of mistreatment of American prisoners plagued Washington at home and Franklin in Paris. In the beginning Lord Germain took the attitude that rebels deserved no consideration as regular prisoners of war, and not until *1782* did the pressure of events compel him to confer belligerent status on captive Americans. Pathetic messages of complaint and nauseating atrocity tales spread wide and deep the horrors of British prison life. In justice it must be added that captives reported kindly treatment at the hands of some ships' captains and prison commissaries; that English civilians dipped into their pockets to aid suffering Americans; and that Loyalists and British seamen in the Simsbury mines or the American prison ships at Boston and New London complained with equal bitterness. The wrangles over amelioration of prison conditions and the emaciated state of exchanged captives lasted as long as the war itself.

Atrocity tales did serve some purpose, as Washington shrewdly recognized in suggesting that officers repeat them in front of their servants. Such tales discouraged desertion and stimulated patriotism. The fortitude of the unfortunate seamen lying in the hulks in Wallabout Bay shone in contrast to the sadism of their captors. Americans steadfastly refused the freedom offered them if they turned coat, preferring to wait for exchange or peace, to attempt an escape, or to die. Frequent escapes were essayed from the Mill and Forton prisons, where guards were susceptible to bribes and walls could be dug under or scaled; by contrast few prisoners fled the poisonous hulks, although Thomas Andros has left us one record of such a feat. Some of the most brutal and heroic moments of the Revolution occurred inside these prisons and along the escape routes leading back to home.

Ethan Allen

A fellow-patriot, musing over his Revolutionary experiences in the vogue of the early nineteenth century, set down this thumbnail sketch of Ethan Allen.

> He used to show a fracture in one of his teeth, occasioned by his twisting off with it, in a fit of anger, the nail which fastened the bar of his handcuffs; and which drew from one of the astonished spectators the exclamation of "damn him, can he eat iron?" I had become well acquainted with him, and have more than once heard him relate his adventures while a prisoner before being brought to New York, exactly corresponding both in substance ·and language with the narrative he gave the public in the year 1779. I have seldom met with a man possessing, in my opinion, a stronger mind, or whose mode of expression was more vehement and oratorical. His style was a singular compound of local barbarisms, Scriptural phrases, and oriental wildness; and though unclassic and sometimes ungrammatical, it was highly animated and forcible. (Alexander Graydon, *Memoirs of a Life Chiefly Passed in Pennsylvania,* Harrisburgh, 1811, p. 223.)

This compressed profile neatly catches the flavor of the man. Ethan Allen (1737/8-1789) belonged to a new breed of American, the ringtailed roarer of the backwoods, who could throttle a bear with his naked hands or conquer a British regiment singlehanded. Allen combined with his physical prowess a curious untamed intellectualism which bore one fruit, his prolix Deistical tract, *Reason the Only Oracle of Man.* In his frontier self-reliance and rationalistic world view, Allen typified the eighteenth-century democrat, confident in his unaided strength and reason to clear the wilderness, conquer tyranny, and create the good society.

Although born in Connecticut, Ethan Allen is always primarily identified with Vermont, where he had by 1770 become the recognized leader and titular Colonel of the Green Mountain Boys. These rugged woodsmen were already battling for independence from the powerful state of New York, whose royal governor, William Tryon, set a price on Ethan's head. "Try on and be damned," said Ethan. Allen might have gone to college, and he had begun to study with the minister of Salisbury to that end, but thrown on his own resources by his father's death in 1755, he continued farming, dabbled in mining, fought for two weeks in the French and Indian War, and speculated in land in the New Hampshire grants (as Vermont was then called). When the Revolution broke out he and his boys attacked Fort Ticonderoga on their own initiative, supported by Connecticut money, and Ethan won immortality by summoning its commander to surrender in the name of Jehovah and the Congress, two authorities he never fully recognized.

Allen's war experiences from May, 1775, to May, 1778, when he was exchanged, are covered in his personal narrative, written in a muscular and expressive prose. In March, 1779, the narrative began to appear serially in the *Pennsylvania Packet,* and was published in book form the same year by Robert Bell in Philadelphia. Like the sensational Indian captivities, it found a ready public, going through eight editions in two years, and undoubtedly helped to whip up national feeling against the British. Through the first half of the nineteenth century the narrative kept appearing in successive editions, and in 1930 it received a modern reissue. Its vigor and realism have attracted high praise, from Moses Coit Tyler to Stewart Holbrook.

Oddly, Allen soon lost his reputation as a patriot, and in 1780 was accused of negotiating with the British for recognition of Vermont. During the Confederation period he remained gloomily aloof from the unionist movement.

There are lively biographies by John Pell (1928) and Stewart Holbrook (1940). A list of editions of the narrative is given in John Pell's reprinting (New York, printed for the Fort Ticonderoga Museum by Richard W. Ellis: the Georgian Press, 1930). The present text is edited from the Burlington, Vermont, 1846 edition, *A Narrative of Col. Ethan Allen's Captivity, and Treatment by the British, from 1775 to 1778. Written by himself. Fourth edition [sic],* with notes. Pp. 9-34, 37-48, 77-83, 117-120.

INDUCED by a sense of duty to my country, and by the application of many of my worthy friends, some of whom are of the first characters, I have concluded to publish the following narrative of the extraordinary scenes of my captivity, and the discoveries which I made in the course of the same, of the cruel and relentless disposition and behavior of the enemy towards the prisoners in their power; from which the state politician, and every gradation of character among the people to the worthy tiller of the soil, may deduce such inferences as they shall think proper to carry into practice. Some men are appointed into office, in these States, who read the history of the cruelties of this war with the same careless indifference as they do the pages of the Roman history; nay, some are preferred to places of trust and profit by the Tory influence.

The instances are (I hope) but rare, and it stands all freemen in hand to prevent their further influence, which, of all other things, would be the most baneful to the liberties and happiness of this country, and, so far as such influence takes place, robs us of the victory we have obtained at the expense of so much blood and treasure.

I should have exhibited to the public a history of the facts herein contained, soon after my exchange, had not the urgency of my private affairs, together with more urgent public business, demanded my attention, till a few weeks before the date hereof. The reader will readily discern that a narrative of this sort could not have been written when I was a prisoner. My trunk and writings were often searched under various pretenses; so that I never wrote a syllable, or made even a rough minute whereon I might predicate this narration, but trusted solely to my memory for the whole. I have, however, taken the greatest care and pains to recollect the facts and arrange them; but as they touch a variety of characters and opposite interests, I am sensible that all will not be pleased with the relation of them. Be this as it will, I have made truth my invariable guide, and stake my honor on the truth of the facts. I have been very generous with the British in giving them full and ample credit for all their good usage, of any considerable consequence, which I met with among them during my captivity; which was easily done, as I met with but little in comparison of the bad, which, by reason of the great plurality of it, could not be contained in so concise a narrative; so that I am certain that I have more fully enumerated the favors which I received than the abuses I suffered. The critic will be pleased to excuse any inaccuracies in the performance itself, as the author has unfortunately missed of a liberal education.

ETHAN ALLEN

Bennington, March 25, 1779

*   *   *   *

Ever since I arrived at the state of manhood, and acquainted myself with the general history of mankind, I have felt a sincere passion for liberty. The history of nations, doomed to perpetual slavery in consequence of yielding up to tyrants their natural-born liberties, I read with a sort of philosophical horror; so that the first systematical and bloody attempt, at Lexington, to enslave America thoroughly electrified my mind, and fully determined me to take part with my country. And, while I was wishing for an opportunity to signalize myself in its behalf, directions were privately sent to me from the then colony (now state) of Connecticut to raise the Green Mountain Boys, and, if possible, with them to surprise and take the fortress of Ticonderoga. This enterprise I cheerfully undertook; and, after first guarding all the several passes that led thither, to cut off all intelligence between the garrison and the country, made a forced march from Bennington, and arrived at the lake opposite to Ticonderoga on the evening of the ninth day of May, 1775, with two hundred and thirty valiant Green Mountain Boys, and it was with the utmost difficulty that I procured boats to cross the lake. However, I landed eighty-three men near the garrison, and sent the boats back for the rear guard, commanded by Colonel Seth Warner, but the day began to dawn, and I found myself under a necessity to attack the fort before the rear could cross the lake; and, as it was viewed hazardous, I harangued the officers and soldiers in the manner following:

"Friends and fellow-soldiers: You have, for a number of years past, been a scourge and terror to arbitrary power. Your valor has been famed abroad, and acknowledged, as appears by the advice and orders to me, from the General Assembly of Connecticut, to surprise and take the garrison now before us. I now propose to advance before you and, in person, conduct you through the wicket-gate; for we must this morning either quit our pretensions to valor or possess ourselves of this fortress in a few minutes; and, inasmuch as it is a desperate attempt, which none but the bravest of men dare undertake, I do not urge it on any contrary to his will. You that will undertake voluntarily, poise your firelocks."

The men being, at this time, drawn up in three ranks, each poised his firelock. I ordered them to face to the right, and at the head of the center file marched them immediately to the wicket-gate aforesaid, where I found a sentry posted, who instantly snapped his fusee at me. I ran immediately towards him, and he retreated through the covered way into the parade within the garrison, gave a halloo, and ran under a bomb-proof. My party, who followed me into the fort, I formed on the parade in such a manner as to face the two barracks which faced each other.

The garrison being asleep, except the sentries, we gave three huzzas which greatly surprised them. One of the sentries made a pass at one of my officers with a charged bayonet, and slightly wounded him. My first thought was to kill him with my sword; but, in an instant, I altered the design and fury of the blow to a slight cut on the side of the head; upon which he dropped his gun and asked quarter, which I readily granted him, and demanded of him the place where the commanding officer kept. He showed me a pair of stairs in the front of a barrack, on the west part of the garrison, which led up to a second story in said barrack, to which I immediately repaired, and ordered the commander, Captain De la Place, to come forth instantly, or I would sacrifice the whole garrison; at which the Captain came immediately to the door, with his breeches in his hand, when I ordered him to deliver me the fort instantly.

He asked me by what authority I demanded it.

I answered him, "In the name of the great Jehovah, and the Continental Congress."

The authority of the Congress being very little known at that time, he began to speak again. But I interrupted him and, with my drawn sword over his head, again demanded an immediate surrender of the garrison; with which he then complied, and ordered his men to be forthwith paraded without arms, as he had given up the garrison. In the meantime some of my officers had given orders, and in consequence thereof, sundry of the barrack doors were beat down, and about one third of the garrison imprisoned, which consisted of the said commander, a Lieutenant Feltham, a conductor of artillery, a gunner, two sergeants, and forty-four rank and file; about one hundred pieces of cannon, one thirteen-inch mortar, and a number of swivels. This surprise was carried into execution in the gray of the morning of the tenth day of May, 1775. The sun seemed to rise that morning with a superior luster, and Ticonderoga and its dependencies smiled on its conquerors, who tossed about the flowing bowl, and wished success to Congress and the liberty and freedom of America. Happy it was for me, at that time, that the then future pages of the book of fate, which afterwards unfolded a miserable scene of two years and eight months' imprisonment, were hid from view.

But to return to my narration. Colonel Warner, with the rear guard, crossed the lake and joined me early in the morning, whom I sent off without loss of time, with about one hundred men, to take possession of Crown Point, which was garrisoned with a sergeant and twelve men; which he took possession of the same day, as also of upwards of one hundred pieces of cannon. But one thing now remained to be done to make ourselves complete masters of Lake Champlain; this was to possess ourselves of a sloop of war which was then lying at St. Johns, to effect which, it was agreed in a council of war to arm and man out a certain schooner which lay at South Bay, and that Captain (now General) Arnold should command her, and that I should command the bateaux. The necessary preparations being made, we set sail from Ticonderoga in quest of the sloop, which was much larger and carried more guns and heavier metal than the schooner. General Arnold with the schooner, sailing faster than the bateaux, arrived at St. Johns and by surprise possessed himself of the sloop before I could arrive with the bateaux. He also made prisoners of a sergeant and twelve men who were garrisoned at that place. It is worthy of remark that as soon as General Arnold had secured the prisoners on board, and had made preparation for sailing, the wind, which but a few hours before was fresh in the south and well served to carry us to St. Johns, now shifted and came fresh from the north; and in about one hour's time, General Arnold sailed with the prize and schooner for Ticonderoga. When I met him with my party, within a few miles of St. Johns, he saluted me with a discharge of cannon, which I returned with a volley of small arms. This being repeated three times, I went on board the sloop with my party, where several loyal Congress healths were drank.

We were now masters of Lake Champlain and the garrison depending thereon. This success I viewed of consequence in the scale of American politics; for if a settlement between the then colonies and Great Britain had soon taken place, it would have been easy to have restored these acquisitions; but viewing the then future consequences of a cruel war, as it has really proved to be, and the command of that lake, garrisons, artillery, etc., it must be viewed to be of signal importance to the American cause, and it is marvelous to me that we ever lost the command of it. Nothing but taking a Burgoyne with a whole British army could, in my opinion, atone for it. And notwithstanding such an extraordinary victory, we must be obliged to regain the command of that lake again, be the cost what it will; by doing this Canada will easily be brought into union and confederacy with the United States of America. Such an event would put it out of the power of the Western tribes of Indians to carry on a war with us, and be a solid and durable bar against any further inhuman barbarities committed on our frontier inhabitants by cruel and bloodthirsty savages; for it is impossible for them to carry on a war, except they are supported by the trade and commerce of some civilized nation, which to them would be impracticable did Canada compose a part of the American empire.

Early in the fall of the year, the little army under the command of the Generals Schuyler and Montgomery were ordered to advance into Canada. I was at Ticonderoga when this order arrived, and the Generals with most of the field officers requested me to attend them in the expedition; and, though at that time I had no commission from Congress, yet they engaged me, that I should be considered as an officer, the same as though I had a commission, and should, as occasion might require, command certain detachments of the army. This I considered as an honorable offer, and did not hesitate to comply with it, and advanced with the army to the Isle-aux-Noix, from whence I was ordered by the General to go in company with Major Brown and certain interpreters through the woods into Canada, with letters to the Canadians, and to let them know that the design of the army was only against the English garrisons, and not the country, their liberties, or religion. And having, through much danger, negotiated this business, I returned to the Isle-aux-Noix in the fore part of September, when General Schuyler returned to Albany; and in consequence the command devolved upon General Montgomery, whom I assisted in laying a line of circumvallation round the fortress of St. Johns. After which I was ordered by the General to make a second tour into Canada, upon nearly the same design as before, and withal to observe the disposition, designs, and movements of the inhabitants of the country. This reconnoiter I undertook reluctantly, choosing rather to assist at the siege of St. Johns, which was then closely invested; but my esteem for the General's person, and opinion of him as a politician and brave officer, induced me to proceed.

I passed through all the parishes on the river Sorel, to a parish at the mouth of the same, which is called by the same name, preaching politics; and went from thence across the Sorel to the river St. Lawrence, and up the river through the parishes to Longueuil, and so far met with good success as an itinerant. In this round my guard were Canadians, my interpreter and some few attendants excepted. On the morning of the twenty-fourth day of September I set out with my guard of about eighty men from Longueuil, to go to Laprairie, from whence I determined to go to General Montgomery's camp; but had not advanced two miles before I met with Major Brown (who has since been advanced to the rank of a Colonel), who desired me to halt, saying that he had something of importance to communicate to me and my confidants; upon which I halted the party, and went into a house and took a private room with him and several of my associates, where Colonel Brown proposed that, "provided I would return to Longueuil and procure some canoes, so as to cross the river St. Lawrence a little north of Montreal, he would cross it a little to the south of the town with near two hundred men, as he had boats sufficient; and that we could make ourselves masters of Montreal." This plan was readily approved by me and those in council; and in consequence of which I returned to Longueuil, collected a few canoes, and added about thirty English-Americans to my party, and crossed the river in the night of the twenty-fourth, agreeably to the before proposed plan.

My whole party at this time consisted of about one hundred and ten men, near eighty of whom were Canadians. We were most of the night crossing the river, as we had so few canoes that they had to pass and repass three times, to carry my party across. Soon after daybreak I set a guard between me and the town, with special orders to let no person whatever pass or repass them, and another guard on the other end of the road with like directions. In the meantime I reconnoitered the best ground to make a defense, expecting Colonel Brown's party was landed on the other side of the town, he having, the day before, agreed to give three huzzas with his men early in the morning, which signal I was to return, that we might each know that both parties were landed. But the sun by this time being nearly two hours high, and the sign failing, I began to conclude myself to be in a praemunire,* and would have crossed the river back again, but I knew the enemy would have discovered such an attempt; and as there could not more than one-third of my troops cross at one time, the other two-thirds would of course fall into their hands. This I could not reconcile to my own feelings as a man, much less as an officer. I therefore concluded to maintain the ground, if possible, and all to fare alike. In consequence of this resolution I dispatched two messengers, one to Laprairie, to Colonel Brown, and the other to l'Assomption, a French settlement, to Mr. Walker, who was in our interest, requesting their speedy assistance, giving them at the same time to understand my critical situation.

In the meantime sundry persons came to my guards, pretending to be friends, but were by them taken prisoners and brought to me. These I ordered to confinement until their friendship could be further confirmed, for I was jealous they were spies, as they proved to be afterwards. One of the principal of them, making his escape, exposed the weakness of my party, which was the final cause of my misfortune; for I have been since informed that Mr. Walker, agreeably to my desire, exerted himself, and had raised a considerable number of men for my assistance, which brought him into difficulty afterwards, but upon hearing of my misfortune he disbanded them again.

The town of Montreal was in a great tumult. General Carleton and the royal party made every preparation to go on board their vessels of force, as I was afterwards informed, but the spy escaped from my guard to the town occasioned an alteration in their policy, and emboldened General Carleton to send the force which he had there collected out against me. I had previously chosen my ground, but when I saw the number of the enemy as they sallied out of the town, I perceived it would be a day of trouble, if not of rebuke; but I had no chance to flee, as Montreal was situated on an island, and the river St. Lawrence cut off my communication to General Montgomery's camp. I encouraged my soldiery to bravely defend themselves, that we should be able to keep the ground, if no more. This, and much more, I affirmed with the

* An act of outlawry.

greatest seeming assurance, and which in reality I thought to be in some degree probable.

The enemy consisted of not more than forty regular troops, together with a mixed multitude, chiefly Canadians, with a number of English who lived in town, and some Indians; in all to the number of near five hundred.

The reader will notice that most of my party were Canadians; indeed, it was a motley parcel of soldiery which composed both parties. However, the enemy began to attack from woodpiles, ditches, buildings, and suchlike places, at a considerable distance, and I returned the fire from a situation more than equally advantageous. The attack began between two and three o'clock in the afternoon, just before which I ordered a volunteer by the name of Richard Young, with a detachment of nine men as a flank guard, which, under the cover of the bank of the river, could not only annoy the enemy but at the same time serve as a flank guard to the left of the main body.

The fire continued for some time on both sides, and I was confident that such a remote method of attack could not carry the ground, provided it should be continued till night. But near half the body of the enemy began to flank round to my right; upon which I ordered a volunteer by the name of John Dugan, who had lived many years in Canada and understood the French language, to detach about fifty of the Canadians and post himself at an advantageous ditch, which was on my right, to prevent my being surrounded. He advanced with the detachment, but instead of occupying the post made his escape, as did likewise Mr. Young upon the left, with their detachments. I soon perceived that the enemy was in possession of the ground which Dugan should have occupied.

At this time I had but about forty-five men with me, some of whom were wounded. The enemy kept closing around me, nor was it in my power to prevent it; by which means my situation, which was advantageous in the first part of the attack, ceased to be so in the last. Being almost entirely surrounded with such vast, unequal numbers, I ordered a retreat, but found that those of the enemy who were of the country, and their Indians, could run as fast as my men, though the regulars could not. Thus I retreated near a mile, and some of the enemy, with the savages, kept flanking me, and others crowded hard in the rear.

In fine I expected, in a very short time, to try the world of spirits, for I was apprehensive that no quarter would be given to me, and therefore had determined to sell my life as dear as I could. One of the enemy's officers, boldly pressing in the rear, discharged his fusee at me; the ball whistled near me, as did many others that day. I returned the salute, and missed him, as running had put us both out of breath; for I conclude we were not frightened. I then saluted him with my tongue in a harsh manner and told him that, inasmuch as his numbers were so far superior to mine, I would surrender provided I could be treated with honor, and be assured of good quarter for myself and the men who were with me; and he answered I should; another officer, coming up directly after, confirmed the treaty; upon which I agreed to surrender with my party, which then consisted of thirty-one effective men and seven wounded. I ordered them to ground their arms, which they did.

The officer I capitulated with then directed me and my party to advance towards him, which was done. I handed him my sword, and in half a minute after, a savage, part of whose head was shaved, being almost naked and painted, with feathers intermixed with the hair of the other side of his head, came running to me with an incredible swiftness; he seemed to advance with more than mortal speed. As he approached near me, his hellish visage was beyond all description; snake's eyes appear innocent in comparison of his; his features distorted; malice, death, murder, and the wrath of devils and damned spirits are the emblems of his countenance; and in less than twelve feet of me, presented his firelock. At the instant of his present, I twitched the officer, to whom I gave my sword, between me and the savage; but he flew round with great fury, trying to single me out to shoot me without killing the officer. By this time I was nearly as nimble as he, keeping the officer in such a position that his danger was my defense; but, in less than half a minute, I was attacked by just such another imp of hell. Then I made the officer fly around with incredible velocity, for a few seconds of time, when I perceived a Canadian, who had lost one eye, as appeared afterwards, taking my part against the savages; and in an instant an Irishman came to my assistance with a fixed bayonet and drove away the fiends, swearing by Jasus he would kill them. This tragic scene composed my mind. The escaping from so awful a death made even imprisonment happy, the more so as my conquerors on the field treated me with great civility and politeness.

The regular officers said that they were very happy to see Colonel Allen. I answered them that I should rather choose to have seen them at General Montgomery's camp. The gentlemen replied that they gave full credit to what I said, and so I walked to the town, which was, as I should guess, more than two miles, a British officer walking at my right hand, and one of the French noblesse at my left, the latter of which, in the action, had his eyebrow carried away by a glancing shot, but was nevertheless very merry and facetious; and no abuse was offered me till I came to the barrack yard at Montreal, where I met General Prescott, who asked me my name, which I told him. He then asked me whether I was that Colonel Allen who took Ticonderoga. I told him I was the very man. Then he shook his cane over my head, calling many hard names, among which he frequently used the word rebel, and put himself in a great rage. I told him he would do well not to cane me, for I was not accustomed to it, and shook my fist at him, telling him that was the beetle of mortality for him, if he offered to strike; upon which Captain M'Cloud of the British pulled him by the skirt and whispered to him, as he afterwards told me, to this import: that it was inconsistent with his honor to strike a prisoner. He then ordered a sergeant's command with fixed bayonets to come forward and kill thirteen Canadians, who were included in the treaty aforesaid.

It cut me to the heart to see the Canadians in so hard a case, in consequence of their having been true to me. They were wringing their hands, saying their prayers, as I concluded, and expected immediate death. I therefore stepped between the executioners and the Canadians, opened my clothes, and told General Prescott to thrust his bayonet into my breast, for I was the sole cause of the Canadians' taking up arms.

The guard, in the meantime, were rolling their eyeballs from the General to me, as though impatiently waiting his dread commands to sheath their bayonets in my heart. I could, however, plainly discern that he was in a suspense and quandary about the matter. This gave me additional hopes of succeeding, for my design was not to die but to save the Canadians by a finesse. The General stood a minute, when he made me the following reply: "I will not execute you now, but you shall grace a halter at Tyburn, God damn you."

I remember I disdained his mentioning such a place. I was, notwithstanding, a little pleased with the expression, as it significantly conveyed to me the idea of postponing the present appearance of death. Besides, his sentence was by no means final as to "gracing a halter," although I had anxiety about it after I landed in England, as the reader will find in the course of this history. General Prescott then ordered one of his officers to take me on board the *Gaspee* schooner of war and confine me, hands and feet, in irons, which was done the same afternoon I was taken.

The action continued an hour and three-quarters by the watch, and I know not to this day how many of my men were killed, though I am certain there were but few. If I remember right, seven were wounded. One of them, William Stewart by name, was wounded by a savage with a tomahawk after he was taken prisoner and disarmed, but was rescued by some of the generous enemy, and so far recovered of his wounds that he afterwards went with the other prisoners to England.

Of the enemy were killed a Major Carden, who had been wounded in eleven different battles, and an eminent merchant, Patterson, of Montreal, and some others, but I never knew their whole loss, as their accounts were different. I am apprehensive that it is rare that so much ammunition was expended and so little execution done by it, though such of my party as stood the ground behaved with great fortitude, much exceeding that of the enemy, but were not the best of marksmen, and, I am apprehensive, were all killed or taken. The wounded were all put into the hospital at Montreal, and those that were not were put on board of different vessels in the river, and shackled together by pairs, viz. two men fastened together by one handcuff being closely fixed to one wrist of each of them, and treated with the greatest severity, nay as criminals.

I now come to the description of the irons which were put on me. The handcuff was of the common size and form, but my leg irons I should imagine would weigh thirty pounds; the bar was eight feet long, and very substantial; the shackles which encompassed my ankles were very tight. I was told by the officer who put them on that it was the King's plate, and I heard other of their officers say that it would weigh forty weight. The irons were so close upon my ankles that I could not lay down in any other manner than on my back. I was put into the lowest and most wretched part of the vessel, where I got the favor of a chest to sit on; the same answered for my bed at night. I procured some little blocks of the guard, who day and night with fixed bayonets watched over me, to lie under each end of the large bar of my leg irons, to preserve my ankles from galling while I sat on the chest, or lay back on the same, though most of the time, night and day, I sat on it. But at length, having a desire to lie down on my side, which the closeness of my irons forbid, I desired the Captain to loosen them for that purpose, but was denied the favor. The Captain's name was Royal, who did not seem to be an ill-natured man, but oftentimes said that his express orders were to treat me with such severity, which was disagreeable to his own feelings; nor did he ever insult me, though many others who came on board did. One of the officers, by the name of Bradley, was very generous to me; he would often send me victuals from his own table, nor did a day fail but he sent me a good drink of grog.

The reader is now invited back to the time I was put into irons. I requested the privilege to write to General Prescott, which was granted. I reminded him of the kind and generous treatment of the prisoners I took at Ticonderoga, compared to the injustice and ungentlemanlike usage I had met with from him, and demanded better usage, but received no answer from him. I soon after wrote to General Carleton, with the same success. In the meanwhile, many of those who were permitted to see me were very insulting.

I was confined in the manner I have related on board the *Gaspee* schooner about six weeks, during which time I was obliged to throw out plenty of extravagant language, which answered certain purposes, at that time, better than to grace a history.

To give an instance, upon being insulted, in a fit of anger I twisted off a nail with my teeth, which I took to be a ten-penny nail; it went through the mortise of the bar of my handcuff, and at the same time I swaggered over those who abused me, particularly a Doctor Dace, who told me that I was outlawed by New York, and deserved death for several years past; was at last fully ripened for the halter, and in a fair way to obtain it. When I challenged him, he excused himself, in consequence, as he said, of my being a criminal; but I flung such a flood of language at him that it shocked him and the spectators, for my anger was very great. I heard one say, "Damn him, can he eat iron?" After that a small padlock was fixed to the handcuff, instead of the nail; and as they were mean-spirited in their treatment to me, so it appeared to me that they were equally timorous and cowardly.

[In the next ten days Allen and the other prisoners were transferred three times to different ships lying off Quebec.]

I was then taken on board a vessel called the *Adamant,* together with the prisoners taken with me, and put under the power of an English merchant from London, whose name was Brook Watson: a man of malicious and cruel disposition, and who was probably excited, in the exercise of his malevolence, by a junto of Tories who sailed with him to England; among whom were Colonel Guy Johnson, Colonel Closs, and their attendants and associates, to the number of about thirty.

All the ship's crew, Colonel Closs in his personal behavior excepted, behaved towards the prisoners with that spirit of bitterness which is the peculiar characteristic of Tories, when they have the friends of America in their power, measuring their loyalty to the English King by the barbarity, fraud, and deceit which they exercise towards the Whigs.

A small place in the vessel, enclosed with white oak plank, was assigned for the prisoners, and for me among the rest. I should imagine that it was not more than twenty feet one way, and twenty-two the other. Into this place we were all, to the number of thirty-four, thrust and handcuffed, two prisoners more being added to our number, and were provided with two excrement tubs. In this circumference we were obliged to eat and perform the offices of evacuation during the voyage to England, and were insulted by every blackguard sailor and Tory on board, in the cruelest manner; but what is the most surprising is, that not one of us died in the passage. When I was first ordered to go into the filthy enclosure, through a small sort of door, I positively refused, and endeavored to reason the before-named Brook Watson out of a conduct so derogatory to every sentiment of honor and humanity, but all to no purpose, my men being forced in the den already; and the rascal who had the charge of the prisoners commanded me to go immediately in among the rest. He further added that the place was good enough for a rebel; that it was impertinent for a capital offender to talk of honor or humanity; that anything short of a halter was too good for me; and that that would be my portion soon after I landed in England, for which purpose only I was sent thither.

About the same time a lieutenant among the Tories insulted me in a grievous manner, saying that I ought to have been executed for my rebellion against New York, and spit in my face. Upon which, though I was handcuffed, I sprang at him with both hands and knocked him partly down, but he scrambled along into the cabin, and I after him; there he got under the protection of some men with fixed bayonets, who were ordered to make ready to drive me into the place aforementioned. I challenged him to fight, notwithstanding the impediments that were on my hands, and had the exalted pleasure to see the rascal tremble for fear. His name I have forgot, but Watson ordered his guard to get me into the place with the other prisoners, dead or alive, and I had almost as lieve die as do it, standing it out until they environed me round with bayonets; and brutish, prejudiced, abandoned wretches they were, from whom I could expect nothing but death or wounds. However, I told them that they were good honest fellows; that I could not blame them; that I was only in dispute with a calico merchant, who knew not how to behave towards a gentleman of the military establishment. This was spoken rather to appease them for my own preservation, as well as to treat Watson with contempt, but still I found they were determined to force me into the wretched circumstances which their prejudiced and depraved minds had prepared for me. Therefore, rather than die, I submitted to their indignities, being drove with bayonets into the filthy dungeon with the other prisoners, where we were denied fresh water, except a small allowance, which was very inadequate to our wants; and in consequence of the stench of the place, each of us was soon followed with a diarrhea and fever, which occasioned an intolerable thirst. When we asked for water we were most commonly, instead of obtaining it, insulted and derided; and to add to all the horrors of the place, it was so dark that we could not see each other, and were overspread with body lice. We had, notwithstanding these severities, full allowance of salt provisions and a gill of rum per day, the latter of which was of the utmost service to us, and probably was the means of saving several of our lives. About forty days we existed in this manner, when the land's end of England was discovered from the mast-head, soon after which the prisoners were taken from their gloomy abode, being permitted to see the light of the sun and breathe fresh air, which to us was very refreshing. The day following we landed at Falmouth.

A few days before I was taken prisoner I shifted my clothes, by which I happened be taken in a Canadian dress, viz. a short fawn-skin jacket, double-breasted, an undervest and breeches of sagathy, worsted stockings, a decent pair of shoes, two plain shirts, and a red worsted cap. This was all the clothing I had, in which I made my appearance in England.

When the prisoners were landed, multitudes of the citizens of Falmouth, excited by curiosity, crowded to see us, which was equally gratifying to us. I saw numbers on the tops of houses, and the rising adjacent grounds were covered with them, of both sexes. The throng was so great that the King's officers were obliged to draw their swords and force a passage to Pendennis Castle, which was near a mile from the town, where we were closely con-fined, in consequence of orders from General Carleton, who then commanded in Canada.

The rascally Brook Watson then set out for London in great haste, expecting the reward of his zeal. But the Ministry received him, as I have been since informed, rather coolly, for the minority in Parliament took advantage, arguing that the opposition of America to Great Britain was not a rebellion. If it is, say they, why do you not execute Colonel Allen according to law? But the majority argued that I ought to be executed, and that the oppo-sition was really a rebellion, but that policy obliged them not to do it, inasmuch as the Congress had then most prisoners in their power; so that my being sent to England for the purpose of being executed, and necessity restraining them, was rather a foil on their laws and authority, and they consequently disapproved of my being sent thither. But I had never heard the least hint of those debates in Parliament, or of the working of their policy, until some time after I left England.

Consequently the reader will readily conceive I was anxious about my preservation, knowing that I was in the power of a haughty and cruel nation, considered as such. Therefore, the first proposition which I determined in my own mind was, that humanity and moral suasion would not be consulted in the determining of my fate; and those that daily came in great numbers out of curiosity to see me, both gentle and simple, united in this, that I would be hanged. A gentleman from America by the name of Temple, and who was friendly to me, just whispered me in the ear and told me that bets were laid in London that I would be executed; he likewise privately gave me a guinea, but durst say but little to me.

However, agreeably to my first negative proposition, that moral virtue would not influence my destiny, I had recourse to stratagem, which I was in hopes would move in the circle of their policy. I requested of the commander of the castle the privilege of writing to Congress, who, after consulting with an officer that lived in town, of a superior rank, permitted me to write. I wrote, in the fore part of the letter, a short narrative of my ill-treatment, but withal let them know that, though I was treated as a criminal in England, and continued in irons, together with those taken with me, yet it was in consequence of the orders which the commander of the castle received from General Carleton. And therefore I desired Congress to desist from matters of retaliation until they should know the result of the government in England respecting their treatment towards me, and the prisoners with me, and govern themselves accordingly; with a particular request, that if retaliation should be found necessary, it might be exercised not according to the smallness of my character in America but in proportion to the importance of the cause for which I suffered. This is, according to my present recollection, the substance of the letter, inscribed "To the illustrious Continental Congress." This letter was written with a view that it should be sent to the Ministry at London rather than to Congress, with a design to intimidate the haughty English government, and screen my neck from the halter.

The next day the officer from whom I obtained license to write came to see me, and frowned on me on account of the impudence of the letter, as he phrased it, and further added, "Do you think that we are fools in England, and would send your letter to Congress, with instructions to retaliate on our own people? I have sent your letter to Lord North." This gave me inward satisfaction, though I carefully concealed it with a pretended resentment, for I found I had come Yankee over him, and that the letter had gone to the identical person I designed it for. Nor do I know to this day but that it had the desired effect, though I have not heard anything of the letter since.

My personal treatment by Lieutenant Hamilton, who commanded the castle, was very generous. He sent me every day a fine breakfast and dinner from his own table, and a bottle of good wine. Another aged gentleman, whose name I cannot recollect, sent me a good supper. But there was no distinction in public support between me and the privates; we all lodged on a sort of Dutch bunks, in one common apartment, and were allowed straw. The privates were well supplied with fresh provisions and, with me, took effectual measures to rid ourselves of lice.

I could not but feel, inwardly, extremely anxious for my fate. This I however concealed from the prisoners, as well as from the enemy, who were perpetually shaking the halter at me. I nevertheless treated them with scorn and contempt and, having sent my letter to the Ministry, could conceive of nothing more in my power but to keep up my spirits, behave in a daring, soldierlike manner, that I might exhibit a good sample of American fortitude. Such a conduct I judged would have a more probable tendency to my preservation than concession and timidity. This therefore was my deportment, and I had lastly determined, in my mind, that if a cruel death must inevitably be my portion, I would face it undaunted; and though I greatly rejoice that I returned to my country and friends, and to see the power and pride of Great Britain humbled, yet I am confident I could then have died without the least appearance of dismay.

Among the great numbers of people who came to the castle to see the prisoners, some gentlemen told me that they had come fifty miles on purpose to see me, and desired to ask me a number of questions, and to make free with me in conversation. I gave for answer that I chose freedom in every sense of the word. Then one of them asked me what my occupation in life had been. I answered him that in my younger days I had studied divinity, but was a conjuror by profession. He replied that I conjured wrong at the time I was taken, and I was obliged to own that I mistook a figure at that time, but that I had conjured them out of Ticonderoga. This was a place of great notoriety in England, so that the joke seemed to go in my favor.

It was a common thing for me to be taken out of close confinement, into a spacious green in the castle, or rather parade, where numbers of gentlemen and ladies were ready to see and hear me. I often entertained such audiences with harangues on the impracticability of Great Britain's conquering the then colonies of America. At one of these times I asked a gentleman for a bowl of punch, and he ordered his servant to bring it, which he did, and offered it to me, but I refused to take it from the hand of his servant. He then gave it to me with his own hand, refusing to drink with me in consequence of my being a state criminal. However, I took the punch and drank it all down at one draught, and handed the gentleman the bowl; this made the spectators as well as myself merry.

I expatiated on American freedom. This gained the resentment of a young beardless gentleman of the company, who gave himself very great airs, and replied that he "knew the Americans very well, and was certain that they could not bear the smell of powder." I replied that I accepted it as a challenge, and was ready to convince him on the spot that an American could bear the smell of powder; at which he answered that he should not put himself on a par with me. I then demanded of him to treat the character of the Americans with due respect. He answered that I was an Irishman; but I assured him that I was a full-blooded Yankee, and in fine bantered him so much that he left me in possession of the ground, and the laugh went against him. Two clergymen came to see me, and, inasmuch as they behaved civilly, I returned the same. We discoursed on several parts of moral philosophy and Christianity, and they seemed to be surprised that I should be acquainted with such topics, or that I should understand a syllogism, or regular mode of argumentation. I am apprehensive my Canadian dress contributed not a little to the surprise and excitement of curiosity: to see a gentleman in England regularly dressed and well-behaved would be no sight at all; but such a rebel, as they were pleased to call me, it is probable was never before seen in England.

[On the eighth of January, 1776, Allen and his fellow-prisoners were taken from prison and placed on an English frigate, which arrived in American waters in May. After spending some months in prison in Halifax, Allen was transported to New York and admitted to parole at the end of November. New York City had meanwhile fallen to the British, and Washington had retreated to White Plains. The Battle of Long Island and the costly loss of Fort Washington on the Hudson left thousands of Continental troops in British hands, and confirmed British expectations of a quick victory. Allen thus saw New York in its darkest hour.]

I now found myself on parole, and restricted to the limits of the city of New York, where I soon projected means to live in some measure agreeably to my rank, though I was destitute of cash. My constitution was almost worn out by such a long and barbarous captivity. The enemy gave out that I was crazy and wholly unmanned, but my vitals held sound, nor was I delirious any more than I had been from youth up; but my extreme circumstances, at certain times, rendered it politic to act in some measure the madman. In consequence of a regular diet and exercise, my blood recruited, and my nerves in a great measure recovered their former tone, strength, and usefulness, in the course of six months.

I next invite the reader to a retrospective sight and consideration of the doleful scene of inhumanity exercised by General Sir William Howe and the army under his command, towards the prisoners taken on Long Island, on the twenty-seventh day of August, 1776, sundry of whom were, in an inhuman and barbarous manner, murdered after they had surrendered their arms; particularly a General Odel, or Woodhull, of the militia, who was hacked to pieces with cutlasses when alive, by the light horsemen, and a Captain Fellows, of the Continental Army, who was thrust through with a bayonet, of which wound he died instantly. Sundry others were hanged up by the neck till they were dead,

five on the limb of a white oak tree, and without any reason
assigned, except that they were fighting in defense of the only
blessing worth preserving. And indeed those who had the misfortune to fall into their hands at Fort Washington, in the month
of November following, met with but very little better usage,
except that they were reserved from immediate death to famish
and die with hunger. In fine, the word rebel, applied to any
vanquished persons, without regard to rank, who were in the
Continental service on the twenty-seventh of August aforesaid,
was thought by the enemy sufficient to sanctify whatever cruelties
they were pleased to inflict, death itself not excepted. But to pass
over particulars which would swell my narrative far beyond my
design.

The private soldiers who were brought to New York were
crowded into churches and environed with slavish Hessian guards,
a people of a strange language who were sent to America for no
other design but cruelty and desolation, and at others by merciless
Britons, whose mode of communicating ideas being intelligible
in this country, served only to tantalize and insult the helpless
and perishing; but above all was the hellish delight and triumph
of the Tories over them, as they were dying by hundreds. This
was too much for me to bear as a spectator, for I saw the Tories
exulting over the dead bodies of their murdered countrymen. I
have gone into the churches and seen sundry of the prisoners in
the agony of death, in consequence of very hunger, and others
speechless and very near death, biting pieces of chips; others
pleading for God's sake for something to eat, and at the same
time shivering with the cold. Hollow groans saluted my ears, and
despair seemed to be imprinted on all of their countenances.
The filth in these churches, in consequence of the fluxes, was
almost beyond description. The floors were covered with excrements. I have carefully sought to direct my steps so as to avoid it,
but could not. They would beg for God's sake for one copper, or
morsel of bread. I have seen in one of these churches seven dead
at the same time, lying among the excrements of their bodies.

It was a common practice with the enemy to convey the dead
from these filthy places in carts, to be slightly buried, and I have
seen whole gangs of Tories making derision, and exulting over the
dead, saying, "There goes another load of damned rebels." I have

observed the British soldiers to be full of their blackguard jokes and vaunting on those occasions, but they appeared to me less malignant than Tories.

The provision dealt out to the prisoners was by no means sufficient for the support of life. It was deficient in quantity and much more so in quality. The prisoners often presented me with a sample of their bread, which I certify was damaged to that degree that it was loathsome and unfit to be eaten, and I am bold to aver it as my opinion that it had been condemned and was of the very worst sort. I have seen and been fed upon damaged bread, in the course of my captivity, and observed the quality of such bread as has been condemned by the enemy, among which was very little so effectually spoiled as what was dealt out to these prisoners. Their allowance of meat (as they told me) was quite trifling, and of the basest sort. I never saw any of it, but was informed that bad as it was, it was swallowed almost as quick as they got hold of it. I saw some of them sucking bones after they were speechless; others, who could yet speak, and had the use of their reason, urged me, in the strongest and most pathetic manner, to use my interest in their behalf. "For you plainly see," said they, "that we are devoted to death and destruction."

And after I had examined more particularly into their truly deplorable condition, and had become more fully apprised of the essential facts, I was persuaded that it was a premeditated and systematical plan of the British council to destroy the youths of our land, with a view thereby to deter the country and make it submit to their despotism. But I could not do them any material service, and by any public attempt for that purpose I might endanger myself, by frequenting places the most nauseous and contagious that could be conceived of. I refrained from going into churches, but frequently conversed with such of the prisoners as were admitted to come out into the yard, and found that the systematical usage still continued. The guard would often drive me away with their fixed bayonets. A Hessian one day followed me five or six rods, but by making use of my legs I got rid of the lubber. Sometimes I could obtain a little conversation, notwithstanding their severities.

I was in one of the churchyards, and it was rumored among those in the church, and sundry of the prisoners came with their usual complaints to me, and among the rest a large-boned, tall young man from Pennsylvania, as he told me, who was reduced to a mere skeleton. He said he was glad to see me before he died, which he expected to have done last night, but was a little revived. He furthermore informed me that he and his brother had been urged to enlist into the British, but both had resolved to die first; that his brother had died last night, in consequence of that resolution, and that he expected shortly to follow him. I made the other prisoners stand a little off, and told him with a low voice to enlist. He then asked whether it was right in the sight of God. I assured him that it was, and that duty to himself obliged him to deceive the British by enlisting and deserting the first opportunity; upon which he answered with transport that he would enlist. I charged him not to mention my name as his adviser, lest it should get air, and I should be closely confined in consequence of it.

The integrity of these suffering prisoners is hardly credible. Many hundreds, I am confident, submitted to death rather than to enlist in the British service, which I am informed they most generally were pressed to do. I was astonished at the resolution of the two brothers particularly; it seems that they could not be stimulated to such exertions of heroism from ambition, as they were but obscure soldiers. Strong indeed must the internal principle of virtue be, which supported them to brave death, and one of them went through the operation, as did many hundred others. I readily grant that instances of public virtue are no excitement to the sordid and vicious, nor, on the other hand, will all the barbarity of Britain and Heshland awaken them to a sense of their duty to the public; but these things will have their proper effect on the generous and brave.

[The battles of Trenton and Princeton on the day after Christmas, 1776, and the third day of 1777, gave Washington British prisoners to exchange for the unfortunate captives in New York. Allen estimated that about two thousand of the American prisoners on Manhattan Island died from their treatment. From January to August, 1777, he lived under the terms of his parole on western Long Island. On August 25th he was seized in a tavern, accused of breaking his parole, and placed in the provost jail in New York City, where he collected still more instances of British inhumanity.]

I was confined in the provost jail at New York, the twenty-

sixth day of August, 1777, and continued there to the third day of
May, 1778, when I was taken out under guard and conducted to
a sloop in the harbor at New York, in which I was guarded to
Staten Island, to General Campbell's quarters, where I was admitted to eat and drink with the General and several other of the
British field officers, and treated for two days in a polite manner.
As I was drinking wine with them one evening, I made an observation on my transition from the provost criminals to the company of gentlemen, adding that I was the same man still, and
should give the British credit, by him (speaking to the General)
for two days' good usage.

The next day Colonel Archibald Campbell, who was exchanged
for me, came to this place, conducted by Mr. Boudinot, the then
American commissary of prisoners, and saluted me in a handsome manner, saying that he never was more glad to see any
gentleman in his life, and I gave him to understand that I was
equally glad to see him, and was apprehensive that it was from
the same motive. The gentlemen present laughed at the fancy,
and conjectured that sweet liberty was the foundation of our
gladness. So we took a glass of wine together, and then I was
accompanied by General Campbell, Colonel Campbell, Mr. Boudinot, and a number of British officers to the boat which was
ready to sail to Elizabethtown-point. Meanwhile I entertained
them with a rehearsal of the cruelties exercised towards our prisoners, and assured them that I should use my influence that their
prisoners should be treated, in future, in the same manner as
they should in future treat ours; that I thought it was right in
such extreme cases that their example should be applied to their
own prisoners. Then we exchanged the decent ceremonies of compliment, and parted. I sailed to the point aforesaid and, in a
transport of joy, landed on liberty ground, and as I advanced
into the country received the acclamations of a grateful people.

I soon fell into company with Colonel Shelden, of the light
horse, who in a polite and obliging manner accompanied me to
headquarters, Valley Forge. There I was courteously received by
General Washington, with peculiar marks of his approbation and
esteem, and was introduced to most of the generals and many of
the principal officers of the army, who treated me with respect.
And after having offered General Washington my further service

in behalf of my country, as soon as my health, which was very much impaired, would admit, and obtained his license to return home, I took my leave of His Excellency, and set out from Valley Forge with General Gates and his suite for Fishkill, where we arrived the latter end of May. In this tour the General was pleased to treat me with the familiarity of a companion and generosity of a lord, and to him I made known some striking circumstances which occurred in the course of my captivity. I then bid farewell to my noble General and the gentlemen of his retinue, and set out for Bennington, the capital of the Green Mountain Boys, where I arrived the evening of the last day of May to their great surprise, for I was thought to be dead, and now both their joy and mine was complete. Three cannon were fired that evening, and next morning Colonel Herrick gave orders and fourteen more were discharged, welcoming me to Bennington, my usual place of abode; thirteen for the United States, and one for the Young Vermont.

After this ceremony was ended we moved the flowing bowl, and rural felicity, sweetened with friendship, glowed in each countenance, and with loyal healths to the rising States of America, concluded that evening, and, with the same loyal spirit, I now conclude my narrative.

Thomas Dring

Thomas Dring (1758-1825), a Rhode Islander, was born in Newport but resided chiefly in Providence. As his story explains, he shipped on a privateer toward the close of the Revolution, and was shortly captured and thrust into the loathsome *Jersey*. Upon his liberation he sailed on American merchantmen, and eventually attained his own command. In 1803 he retired from the sea and entered business. The last year of his life he began writing his prison-ship memories, and left at his death a valuable but jumbled and ungrammatical manuscript. With the approval of "several gentlemen of high respectability" who had themselves seen the inside of the *Jersey*, Albert G. Greene prepared the material for publication, by arranging it topically, eliminating redundancies, and observing the rules of syntax, but withal adhering faithfully to the emphases and descriptions of Captain Dring. In this form the work appeared under the title *Recollections of the Jersey Prison-Ship; taken, and prepared for publication, from the original manuscript of the late Captain Thomas Dring, of Providence, R.I., one of the prisoners,* by Albert G. Greene (Providence, published by H. H. Brown, 1829). It was reprinted in 1831 in New York, and in 1865 in Morrisania, N. Y., in a limited edition edited by Henry B. Dawson, with useful supplementary materials.

The present text is edited from the first edition, pp. 17-53, 58-68, 116-136, 145-152, 165-167.

CHAPTER ONE

OUR CAPTURE

THE NUMBER of those who perished on board the prison and hospital ships at the Wallabout has never been, and never can be, known. It has been ascertained, however, with as much precision as the nature of the case will admit, that more than *ten thousand* died on board the *Jersey,* and the hospital ships *Scorpion, Strombolo,* and *Hunter.* Thousands there suffered, and pined and died, whose names have never been known by their countrymen. They died where no eye could admire their fortitude, no tongue could praise their devotion to their country's cause.

For years the very name of "the old *Jersey*" seemed to strike a

3. THOMAS DRING

terror to the hearts of those whose necessities required them to venture upon the ocean. The mortality which prevailed on board her was well known throughout the country, and to be confined within her dungeons was considered equal to a sentence of death, from which but little hope of escape remained.

It was my hard fortune, in the course of the war, to be twice confined on board the prison ships of the enemy. I was first immured in the year 1779 on board the *Good Hope,* then lying in the North River, opposite the city of New York; but after a confinement of more than four months, I succeeded in making my escape to the Jersey shore. Afterwards, in the year 1782, I was again captured and conveyed on board the *Jersey,* where for nearly five months I was a witness and a partaker of the unspeakable sufferings of that wretched class of American prisoners, who were there taught the utmost extent of human misery.

I am now far advanced in years, and am the only survivor (with the exception of two) of a crew of sixty-five men. I often pass some descendant of one of my old companions in captivity, and the recollection comes fresh to my mind that his father was my comrade and fellow-sufferer in prison; that I saw him breathe his last upon the deck of the *Jersey,* and assisted at his interment at the Wallabout: circumstances probably wholly unknown to the person the sight of whom had excited the recollection.

In the month of May, 1782, I sailed from Providence (Rhode Island) as Master's Mate, on board a privateer called *The Chance.* This was a new vessel, on her first cruise. She was owned in Providence by Messrs. Clarke and Nightingale, and manned chiefly from that place and vicinity. She was commanded by Captain Daniel Aborn, mounted twelve six-pound cannon, and sailed with a complement of about sixty-five men.

Our cruise was but a short one, for in a few days after sailing we were captured by the British ship of war *Belisarius,* Captain Graves, of twenty-six guns. We were captured in the night and our crew, having been conveyed on board the enemy's ship, were put in irons the next morning. During the next day the *Belisarius* made two other prizes, a privateer brig from New London or Stonington (Connecticut), called the *Samson,* of twelve guns, commanded by Captain Brooks, and a merchant schooner from Warren (Rhode Island) commanded by Captain Charles Collins.

4. **THE BRITISH ENTER NEW YORK HARBOR**

A. The British Fleet Anchored between
Long Island and Staten Island, July 12, 1776

B. The British Battery Firing from Hell Gate, Sept. 8, 1776

The crews of these two vessels, except the principal officers, were also put in irons. These captures were all made on soundings south of Long Island. The putting their prisoners in irons was a necessary precaution on the part of the captors. We were kept confined in the cable tier of the ship, but were occasionally permitted to go on deck during the day in small parties. The *Belisarius,* then having on board upwards of one hundred and thirty prisoners, soon made her way for New York, in company with her prizes.

Our situation on board this ship was not, indeed, a very enviable one, but uncomfortable as it was, it was far preferable to that in which we soon expected to be placed, and which we soon found it was our doom to experience. The ship dropped her anchor abreast of the city, and signals were immediately made that she had prisoners on board. Soon after, two large gondolas or boats came alongside, in one of which was seated the notorious David Sproat, the Commissary of Prisoners. This man was an American refugee, universally detested for the cruelty of his conduct and the insolence of his manners.

We were then called on deck, and, having been released from our irons, were ordered into the boats. This being accomplished, we put off from the ship, under a guard of marines, and proceeded towards our much-dreaded place of confinement, which was not then in sight. As we passed along the Long Island shore, against the tide, our progress was very slow. The prisoners were ordered by Sproat to apply themselves to the oars, but not feeling any particular anxiety to expedite our progress, we declined obeying the command. His only reply was, "I'll soon fix you, my lads."

We at length doubled a point and came in view of the Wallabout, where lay before us the black hulk of the old *Jersey,* with her satellites the three hospital ships, to which Sproat pointed in an exulting manner and said, "There, rebels, *there* is the *cage* for you." Oh! how I wished to be standing alone with that inhuman wretch upon the green turf, at that moment!

As he spoke, my eye was instantly turned from the dreaded hulk, but a single glance had shown us a multitude of human beings moving upon her upper deck. Many were on her bowsprit, for the purpose, as I afterwards learned, of getting without the limits.

It was then nearly sunset, and before we were alongside every man except the sentinels on the gangway had disappeared. Previous to their being sent below, some of the prisoners, seeing us approaching, waved their hats, as if they would say, Approach us not; and we soon found fearful reason for the warning.

CHAPTER TWO

THE FIRST NIGHT ON BOARD

WE HAD now reached the accommodation ladder which led to the gangway on the larboard side of the *Jersey,* and my station in the boat, as she hauled alongside, was exactly opposite to one of the air ports in the side of the ship. From this aperture proceeded a strong current of foul vapor, of a kind to which I had been before accustomed while confined on board the *Good Hope,* the peculiarly disgusting smell of which I then recollected, after a lapse of three years. This was, however, far more foul and loathsome than anything which I had ever met with on board that ship, and produced a sensation of nausea far beyond my powers of description.

Here, while waiting for orders to ascend on board, we were addressed by some of the prisoners, from the air ports. We could not, however, discern their features, as it had now become so dark that we could not distinctly see any object in the interior of the ship. After some questions whence we came and respecting the manner of our capture, one of the prisoners said to me that it was "a lamentable thing to see so many young men in full strength, with the flush of health upon their countenances, about to enter that infernal place of abode." He then added in a tone and manner but little fitted to afford us much consolation: "Death has no relish for such skeleton carcasses as we are, but he will now have a feast upon you fresh comers."

After lanterns had been lighted on board, for our examination, we ascended the accommodation ladder to the upper deck and passed through the barricado door, where we were examined and our bags of clothes inspected. These we were permitted to retain, provided they contained no money or weapons of any kind.

After each man had given his name and the capacity in which he had served on board the vessel in which he was captured, and the same had been duly registered, we were directed to pass through the other barricado door, on the starboard side, down the ladder leading to the main hatchway. I was detained but a short time with the examination, and was permitted to take my bag of clothes with me below; and passing down the hatchway, which was still open, through a guard of soldiers, I found myself among the wretched and disgusting multitude, a prisoner on board the *Jersey*.

The gratings were soon after placed over the hatchways and fastened down for the night, and I seated myself on the deck, holding my bag with a firm grasp, fearful of losing it among the crowd. I had now ample time to reflect on the horrors of the scene, and to consider the prospect before me. It was impossible to find one of my former shipmates in the darkness, and I had, of course, no one with whom to speak during the long hours of that dreadful night—surrounded by I knew not whom, except that they were beings as wretched as myself; with dismal sounds meeting my ears from every direction; a nauseous and putrid atmosphere filling my lungs, at every breath; and a stifling and suffocating heat, which almost deprived me of sense, and even of life.

Previous to leaving the boat, I had put on several additional articles of apparel for the purpose of security, but I was soon compelled to disencumber myself of these, and was willing to hazard their loss, for a relief from the intolerable heat.

The thought of sleep did not enter my mind. At length, discovering a glimmering of light through the iron gratings of one of the air ports, I felt that it would be indeed a luxury if I could but obtain a situation near that place, in order to gain one breath of the exterior air. Clenching my hand firmly around my bag, which I dared not leave, I began to advance towards the side of the ship, but was soon greeted with the curses and imprecations of those who were lying on the deck, and whom I had disturbed in attempting to pass over them. I, however, persevered and at length arrived near the desired spot, but found it already occupied, and no persuasion would induce a single individual to relinquish his place for a moment.

Thus I passed the first dreadful night, waiting with sorrowful forebodings for the coming day. The dawn at length appeared, but came only to present new scenes of wretchedness, disease, and woe. I found myself surrounded by a crowd of strange and unknown forms, with the lines of death and famine upon their faces. My former shipmates were all lost and mingled among the multitude, and it was not until we were permitted to ascend the deck, at eight o'clock, that I could discern a single individual whom I had ever seen before. Pale and meager, the throng came upon deck to view, for a few moments, the morning sun, and then to descend again, to pass another day of misery and wretchedness.

CHAPTER THREE

THE FIRST DAY

AFTER PASSING the weary and tedious night, to whose accumulated horrors I have but slightly alluded, I was permitted to ascend to the upper deck, where other objects even more disgusting and loathsome met my view. I found myself surrounded by a motley crew of wretches with tattered garments and pallid visages, who had hurried from below for the luxury of a little fresh air. Among them I saw one ruddy and healthful countenance, and recognized the features of one of my late fellow-prisoners on board the *Belisarius*. But how different did he appear from the group around him, who had here been doomed to combat with disease and death! Men who, shrunken and decayed as they stood around him, had been but a short time before as strong, as healthful, and as vigorous as himself. Men who had breathed the pure breezes of the ocean, or danced lightly in the flower-scented air of the meadow and the hill, and had from thence been hurried into the pent-up air of a crowded prison ship, pregnant with putrid fever, foul with deadly contagion—here to linger out the tedious and weary day, the disturbed and anxious night; to count over the days and weeks and months of a wearying and degrading captivity, unvaried but by new scenes of painful suffering, and new inflictions of remorseless cruelty; their brightest hope and their daily prayer, that death would not long delay to release them from their torments.

In the wretched groups around me I saw but too faithful a picture of our own almost certain fate, and found that all which we had been taught to fear of this terrible place of abode was more than realized.

During the night, in addition to my other sufferings, I had been tormented with what I supposed to be vermin, and on coming upon deck I found that a black silk handkerchief which I wore around my neck was completely spotted with them. Although this had often been mentioned as one of the miseries of the place, yet as I had never before been in a situation to witness anything of the kind, the sight made me shudder; as I knew at once that so long as I should remain on board, these loathsome creatures would be my constant companions and unceasing tormentors.

The next disgusting object which met my sight was a man suffering with the smallpox, and in a few minutes I found myself surrounded by many others laboring under the same disease, in every stage of its progress.

As I had never had the smallpox, it became necessary that I should be inoculated, and there being no proper person on board to perform the operation, I concluded to act as my own physician. On looking about me I soon found a man in the proper stage of the disease, and desired him to favor me with some of the matter for the purpose. He readily complied, observing that it was a necessary precaution on my part, and that my situation was an excellent one in regard to *diet,* as I might depend upon finding that *extremely moderate.* The only instrument which I could procure for the purpose of inoculation was a common pin. With this, having scarified the skin of my hand between the thumb and forefinger, I applied the matter and bound up my hand. The next morning I found that the wound had begun to fester, a sure symptom that the application had taken effect. Many of my former shipmates took the same precaution, and were inoculated during the day. In my case the disorder came on but lightly and its progress was favorable, and without the least medical advice or attention, by the blessing of Divine Providence, I soon recovered.

Since that time more than forty years have passed away, but the scar on my hand is still plainly to be seen. I often look upon it when alone, and it brings fresh to my recollection the fearful scene in which I was then placed, the circumstances by which it was attended, and the feelings which I then experienced.

CHAPTER FOUR

THE GUN ROOM AND MESSES

ON THE arrival of prisoners on board the *Jersey*, the first thing necessary to be done was, as soon as possible, to form, or be admitted into, some regular *mess*. On the day of a prisoner's arrival it was impossible for him to procure any food, and even on the second day he could not procure any in time to have it cooked. No matter how long he had fasted, nor how acute might be his sufferings from hunger and privation, his petty tyrants would on no occasion deviate from their rule of delivering the prisoner's morsel at a particular hour and at no other. And the poor, half-famished wretch must absolutely wait until the coming day, before his pittance of food could be boiled with that of his fellow-captives. It was therefore most prudent for a newly arrived prisoner to gain admittance into some old established mess (which was not attended with much difficulty, as death was daily providing vacancies), for he would thereby be associated with those who were acquainted with the mode of procuring their allowance in time, and be also protected from many impositions, to which as a stranger he otherwise would be liable during the first days of his confinement.

The cruel tyrants to whose petty sway we were subjected on board this hulk knew no distinction among their prisoners. Whether taken on the land or on the ocean, in arms or from our own firesides, it was the same to them. No matter in what rank or capacity a prisoner might have been known before his capture, no distinction was here made; we were "all *rebels*." Our treatment, our fare, its allowance, and its quality were the same. They did not, of course, interfere in our private arrangements, but left us to manage our affairs in our own way.

The extreme after part of the ship, between decks, was called the *gun room*. Although no distinction was made by our masters, yet those among the prisoners who had been officers previous to their capture had taken possession of this room as their own place of abode, and from custom it was considered as belonging exclusively to them. As an officer I found my way into this apartment and, with such of my late companions as had been officers, was received with civility by those who were already in possession of it, who humanely tendered us such little services as were in their power to offer. We soon became incorporated with them, and having formed ourselves into messes as nearly as possible according to our grades, we were considered as a part of this family of sufferers.

The different messes of the prisoners were all numbered, and every morning at nine o'clock, the Steward and his assistants having taken their station at the window in the bulkhead of the Steward's room, the bell was rung, and the messes called in rotation.

An individual belonging to each mess stood ready in order to be in time to answer when its number was called. As the number of each mess was spoken, its allowance was handed from the window to the person waiting to receive it, the rations being all prepared previous to the hour of delivery. The prisoner must receive for his mess whatever was offered, and be its quantity or quality what it might, no alteration or change was ever allowed. We as prisoners were allowed each day for *six* men what was equal in quantity to the rations of *four* men at *full allowance*. That is, each prisoner was furnished in quantity with two-thirds of the allowance of a seaman in the British Navy, which was as follows:

On Sunday.   1 lb. of biscuit, 1 lb. of pork, and half a pint of peas.

" Monday.   1 lb. of biscuit, 1 pint of oatmeal, 2 ounces of butter.

" Tuesday.   1 lb. of biscuit and two lbs. of beef.

" Wednesday.   1½ lbs. of flour and two ounces of suet.

" Thursday.   The same as Sunday.

" Friday.   The same as Monday.

" Saturday.   The same as Tuesday.

Hence as prisoners, whenever we had our due, we received (as they said) two-thirds of the ordinary allowance of their own seamen, and even this was of a very inferior quality. We never received any butter, but in its stead they gave us a substance which they called sweet oil. This was so rancid and even putrid that the smell of it, accustomed as we were to everything foul and nauseous, was more than we could endure. We, however, always received and gave it to the poor, half-starved Frenchmen who were on board, who took it gratefully and swallowed it with a little salt and their wormy bread. Oil of a similar quality was given to the prisoners on board the *Good Hope,* where I was confined in 1779. There, however, it was of some use to us as we burnt it in our lamps, being there indulged with the privilege of using lights until nine o'clock at night. But here it was of no service, as we were allowed on board the *Jersey* no light or fire on any occasion whatever.

CHAPTER FIVE

THE COOK'S QUARTERS

HAVING RECEIVED our daily rations, which were frequently not delivered to us in time to be boiled on the same day, we were consequently often under the necessity of fasting for the next twenty-four hours if we had not a stock of provisions on hand or were obliged at times to consume our food in its raw state, when the cravings of hunger could no longer be resisted.

The cooking for the great mass of the prisoners was done under the forecastle or, as it was usually called, the galley, in a boiler or "great copper" which was enclosed in brickwork about eight feet square. This copper was large enough to contain two or three hogsheads of water. It was made in a square form, and divided into two separate compartments by a partition. In one side of the copper the peas and oatmeal for the prisoners were boiled, which was done in fresh water. In the other side the meat was boiled. This side of the boiler was filled with salt water from alongside the ship, by which means the copper became soon corroded and poisonous, the fatal consequences of which are so obvious that I need not enlarge upon the subject.

After the daily rations had been furnished to the different messes, the portion of each mess was designated by a tally fastened to it by a string. Being thus prepared, every ear was anxiously waiting for the summons of the *cook's bell.* As soon as this was heard to sound, the persons having charge of the different portions of food thronged to the galley; and in a few minutes after, hundreds of tallies were seen hanging over the sides of the brickwork by their respective strings, each eagerly watched by some individual of the mess, who always waited to receive it. The meat was suffered thus to remain in the boiler but a certain time; and when this had elapsed, the cook's bell was again rung, and the pittance of food must be immediately removed. Whether sufficiently cooked or not, it could remain no longer. The proportions of peas and oatmeal belonging to each mess were measured out from the copper, after they were boiled.

Among the emaciated crowd of living skeletons who had remained on board for any length of time, the cook was the only person who appeared to have much flesh upon his bones. He perhaps contrived to obtain a greater quantity of provisions than any of ourselves; but if they were of the same quality with our own, it is obvious that his plumpness of appearance could not be the result of *good living*. He had himself been formerly a prisoner, but seeing no prospect of ever being liberated, he had entered in his present capacity, and his mates and scullions had followed his example, they having also been prisoners at first. I attributed the appearance of our cook merely to the fact that he was more content with his situation than any other person on board appeared to be. He indeed possessed a considerable share of good humor, and although often cursed by the prisoners (but not in his hearing) for his refusals to comply with their requests, yet considering the many applications which were made to him for favors, and the encumbrances which were around "his palace," he really displayed a degree of fortitude and forbearance far beyond what most men would have been capable of exhibiting under similar circumstances. He did, indeed, at times, when his patience was exhausted, "make the hot water fly among us," but a reconciliation was usually effected with but little difficulty.

In consequence of the poisonous effects produced by the use of the sea water for boiling our meat in the great copper, many of the different messes had obtained permission from "His Majesty the cook" to prepare their own rations separate from the general mess in the great boiler. For this purpose, a great number of spikes and hooks had been driven into the brickwork by which the boiler was enclosed, on which to suspend their tin kettles. As soon as we were permitted to go on deck in the morning, someone took the tin kettle belonging to the mess, with as much water and such splinters of wood as we had been able to procure during the

previous day, and carried them to the galley; and there, having
suspended his kettle on one of the hooks or spikes in the brickwork, he stood ready to kindle his little fire as soon as the cook
or his mates would permit it to be done. It required but little
fuel to boil our food in these kettles, for their bottoms were
made in a concave form, and the fire was applied directly in the
center. And let the remaining brands be ever so small, they were
all carefully quenched, and having been conveyed below, were
kept for use on a future occasion. Much contention often arose
through our endeavors to obtain places round the brickwork, but
these disputes were always promptly decided by the cook, from
whose mandate there was no appeal. No sooner had one prisoner
completed the cooking for his mess than another supplicant stood
ready to take his place; and they thus continued to throng the
galley during the whole time that the fire was allowed to remain
under the great copper, unless it happened to be the pleasure of
the cook to drive them away.   .

I have said that but little wood was requisite for our purpose,
but the great difficulty was to procure a sufficient quantity of fresh
water for this manner of cooking. The arrangement by which we
effected this was by agreeing that each man in the mess should
during the day previous procure and save as much water as possible, as no prisoner was ever allowed to take more than a pint at
one time from the scuttle cask in which it was kept. Every individual was, therefore, obliged each day to save a little for the
common use of the mess on the next morning. By this arrangement, the mess to which I belonged had always a small quantity of
fresh water in store, which we carefully kept, with a few other
necessaries, in a chest which we used in common.

During the whole period of my confinement, I never partook of
any food which had been cooked in the great copper. It is to this
fact that I have always attributed, under Divine Providence, the
degree of health which I preserved while on board. I was thereby
also, at times, enabled to procure several necessary and comfortable things, such as tea, sugar, etc., so that, wretchedly as I was
situated, my condition was far preferable to that of most of my
fellow-sufferers, which has ever been with me a theme of sincere
and lasting gratitude to Heaven.

But terrible indeed was the condition of most of my fellow-captives. Memory still brings before me those emaciated beings, moving from the galley with their wretched pittance of meat, each creeping to the spot where his mess were assembled, to divide it with a group of haggard and sickly creatures, their garments hanging in tatters around their meager limbs, and the hue of death upon their careworn faces. With the meat they consumed their scanty remnants of bread, which was often moldy and filled with worms. And even from this vile fare they would rise up in torments from the cravings of unsatisfied hunger and thirst.

No vegetables of any description were ever afforded us by our inhuman keepers. Good Heaven, what a luxury to us would then have been even a few potatoes, if but the very leavings of the swine of our country!

CHAPTER SIX

BELOW DECKS

THE PRISONERS, as before stated, were confined on the two main decks below. My usual place of abode being in the gun room on the center deck, I was never under the necessity of descending to the lower dungeon, and during my confinement I had no disposition to visit it. It was inhabited by the most wretched in appearance of all our miserable company. From the disgusting and squalid appearance of the groups which I saw ascending the stairs from below, it must have been more dismal, if possible, than that part of the hulk where I resided. Its occupants appeared to be mostly foreigners, who had seen and survived every variety of human suffering. The faces of many of them were covered with dirt and filth; their long hair and beards matted and foul; clothed in rags, and with scarcely a sufficient supply of these to cover their disgusting bodies. Many among them possessed no clothing except the remnants of those garments which they wore when first brought on board, and were unable to procure even any materials for patching these together, when they had been worn to tatters by constant use! And had this been in their power, they had not the means of procuring a piece of thread, or even a needle. Some, and indeed many of them, had not the means of procuring a razor or an ounce of soap.

Their beards were occasionally reduced by each other with a

pair of shears or scissors, but this operation, though conducive to cleanliness, was not productive of much improvement in their personal appearance. The skins of many of them were discolored by continual washing in salt water, added to the circumstance that it was impossible for them to wash their linen in any other manner than by laying it on the deck and stamping on it with their feet, after it had been immersed in salt water—their bodies remaining naked during the operation.

To men thus situated, everything like ordinary cleanliness was impossible. Much that was disgusting in their appearance undoubtedly originated from neglect, which long confinement had rendered habitual, until it created a confirmed indifference to personal appearance.

As soon as the gratings had been fastened over the hatchways for the night, we generally went to our sleeping places. It was, of course, always desirable to obtain a station as near as possible to the side of the ship and, if practicable, in the immediate vicinity of one of the air ports, as this not only afforded us a better air but also rendered us less liable to be trodden upon by those who were moving about the decks during the night.

But silence was a stranger to our dark abode. There were continual noises during the night. The groans of the sick and the dying; the curses poured out by the weary and exhausted upon our inhuman keepers; the restlessness caused by the suffocating heat and the confined and poisoned air, mingled with the wild and incoherent ravings of delirium—these were the sounds which, every night, were raised around us in all directions. Such was our ordinary situation, but at times the consequences of our crowded condition were still more terrible and proved fatal to many of our number in a single night.

But strange as it may appear, notwithstanding all the maladies and sufferings which were there endured, I knew many who had been inmates of that abode for two years, who were apparently well. They had, as they expressed it, "been through the furnace, and become *seasoned*." Most of these, however, were foreigners, who appeared to have abandoned all hope of ever being exchanged, and had become quite indifferent in regard to their place of abode.

Far different was the condition of that portion of our number who were natives of the Northern States. These formed by far the most numerous class of the prisoners. Most of these were young men who had been induced by necessity or inclination to try the perils of the sea and had, in many instances, been captured soon after leaving their homes, and during their first voyage. After they had been here immured, the sudden change in their situation was like a sentence of death. Many a one was crushed down beneath that sickness of the heart, so well described by the poet,

> "Night and day,
> Brooding on what he had been, what he was;
> 'Twas more than he could bear. His longing fits
> Thickened upon him. *His desire for Home*
> *Became a madness.*"

Many of these poor creatures had, in addition, been plundered of their wearing apparel by their captors. And here, the dismal and disgusting objects by which they were surrounded; the vermin which infested them; their vile and loathsome food; and what, with *them,* was far from being the lightest of their trials, their ceaseless longing after their *homes* and the scenes to which they had been accustomed—all combined to produce a wonderful effect upon them. Dejection and anguish were soon visible in their countenances. They became dismayed and terror-stricken, and many of them absolutely died that most awful of all human deaths, the effects of a *broken heart.*

> "Denied the comforts of a dying bed,
> With not a pillow to support the head:
> How could they else, but pine and grieve and sigh,
> Detest that wretched life, and *wish* to die?"

CHAPTER SEVEN

THE WORKING PARTY

A custom had long been established that certain labor which it was necessary should be performed daily should be done by a company, usually called the "working party." This consisted of about twenty able-bodied men, chosen from among the prisoners, and was commanded, in daily rotation, by those of our number who had formerly been officers of vessels. The commander of the party for the day bore the title of *Boatswain*. The members of the working party received, as a compensation for their services, a full allowance of provisions and a half pint of rum each, per day, with the privilege of going on deck early in the morning to breathe the pure air. This privilege alone was a sufficient compensation for all the duty which was required of them.

Their routine of service was to wash down that part of the upper deck and gangways where the prisoners were permitted to walk, to spread the awning, and to hoist on board the wood, water, and other supplies from the boats in which they were brought alongside the ship.

When the prisoners ascended the upper deck in the morning, if the day was fair each carried up his hammock and bedding, which were all placed upon the spar deck or booms. The working party then took the sick and disabled who remained below and placed them in the bunks prepared for them upon the center deck; they then, if any of the prisoners had died during the night, carried up the dead bodies, and laid them upon the booms. After this it was their duty to wash down the main decks below, during which operation the prisoners remained upon the upper deck, except such as chose to go below and volunteer their services in the performance of this duty.

Around the railing of the hatchway leading from the center to the lower deck were placed a number of large tubs for the occasional use of the prisoners during the night, and as general receptacles of filth. Although these were indispensably necessary to us, yet they were highly offensive. Nevertheless, on account of our crowded situation, many of the prisoners were obliged to sleep in their immediate vicinity. It was a part of the duty of the working party to carry these tubs on deck, at the time when the prisoners ascended in the morning, and to return them between decks in the afternoon.

Our beds and clothing were kept on deck until it was nearly the hour when we were to be ordered below for the night. During this interval the chests, etc., on the lower decks being piled up and the hammocks removed, the decks washed and cleared of all encumbrances except the poor wretches who lay in the bunks, it was quite refreshing, after the suffocating heat and foul vapors of the night, to walk between decks. There was then some circulation of air through the ship, and for a few hours our existence was, in some degree, tolerable.

About two hours before sunset the order was generally issued for the prisoners to carry their hammocks below. After this had been done we were allowed either to retire between decks or to remain above until sunset, according to our own pleasure. Everything which we could do conducive to cleanliness had then been performed. If we ever felt anything like enjoyment in this wretched abode, it was during this brief interval, when we breathed the cool air of the approaching night, and felt the luxury of our evening pipe. But short indeed was this period of repose. The working party were soon ordered to carry the tubs below, and we prepared to descend to our gloomy and crowded dungeons. This was no sooner done than the gratings were closed over the hatchways, the sentinels stationed, and we left to sicken and pine beneath our accumulated torments, with our guards above crying aloud, through the long night, "All's well!"

CHAPTER SIXTEEN

THE FOURTH OF JULY

A few days before the Fourth of July we had made such preparations as our circumstances would admit for an observance of the anniversary of American Independence. We had procured some supplies wherewith to make ourselves merry on the occasion and intended to spend the day in such innocent pastime and amusement as our situation would afford, not dreaming that our proceedings would give umbrage to our keepers, as it was far from our intention to trouble or insult them. We thought that, although prisoners, we had a right on that day at least to sing and be merry. As soon as we were permitted to go on deck in the morning, thirteen little national flags were displayed in a row upon the booms. We were soon ordered by the guard to take them away, and as we neglected to obey the command, they triumphantly demolished and trampled them underfoot.

Unfortunately for us, our guards at that time were Scotchmen, who next to the refugees were the objects of our greatest hatred;

but their destruction of our flags was merely viewed in silence, with the contempt which it merited.

During the time we remained on deck several patriotic songs were sung and choruses were repeated, but not a word was intentionally spoken to give offense to our guards. They were, nevertheless, evidently dissatisfied with our proceedings, as will soon appear. Their moroseness was a prelude to what was to follow. We were in a short time forbidden to pass along the common gangways, and every attempt to do so was repelled by the bayonet. Although thus incommoded, our mirth still continued. Songs were still sung, accompanied with occasional cheers. Things thus proceeded until about four o'clock, when the guards were turned out, and we received orders to descend between decks, where we were immediately driven, at the point of the bayonet.

After being thus sent below in the greatest confusion, at that early and unusual hour, and having heard the gratings closed and fastened above us, we supposed that the barbarous resentment of our guards was fully satisfied. But we were mistaken, for they had further vengeance in store, and merely waited for an opportunity to make us feel its weight.

The prisoners continued their singing between decks, and were of course more noisy than usual, but forbore, even under their existing temptations, to utter any insulting or aggravating expressions. At least, I heard nothing of the kind, unless our patriotic songs could be so construed.

In the course of the evening we were ordered to desist from making any further noise. This order not being fully complied with, at about nine o'clock the gratings were removed and the guards descended among us, with lanterns and drawn cutlasses in their hands. The poor helpless prisoners retreated from the hatchways, as far as their crowded situation would permit, while their cowardly assailants followed as far as they dared, cutting and wounding everyone within their reach, and then ascended to the upper deck, exulting in the gratification of their revenge.

Many of the prisoners were wounded, but from the total darkness neither their number nor their situation could be ascertained; and if this had been possible, it was not in the power of their companions to afford them the least relief. During the whole of that tragical night, their groans and lamentations were dreadful in the extreme. Being in the gun room, I was at some distance from the immediate scene of this bloody outrage, but the distance was by no means far enough to prevent my hearing their continual cries from the extremity of pain, their applications for assistance, and their curses upon the heads of their brutal assailants.

It had been the usual custom for each prisoner to carry below, when he descended at sunset, a pint of water, to quench his thirst during the night. But on this occasion we had thus been driven to our dungeons three hours before the setting of the sun, and without our usual supply of water.

Of this night I cannot describe the horrors. The day had been very sultry, and the heat was extreme throughout the ship. The unusual number of hours during which we had been crowded together between decks; the foul atmosphere and sickening heat; the additional excitement and restlessness caused by the wanton attack which had been made; above all the want of water, not a drop of which could we obtain during the whole night to cool our parched tongues; the imprecations of those who were half distracted with their burning thirst; the shrieks and wailings of the wounded; the struggles and groans of the dying—all together formed a combination of horrors which no pen can describe.

In the agonies of their suffering the prisoners invited, and even challenged, their inhuman guards to descend once more among them; but this they were prudent enough not to attempt.

Their cries and supplications for water were terrible, and were of themselves sufficient to render sleep impossible. Oppressed with the heat, I found my way to the grating of the main hatchway, where on former nights I had frequently passed some time for the benefit of the little current of air which circulated through the bars. I obtained a place on the larboard side of the hatchway, where I stood facing the east, and endeavored as much as possible to draw my attention from the terrific sounds below me, by watching through the grating the progress of the stars. I there spent hour after hour in following with my eye the motion of a particular star as it rose and ascended, until it passed over beyond my sight.

How I longed for the day to dawn! At length the morning light began to appear, but still our torments were increasing every moment. As the usual hour for us to ascend to the upper deck approached, the working party were mustered near the hatchway; and we were all anxiously waiting for the opportunity to cool our weary frames, to breathe for a while the pure air, and above all to procure water to quench our intolerable thirst. The time arrived, but still the gratings were not removed. Hour after hour passed on, and still we were not released. Our minds were at length seized with the horrible suspicion that our tyrants had determined to make a finishing stroke of their cruelty, and rid themselves of us altogether.

It was not until ten o'clock in the forenoon that the gratings were at length removed. We hurried on deck and thronged to the water cask, which was completely exhausted before our thirst was allayed. So great was the struggle around the cask that the guards were again turned out to disperse the crowd. In a few hours, however, we received a new supply of water, but it seemed impossible to allay our thirst, and the applications at the cask were incessant until sunset.

Our rations were delivered to us, but of course not until long after the usual hour. During the whole day, however, no fire was kindled for cooking in the galley. All the food which we consumed that day we were obliged to swallow raw. Everything indeed had been entirely deranged by the events of the past night, and several days elapsed before order was restored. This was at length obtained by a change of the guard, who, to our great joy, were relieved by a party of Hessians.

The average number who died on board, during the period of twenty-four hours, was about five, but on the morning of the fifth of July, eight or ten corpses were found below. Many had been badly wounded, to whom, in the total darkness of the night, it was impossible for their companions to render any assistance; and even during the next day they received no attention, except that which was afforded by their fellow-prisoners, who had nothing to administer to their comfort, not even bandages for their wounds.

CHAPTER SEVENTEEN

AN ATTEMPT TO ESCAPE

IT HAD been some time in contemplation, among a few of the inmates of the gun room, to make a desperate attempt to escape, by
cutting a hole through the stern or counter of the ship. In order
that their operations might proceed with even the least probability of success, it was absolutely necessary that but few of the
prisoners should be admitted to the secret. At the same time it
was impossible for them to make any progress in their labor unless
they first confided their plan to all the other occupants of the
gun room, which was accordingly done.

In this part of the ship, each mess was on terms of more or less
intimacy with those whose little sleeping enclosures were immediately adjacent to their own; and the members of each mess
frequently interchanged good offices with those in their vicinity,
and borrowed and lent such little articles as they possessed, like
the good housewives of a sociable neighborhood. I never knew
any contention in this apartment during the whole period of my
confinement. Each individual in the gun room, therefore, was
willing to assist his comrades, as far as he had the power to do so.
When the proposed plan of escape was laid before us, although it
met the disapprobation of by far the greater number, still we were
all perfectly ready to assist those who thought it practicable.

We, however, described to them the difficulties and dangers
which must unavoidably attend their undertaking: the prospect
of detection while making the aperture, in the immediate vicinity
of such a multitude of idle men crowded together, a large proportion of whom were always kept awake by their restlessness and
sufferings during the night; the little probability that they would
be able to travel, undiscovered, on Long Island, even should they
succeed in reaching the shore in safety; and, above all, the almost
absolute impossibility of obtaining food for their subsistence, as
an application for that to our keepers would certainly lead to detection. But notwithstanding all our arguments, a few remained
determined to make the attempt. Their only reply to our reason-
ing was that they must die if they remained, and that nothing
worse could befall them if they failed in their undertaking.

One of the most sanguine among the adventurers was a young man named Lawrence, the mate of a ship from Philadelphia. He was a member of the mess next to my own, and I had formed with him a very intimate acquaintance. He frequently explained his plans to me, and dwelt much upon his hopes of success. But ardently as I desired to obtain my liberty, and great as were the exertions I would have made had I seen any probable mode of gaining it, yet it was not my intention to join in this attempt. I nevertheless agreed to assist in the labor of cutting through the planks, and heartily wished, although I had no hope, that the enterprise might prove successful.

The work was accordingly commenced, and the laborers concealed by placing a blanket between them and the prisoners without. The counter of the ship was covered with hard oak plank four inches thick, and through this we undertook to cut an opening sufficiently large for a man to descend, and to do this with no other tools than our jackknives and a single gimlet.

All the occupants of the gun room assisted in this labor in rotation: some in confidence that the plan was practicable, and the rest merely for amusement, or for the sake of being employed. Some one of our number was constantly at work; and we thus continued, wearing a hole through the hard planks from seam to seam, until at length the solid oak was worn away piecemeal and nothing remained but a thin sheathing on the outside, which could be cut away at any time in a few minutes, whenever a suitable opportunity should occur for making the bold attempt to leave the ship.

It had been previously agreed that those who should first descend through the aperture should drop into the water and there remain until all those among the inmates of the gun room who chose to make the attempt could join them, and that the whole band of adventurers should then swim together to the shore, which was about a quarter of a mile from the ship.

A proper time at length arrived. On a very dark and rainy night, the exterior sheathing was cut away; and at midnight four of our number, having disencumbered themselves of their clothes and tied them across their shoulders, were assisted through the opening and dropped, one after another, into the water.

Ill-fated men! Our guards had long been acquainted with the

enterprise. But instead of taking any measures to prevent it they had permitted us to go on with our labor, keeping a vigilant watch for the moment of our projected escape, in order to gratify their bloodthirsty wishes. No other motive than this could have prompted them to the course which they pursued. A boat was in waiting, under the ship's quarter, manned with rowers and a party of the guards. They maintained a perfect silence, after hearing the prisoners drop from the opening, until having ascertained that no more would probably descend; then they pursued the swimmers, whose course they could easily follow by the sparkling of the water, an effect always produced by the agitation of the waves in a stormy night.

We were all profoundly silent in the gun room after the departure of our companions, and in anxious suspense as to the issue of their adventure. In a few minutes we were startled by the report of a gun, which was instantly succeeded by a quick and scattering fire of musketry. In the darkness of the night we could not see the unfortunate victims, but could distinctly hear their shrieks and cries for mercy.

The noise of the firing had alarmed the prisoners generally, and the report of the attempted escape, and its defeat, ran like wildfire through the gloomy and crowded dungeons of the hulk, and produced much commotion among the whole body of the prisoners. In a few moments the gratings were raised and the guards descended, bearing a naked and bleeding man, whom they placed in one of the bunks; and after having left a piece of burning candle by his side, they again ascended to the deck and secured the gratings.

Information of this circumstance soon reached the gun room, and I with several others of our number succeeded in making our way through the crowd to the bunks. The wounded man was my friend Lawrence. He was severely injured in many places, and one of his arms had been nearly severed from his body by the stroke of a cutlass. This, he said, was done in wanton barbarity, while he was crying for mercy, with his hand on the gunwale of the boat. He was too much exhausted to answer any of our questions and uttered nothing further, except a single inquiry respecting the fate of Nelson, one of his fellow-adventurers. This we could not answer. Indeed, what became of the rest we never knew. They were probably all murdered, in the water.

This was the first time that I had ever seen a light between decks. The piece of candle had been left by the side of the bunk in order to produce an additional effect upon the prisoners. Many had been suddenly awakened from their slumbers, and had crowded round the bunk where the sufferer lay. The effect of the partial light upon his bleeding and naked limbs, and upon the pale and haggard countenances and tattered garments of the wild and crowded groups by which he was surrounded, was horrid beyond description.

We could render the sufferer but little assistance, being only able to furnish him with a few articles of apparel, and to bind a handkerchief around his head. His body was completely covered and his hair filled with clotted blood; yet we had not the means of washing the gore from his wounds during the night. We had seen many die, but to view this wretched man expiring in that situation where he had been placed beyond the reach of surgical aid, merely to strike us with terror, was dreadful.

The gratings were not removed at the usual hour in the morning, but we were all kept below until ten o'clock. This mode of punishment had now become habitual with our keepers, and we were all frequently detained between decks until a late hour in the day, in revenge for the most trifling occurrence. This cruelty never failed to produce the torments arising from heat and thirst, with all their attendant miseries.

The immediate object of our tyrants having been answered by leaving Mr. Lawrence below in that situation, they promised in the morning that he should have the assistance of a surgeon; but this promise was not fulfilled. The prisoners rendered him every attention in their power. They washed and dressed his wounds, but in vain. Mortification soon commenced; he became delirious, and died.

No inquiry was made by our keepers respecting his situation. They evidently left him thus to suffer in order that the sight of his agonies might deter the rest of the prisoners from following his example.

We received not the least reprimand for this transaction. The aperture was again filled up with plank and made perfectly secure, and no similar attempt to escape was made, at least so long as I remained on board.

It was always in our power to knock down the guards and throw them overboard. But this would have been of no avail. If we had done so, and had effected our escape to Long Island, it would have been next to impossible for us to have proceeded any farther among the number of troops there quartered. Of these there were several regiments, and among them the regiment of Refugees before mentioned, who were vigilant in the highest degree, and would have been delighted at the opportunity of apprehending and returning us to our dungeons.

CHAPTER NINETEEN

THE EXCHANGE

SOON AFTER Captain Aborn had been permitted to go to Long Island on his parole, he sent a message on board the *Jersey* informing us that his parole had been extended so far as to allow his return home, but that he should visit us previous to his departure. He requested our First Lieutenant, Mr. John Tillinghast, to provide a list of the names of those captured in the *Chance* who had died, and also a list of the survivors, noting where each survivor was then confined, whether on board the *Jersey* or on one of the hospital ships.

He also requested that those of our number who desired to write to their friends at home would have their letters ready for delivery to him, whenever he should come on board. The occupants of the gun room, and such of the other prisoners as could procure the necessary materials, were, therefore, soon busily engaged in writing as particular descriptions of our situation as they thought it prudent to do, without the risk of the destruction of their letters, as we were always obliged to submit our writing for inspection previous to its being allowed to pass from the ship. We, however, afterwards regretted that, on this occasion, our descriptions were not more minute, as these letters were not examined.

The next day Captain Aborn came on board, accompanied by several other persons who had also been liberated on parole; but they came no nearer to the prisoners than the head of the gang-way ladder, and passed through the door of the barricade to the quarter deck. This was perhaps a necessary precaution against the contagion, as they were more liable to be affected by it than if they had always remained on board; but we were much dis-appointed at not having an opportunity to speak to them. Our letters were delivered to Captain Aborn by our Lieutenant, through whom he sent us assurances of his determination to do everything in his power for our relief, and that if a sufficient number of British prisoners could be procured, every survivor of his vessel's crew should be exchanged; and if this could not be effected, we might depend on receiving clothing and such other necessary articles as could be sent for our use.

About this time, some of the sick were sent ashore on Black-well's Island. This was considered a great indulgence. I en-deavored to obtain leave to join them, by feigning sickness, but did not succeed. The removal of the sick was a great relief to us, as the air was less foul between decks, and we had more room for motion. Some of the bunks were removed, and the sick were carried on shore as soon as their condition was known. Still, how-ever, the pestilence did not abate on board, as the weather was extremely warm. In the daytime the heat was excessive, but at night it was intolerable.

But we lived on hope, knowing that in all probability our friends at home had ere then been apprised of our condition, and that some relief might perhaps be soon afforded us.

Such was our situation when one day, a short time before sun-set, we descried a sloop approaching us with a white flag at her masthead and knew, by that signal, that she was a cartel, and from the direction in which she came supposed her to be from some of the Eastern States. She did not approach near enough to satisfy our curiosity until we were ordered below for the night.

Long were the hours of that night to the survivors of our crew. Slight as was the foundation on which our hopes had been raised, we had clung to them as our last resource. No sooner were the gratings removed in the morning than we were all upon deck, gazing at the cartel. Her deck was crowded with men, whom we supposed to be British prisoners. In a few minutes they began to enter the Commissary's boats, and proceeded to New York.

In the afternoon a boat from the cartel came alongside the hulk, having on board the Commissary of Prisoners, and by his side sat our townsman, Captain William Corey, who came on board with the joyful information that the sloop was from Providence, with English prisoners to be exchanged for the crew of the *Chance*. The number which she had brought was forty, being more than sufficient to redeem every survivor of our crew then on board the *Jersey*.

I immediately began to prepare for my departure. Having placed the few articles of clothing which I possessed in a bag (for by one of our by-laws, no prisoner, when liberated, could remove his chest), I proceeded to dispose of my other property on board; and after having made sundry small donations of less value, I concluded by giving my tin kettle to one of my friends, and to another the remnant of my cleft of firewood.

I then hurried to the upper deck, in order to be ready to answer to my name, well knowing that I should hear no second call, and that no delay would be allowed.

The Commissary and Captain Corey were standing together on the quarter deck, and as the list of names was read, our Lieutenant, Mr. Tillinghast, was directed to say whether the person called was one of the crew of the *Chance*. As soon as this assurance was given, the individual was ordered to pass down the accommodation ladder into the boat. Cheerfully was the word "Here!" responded by each survivor, as his name was called. My own turn at length came, and the Commissary pointed to the boat. I never moved with a lighter step, for that moment was the happiest of my life. In the excess and overflowing of my joy I forgot, for a while, the detestable character of the Commissary himself, and even, Heaven forgive me, bestowed a bow upon him as I passed.

We took our stations in the boat in silence. No congratulations were heard among us. Our feelings were too deep for utterance. For my own part, I could not refrain from bursting into tears of joy.

Still there were intervals when it seemed impossible that we were in reality without the limits of the old *Jersey*. We dreaded the idea that some unforeseen event might still detain us, and shuddered with the apprehension that we might yet be returned to our dungeons.

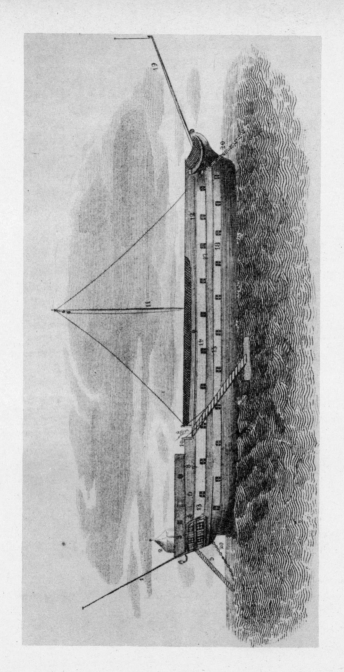

5. THE "OLD JERSEY" PRISON SHIP, 1782

When the cartel arrived, the surviving number of our crew on board the *Jersey* was but thirty-five. This fact being well known to Mr. Tillinghast, and finding that the cartel had brought forty prisoners, he allowed five of our companions in the gun room, to answer to the names of the same number of our crew who had died; and having disguised themselves in the garb of common seamen, they passed unsuspected.

It was nearly sunset when we had all arrived on board the cartel. No sooner had the exchange been completed than the Commissary left us, with our prayers that we might never behold him more. I then cast my eyes towards the hulk, as the horizontal rays of the setting sun glanced on her polluted sides, where from the bends upwards, filth of every description had been permitted to accumulate for years; and the feelings of disgust which the sight occasioned are indescribable. The multitude on her spar deck and forecastle were in motion, and in the act of descending for the night, presenting the same appearance that met my sight when, nearly five months before, I had, at the same hour, approached her as a prisoner.

CONCLUSION

I CANNOT close these sketches without referring to the fate of the old *Jersey*. At the expiration of the war, in 1783, the prisoners remaining on board were liberated, and the hulk, being considered unfit for further use, was abandoned where she lay. The dread of contagion prevented everyone from venturing on board, and even from approaching her polluted frame. But the ministers of destruction were at work. Her planks were soon filled with worms, who, as if sent to remove this disgrace to the name of common humanity, ceased not from their labor until they had penetrated through her decaying bottom, through which the water rushed in, and she sank. With her went down the names of many thousands of our countrymen with which her inner planks and sheathing were literally covered, for but few of her inmates had ever neglected to add their own names to the almost innumerable catalogue. Could these be counted, some estimate might now be made of the whole number who were there immured, but this record has long since been consigned to eternal oblivion. It is supposed that more men perished on her decks than ever died in any other place of confinement on the face of the earth, in the same number of years.

Notwithstanding the lapse of time and the consequent decay and dissolution of the remains of the multitudes who were buried on the shore, which were continually washed from the sand and wasted by the elements, in the year 1803, when the bank at the Wallabout was removed for the purpose of building a Navy Yard, a very great quantity of bones were collected. A memorial was presented to Congress, requesting an appropriation sufficient to defray the expenses necessary for their interment, and for the erection of a suitable monument upon the spot, but the application was unsuccessful. In the year 1808 the bones were interred under the direction of the Tammany Society of New York, attended by a solemn funeral procession, in the presence of a vast concourse of citizens, and the cornerstone of a monument was laid (to use the impressive words which are inscribed upon it) "in the name of the Spirits of the Departed Free."

Thomas Andros

The hazards endured by Thomas Andros (1759-1845) in escaping from the *Jersey*, and the fever that resulted, led him to think of God. Prior to his imprisonment he had worked on his father's farm in Norwich, Connecticut, turned a lathe in a workshop, and drifted from one type of armed service to another. After recovering from his serious illness, he resolved to study for the ministry, and read so zealously that by 1788 he could be ordained. He served his church even longer than did Jonas Clark, passing fifty-seven years as the Congregational minister in Berkley, Massachusetts. Like Clark, he worked on his farm to supplement his parish income, and also taught in the local school. In his later career Andros developed into a vigorous theological polemicist, endeavoring to uphold the Calvinistic tradition of Jonathan Edwards. He found himself in philosophical difficulties with the exponents of the New Divinity, for imputing the power of evil to the Devil, and so limiting the power of God. Nineteenth-century Congregationalism preferred a less mechanistic doctrine, and ultimately Andros was obliged to resign from his parish in 1834. He continued his active life, however, and served two terms in the state legislature. Politically Andros followed the view of commercial New England in vehemently opposing the War of 1812 with England, and seems to have forgotten his earlier animosity against the British. (See his discourse, "The Grand Era of Ruin to Nations from Foreign Influence," Boston, 1812.)

His published writings include a number of sermons and doctrinal essays, besides his captivity narrative. Even this shows the marks of his conversion, for he subtitled it "a series of letters to a friend, suited to inspire faith and confidence in a particular Divine Providence," and in two footnotes he deplored his earlier bellicosity against the enemy, and his partial falsehoods when concealing his escape from potential Tories. This somewhat belated trust in Providence further links the Revolutionary captivity of Andros with the seventeenth-century Puritan captivities, such as the well-known relation of Mary Rowlandson, who regarded her deliverance as a manifestation of God's providential agency.

Biographical sketches of Andros can be found in Samuel H. Emery, *The Ministry of Taunton* (Boston, 1853), II, 254-277, written in part by his son Richard S. Storrs Andros, and in Enoch Sanford, *History of the Town of Berkley* (New York, 1872), 9-27. *The Old Jersey Captive: or, A Narrative of the Captivity of Thomas Andros, (now Pastor of the Church in Berkley) on board the old Jersey Prison Ship at New York, 1781,* was published in Boston by W. Peirce, 1833. It was reprinted in the *Magazine of History*, Extra Number 46 (1916), pp. 5-80, the text here edited.

LETTER ONE

IN THE SUMMER of 1781 the ship *Hannah*, a very rich prize, was captured and brought into the port of New London. But in this case it was far worse than in common lottery gambling, for it followed that there were thousands of fearful blanks to this one prize. It infatuated great numbers of young men who flocked on board our private armed ships, fancying the same success would attend their adventures; but no such prize was ever after brought into that port.

But New London became such a nest of privateers that the English determined on its destruction, and sent an armament and laid it in ashes, and took Fort Griswold on the Groton side of the river, and with savage cruelty put the garrison to the sword, after they had surrendered. Another mighty blank to this prize was that our privateers so swarmed on the ocean that the British cruisers, who were everywhere in pursuit of them, soon filled their prisons at New York to overflowing with captured American seamen.

Among these deluded and infatuated youth, I was one. I entered a volunteer on board a new brig, called the *Fair American*, built on purpose to prey upon the British commerce. She mounted sixteen carriage guns and was manned with a crew whose numbers exceeded what was really her complement. The quarter deck, tops, and longboat were crowded with musketry, so that in action she was a complete flame of fire.

We had not been long at sea before we discovered and gave chase to an English brig, as large as ours, who in appearance mounted as many guns. As we approached her she saluted us with her stern chases, but after exchanging a few shots we ran directly alongside, as near as we could and not get entangled in her top hamper, and with one salute of all the fire we could display put her to silence. And thanks be to God, no lives were lost.

I, with others, went on board to man the prize and to take her into port. But the prize master disobeyed orders. His orders were not to approach the American coast till we had reached the longitude of New Bedford, and then to haul up to the northward, and with a press of sail to make for that port; but he aimed to make land on the back of Long Island. The consequence was, we were captured on the twenty-seventh of August by the *Solebay* frigate, and safely stowed away in the old *Jersey* prison ship at New York.

[Andros here describes conditions aboard the *Jersey* in much the same terms as Dring.]

While on board almost every thought was occupied to invent some plan of escape, but day after day passed, and none presented that I dared to put in execution. But the time had now come when I must be delivered from the ship or die. It could not be delayed even a few days longer; but no plan could I think of that offered even a gleam of hope. If I did escape with my life, I could see no way for it but by miracle.

LETTER TWO

MR. EMERY, the sailing master, was just now going ashore after water. Without really considering what I said, and without the least expectation of success, I thus addressed him, "Mr. Emery, may I go on shore with you after water?" My lips seemed to move almost involuntarily, for no such thing to my knowledge had ever been granted to such a prisoner.

To my surprise and the astonishment of all that heard him, he replied, "Yes, with all my heart."

I then descended immediately into the boat which was in waiting for him. But the prisoners came to the ship's side and queried, "What is that sick man going on shore for?" And the British sailors endeavored to dissuade me from it, though never was counsel so little relished as theirs. To put them all to silence I again ascended on board; but even this was an interposition of a kind Providence, for I had neglected to take my greatcoat, without which I must have perished in cold and storms. I now put it on and waited for the sailing master, meaning to step down again into the boat just before him. This I did, and turned my face away, that I might not be recognized and another attempt be made to prevent my going. The boat was pushed off and we were soon clear of the ship.

I took an oar and attempted to row, but an English sailor took it from me, and very kindly said, "Give me the oar, you are not able to use it, you are too unwell."

I resigned it and gave up myself to the most intense thought upon my situation. I had commenced the execution of a plan in which, if I failed, my life was gone, but if I succeeded, it was possible I might live. I looked back to the black and unsightly old ship, as an object of the greatest horror. "Am I to escape, or return there and perish?" was with me the all-absorbing question. I believed in a God whose plans and purposes were eternal and immutable, and I had no doubt but that with him my bounds were set and my destiny unalterably fixed. Oh that I could know how he intended to dispose of me, that I might struggle with the hope of success or resign myself to my fate!

But this train of thought was soon terminated by the consideration "that secret things belong to God," and that all my present concern was action, or the application of the proper means of escape. Now we had ascended the creek and arrived at the spring where the casks were to be filled, and I proposed to the sailors to go in quest of apples. I had before told them that this was my object in coming on shore, but they chose to defer it till the boat was loaded, and as they did not exact any labor of me, this was just as I would have it. I thought I could do quite as well without their company as with it.

The sailing master passing by me very kindly remarked, "This fresh air will be of service to you." This emboldened me to ask leave to ascend the bank, a slope of about forty-five degrees and thirty feet in height, terminating in a plain of considerable extent, and to call at a house nearby for some refreshment.

He said "Go, but take care and not be out of the way."

I replied, "My state of health is such that there is nothing to fear on that score."

But here, I confess, I violated a principle of honor for which I could not then, nor can I now, entirely excuse myself. I feel a degree of conscious meanness for treating a man thus who put confidence in me, and treated me in such a manner as showed he was a gentleman of sensibility and kindness. The love of life was my temptation, but this principle is always too great, when it tempts us to violate any principle of moral rectitude and honor.

And should I even now learn that my escape involved him in any trouble, it would be a matter of deep regret. Not long after my arrival at home, I sent him my apology for what I did by a British officer, who was exchanged and going directly to New York.

I consider him as God's chosen instrument to save me, and to him as such I owe my life.

When the boat returned, the inquiry was made by the prisoners (as I was afterwards informed), "Where is the sick man that went with you?" The English sailors consoled themselves with this reply, "Ah, he is safe enough, he will never live to go a mile." They did not know what the Sovereign of life and death could enable a sick man to do.

Intent on the business of escape, I surveyed the landscape all around. I discovered at the distance of half a mile what appeared to be a dense swamp of young maples and other bushes. On this I fixed as my hiding place. But how should I get to it, without being discovered and apprehended before I could reach it? I had reason to think the boat's crew would keep an eye upon me; and people were to be seen at a distance in almost every direction. But there was an orchard which extended a good way toward the swamp, and while I wandered from tree to tree in this orchard I should not be suspected of anything more than searching after fruit. At my first entrance into it I found a soldier on sentry, and I had to find out what his business was, and soon discovered he had nothing to do with me, but only to guard a heap of apples. Now I gradually worked myself off to the end of the orchard next to the swamp, and looking round on every side, I saw no person from whom I might apprehend immediate danger.

The boat's crew being yet at work under the bank of the creek and out of sight, I stepped off deliberately. (For I was unable to run, and had I been able, it would have tended to excite suspicion in anyone that might have seen me, even at a distance.) Having forded the creek once or twice, I reached the swamp in safety, and soon found a place which seemed to have been formed by nature on purpose for concealment. A huge log, twenty feet in length, having lain there for many years, was spread over on both sides with such a dense covering of green running briars as to be impervious to the eye. Lifting up this covering at one end, I crept in close by the log, and rested comfortably and securely, for I was well defended from the northeast storm which soon commenced.

When the complete darkness of the night had shut in, and while rain fell in torrents, I began to feel my way out. Though but just able to walk, and though oft thrown into the water by my clothes getting entangled with the bushes, yet I reached the dry land, and endeavored to shape my course for the east end of Long Island. In this I was assisted by finding how New York bore from me, by the sound of ship bells, and the din of labor and activity, even at that time of night.

Here let me remark how easy it is with God to cause men to do good, when they intend no such thing. Without my greatcoat, it would have been scarcely possible to have survived the tempest, rain, and cold of this night in the month of October. But had not the prisoners endeavored to prevent my going in the boat, and caused me to ascend again into the ship, I should have left it behind. Little did I then think for what good Heaven meant to bestow on me, by the trouble they then gave me.

I soon fell into a road that seemed to lead the right way, and when during the night I perceived I was about to meet anyone, my constant plan was to retire to a small distance from the path, and roll myself up as well as I could to resemble a small bunch of bushes or fern. By this expedient I was often saved from recapture.

This road soon brought me into quite a populous village, which was resounding with drums and fifes, and full of soldiers, but in great mercy to me it rained in torrents, so I passed through in the midst of the street in safety. Here I would remark, once for all, that I was then so entirely unacquainted with the particular geography of Long Island that I could not name the places where the events of my narrative happened, nor shall I now attempt to do it. By an accurate map before me, it is possible I might decide what village this was, but I shall let it pass without a name. It would not have been any great mark of wisdom to have stopped when passing through it, and inquired of these fifers and drummers what was the name of the place!

Being sick and greatly exhausted by the adventures of the day and night, it now became absolutely necessary to seek a place of rest, and a barn to me was now the only place in which I dared to enter. I stepped up to the door of what I took to be such a building, and was just about to open it when my eye was arrested by a white streak on the threshold, which I found to be the light reflected from a candle, and I heard human voices within. But human voices were now to me the objects of the greatest terror, and I fled with all the speed I possessed.

Coming to another barn, I discovered a high stack of hay in the yard covered with a Dutch cap. I ascended and sunk myself down deep in the hay, supposing I had found a most comfortable retreat. But how miserably was I deceived! The weather had now cleared up, and the wind blew strong and cold from the northwest. The hay was nothing but coarse sedge, and the wind passed into it and reached me as if I had no protection from it. I had not a dry thread in my clothes, and my sufferings from this time to about eleven o'clock the next day were great—too great even for one in health—but I had to encounter them under the operation of a malignant fever, which would have confined me to my room, if not to my bed, had I been at home.

A young woman came into the yard and milked a cow, just at the foot of the tower where I lay concealed; but I had no eye to pity or kind hand to alleviate my distress. This brought home, with all the tender charities of mother, sister, and brothers, to my recollection, with a sensibility I could feel but cannot describe. The day was clear and grew more moderate, and the coast being clear also, I left my cold and wretched retreat and deliberately made off for the woods, at the distance of half a mile. However, before I descended I had seen prisoners who had escaped from the ship retaken and carried back, and I realized their mistake was, they would go two or more in company. But I would have no companion, as it would excite suspicion and render concealment more difficult, and under the kind Providence of God I chose to be my own counselor, and to have none to fall out with in the way, over what course we should pursue.

Having entered the woods, I found a small but deep dry hollow, clear of bush in the center, though surrounded with a thicket on every side. Into this the sun shone with a most delightful warmth. Here I stripped myself naked, and spread out my clothes to dry.

Being too impatient of delay, I regained the road just as the sun was setting, but this came near to proving fatal, for I discovered just ahead two light dragoons coming down upon me. At first it seemed escape was impossible, but that God who gave me a quickness of thought in expedients that seemed to go quite beyond myself was present with his kind aid.

I now happened to be near a small cottage and a cornfield adjoining the road. I feigned myself to be the man of that cottage, the owner of that cornfield, and getting over the fence, I went about the field deliberately picking up ears of corn that had fallen down, and righting up the cap sheaf of a stack of stalks. The dragoons came nigh, eyed me carefully, though I affected to take no notice of them, and passed on. They were probably in search of me.

I had lost my hat overboard, when in the old *Jersey,* and had thenceforward to cover my head with a handkerchief. I deemed it a calamity at the time, but as an act of Providence the mystery now began to be unfolded. Having no hat but a handkerchief about my head helped to deceive the dragoons, and cause them to think I was the cottager who owned that cornfield.

LETTER THREE

To LIE CONCEALED during the day and to travel at night was my practice, till I had got far towards the east end of the Island. For several days I had not taken any nourishment but water and apples. I found late pears and was pleased with their taste, but they operated as an emetic, quicker than ipecac. A subacid apple sat well on my stomach and was very refreshing, though had I been sick at home with the same disease I should have probably been denied this favor. Indeed, from what I experienced in the free use of water, ripe fruit, unfermented cider found at the presses, etc., I was led to suspect that a great deal of the kind nursing of persons in fever was an unnecessary and cruel kind of self-denial. But I supposed nature would sink without some other kind of aliment. My first attempt to act upon this principle would have proved fatal had it not been for a kind providential interference.

Late in the evening I stepped up to a house on the road and

lifted my hand to rap, but the door folded inward and evaded my stroke, and a lady appeared with a light in her hand. I besought of her a draught of milk. She replied "that there was then a guard of soldiers in the house, and they had consumed it all." The business of this guard was to keep a lookout towards Long Island Sound, and their sentries were on the opposite side of the house. Had I rapped and been met by one of this guard instead of the lady, what would have been the result? And by whose arrangement did the incident so happen that I escaped?

Pursuing my journey, I came to a place where the road parted. One branch turned off through a lofty grove of wood; the other ascended a gentle rise towards a house nearby. I knew not which to take, but that leading towards the house best suited my general course. On coming up near the house, there issued forth from the outbuildings a greater kennel of dogs than I had ever before seen, and assaulted me with a furious yelling. I stopped short, drew up my hands as far as I could out of their reach, and stood still. They snapped at me very spitefully with their jaws within a few inches of my body. And now what should I do? To have attacked them, or fled precipitately, would have been instant destruction. I concluded to take no notice of them, but to turn about gently and take the other road, as if there was no such creature in the world as a dog. I did so, and they followed me for about twenty rods, snapping at me, and seeming to say, "You shall not escape, we will have a taste of your blood." And in this design there seemed to be a perfect union, from the great bowwow down to the yelping spaniel. But at last they all ceased to roar, bid me good night, and disappeared; and I was not much grieved at the loss of their company and their music. It was a concert in which all the discords in the whole staff were put in requisition.

The next place where the reader will find me is a barn. And indeed, I never knew the full value of such a fabric till then. Who can sufficiently eulogize its utility? Were I a poet, its praises should not go unsung. In a feeling personification, I would hail thee as full of mercy to the brute creation, defending them from the stormy blasts and chilling frosts of winter. Nor would I stop here; for to how many wretched wandering human beings hast thou been a kind retreat? Denied even a hearth by hard-hearted avarice and proud unfeeling luxury, they had perished in the

highway had not thy hospitable doors been open for their reception. To thee, as the means of protection from floods of rain and
cold, I owe the preservation of my life.

Had I ventured into the habitations of men, instead of those of
the horned ox, my escape had been impossible. Soon after escaping
the fury of the dogs, in this peaceful abode I took up my lodgings
for the night. A man coming into it in the morning, I made bold
to slide down from the hay loft; and after making some apology
for trespassing upon his premises, I asked him if it was probable
I could get some refreshment in the house. He seemed to think I
could. I then entered the house and stated my wants; but as I did
not design to be a mean, dishonest beggar, first get what I wanted,
and then say I had nothing to pay, or sneak off and say nothing
about pay, I told the family I had but three coppers with me, so
that if they gave me meat or drink, it must be done merely on the
score of charity. The woman seemed to be thinking more about
providing something for the relief of a wretched sufferer, as I
must have appeared to her, than about money. But the old man
was troublesome with his questions. He said it was but a few days
ago two men called at his house and told a story which was found
to be all false; and at last he observed, outright, "I believe *thee*
also is a rogue." Now and then as he pressed hard upon me the
woman would check him and say, "Do let him alone." She had no
questions to ask. All she wanted was to feed me, and had it not
been for her, I know not what the crabbed old man would have
done with me.

And here, O woman, in gratitude to thy sex, let me, with the
famous Ledyard, remark that while I have found man too often
rough and cruel, when I have been a suffering stranger or have
been borne down with discouragement and sorrow at home, I
have seldom found thee otherwise than gentle, kind, and humane.

After I had taken my refreshment I said to the old man, "I
thank you for your kindness. Here are the three coppers, all I
have to carry me a long journey." He did not take them, but said,
"You may give them to that little girl." She took them, but if she
was illiberal and mean, the old man made her so.

I left the house and, going a short distance, a spacious plain
opened to view, and on it, by the tents I saw, I concluded there
was an encampment of soldiers. I therefore turned aside into the

field, ascended a stack of rye covered with a Dutch cap, and here
I remained all the day, it being very stormy; but in the evening I
looked out from my hiding place, and beheld a most lovely moon-
shine that had succeeded the storm. The tents had all disappeared, and I took up my journey over the plain.

Some time in the latter part of the night I reached the eastern
end, and saw before me a number of buildings, though before this
I had not seen any on the plain. But no sooner had I come up to
the first house than I was drawn into a scene of the utmost peril.
In the midst of the road there was a blacksmith's shop; on the
north side there was a lane forming a right angle with the road,
and leading up to a house about twelve rods from it. To the westward of the house, about eight rods distant, stood the barn, and
a lane leading from the house to it; and in the square, three sides
of which were formed by the road and these two lanes, was the
garden. In the corner of this garden near to the house I discovered
a number of beehives, and I coveted some of the honey. I went
first up to the house, and though the door was open, I saw no
light and heard no noise. But I deemed it prudent not to climb
over the fence just at the door of the house to get at the bees, but
to take the lane down to the barn, and there to get into the garden and come up under the cover of the fence to the bee-house.
This I did not then call stealing, for I was in an enemy's land and
might make prize of whatever I could lay my hand upon. (But this
opinion I now fear will not stand the test of the Day of Judgment.)

Having just stepped into the barnyard, and not suspecting the
least danger, I saw a great number of horses tied all round the
yard with their manes and docks cut in uniform. I stood motionless for a moment and began to say to myself, "What does this
mean? Can one farmer own so many horses?" But before the
thought was finished, and as unexpected as a flash of lightning in
a clear day, a dragoon coming out of the barn with his burnished
steel glittering in the bright rays of the moon stepped up to me
and challenged, "Who comes there?" I answered, "A friend." But
before he could say "A friend to whom?" I roared out as if I
were angry, "Where is the well? I want to get some water." Taking me from this seemingly honest and fearless query to be one of
the party, he showed me the well, and I went to it deliberately,

6. **BRITISH FRIGATES PENETRATE THE HUDSON AND DELAWARE RIVERS**

A. The Phoenix and the Rose Engaged by American
Fire Ships and Galleys, August 16, 1776
B. The Action off Mud Ford on the Delaware, Nov. 15, 1777

drew water, and escaped out of his hands. The fact was, as I soon found, this was a detachment of horse and foot going out on the Island for forage to be conveyed to the army at New York, and doubtless he supposed me to be some person, a wagoner perhaps, attached to it. And here again I found the great advantage of losing my hat. Having a handkerchief tied about my head helped on the deception.

The hand of Providence was here very striking in two things, in allowing the instantaneous invention of a plan of escape in such an unexpected emergency, and in taking from me every emotion of fear. I was naturally timid, yet there I knew not what fear was, but had the most perfect command of myself. A little hesitancy, a little faltering through fear, would have been fatal.

After leaving the well, I went down the lane into the road near to the blacksmith's shop. At this moment four of the party came out from behind the opposite side of the shop in full view, at the distance of about three rods from me. I stood motionless and said to myself, "All is now lost!"

But their attention was taken up with a small dog, with which they were sporting. As they did not come at once and seize me in the brightness of the moonlight, I began again to conceive hope, edged away to the fence, and rolled through between the two lower rails. Soon afterward the men said, "Let us go to the barn and turn in," and immediately disappeared. Their sporting with the dog in itself was a trifling circumstance, but to me it was a great event. It saved my life—in the hour of despair it brought me deliverance.

Stretched along as close as I could lie to the lower rail of the fence, I took a little time to survey my situation on all sides, and to discover, if I could, any opening for escape. If I attempted to save myself by going out into the open field, I must be discovered by the sentries and picked up by a dragoon. If I remained where I was, it would soon be daylight, and I could not be mistaken for one of the party. About thirty rods ahead I discovered a large house illuminated from the ground floor to the garret. This I was sure must be the main bivouac of both infantry and horse, and wagons were in numbers passing on to this house. At last I hit upon this plan. When another wagon should pass I would rise and lay hold of it behind, and let it carry me forward into the midst of the party, and they would suppose me to belong to it. The driver sitting under cover forward would not be able to see me. When the next wagon passed I attempted to get hold of it, but could not overtake it, and was left alone in the midst of the road and considerably advanced towards the house just mentioned as the general rendezvous. And now as no other mode of escape offered, I resolved to walk boldly and leisurely among the throng of men and horses, and wagons, and sentries, and pass away if I could. The plan succeeded. I passed fearlessly, with great deliberation, erect and firm, without any shyness, through the midst of them. Some eyed me carefully, yet no one said, "Who art thou?" I was soon out of sight and hid in a dense prim-bush fence, lest a suspicion should arise that a strange man had passed, and a dragoon should pursue me.

Twenty miles farther to the eastward I narrowly escaped falling again into the hands of this same party. Had I not without any knowledge or intention of my own happened to take another road, I should have met them in full march on their return, and it being in the daytime, escape would have been next to impossible. As it was, my road brought me on to the ground where the night before they had chosen to bivouac, and I found their fires still burning.

After leaving my hiding place in the prim fence, I soon found myself in a large orchard. In quest of fruit, I had examined nearly every tree and found none, but just as I was about to give up the search I lit upon a tree where the ground was covered with the fairest and the richest species of apple I ever tasted. They refreshed me as if they had been gathered from Paradise, for I had neither eaten nor drunk anything for a considerable time. How all the other fruit in the orchard should have been gathered in, and the produce of this uncommonly excellent tree left, struck me as a kind of mystery. It was no miracle, but it was a mercy to a wretched sufferer then burning up with fever and thirst. I now sought for and took up my lodgings in the birthplace of my Savior.

Prosecuting my journey on a succeeding evening, I happened to be opposite to a house standing a little out of the road. Before I was aware of the danger a dragoon met me and stopped so near, I could have put my hand on his holsters. "Now," thought I to myself, "I am taken." But what a blessed thing it was I had lost my hat. The old dirty handkerchief about my head saved me again. From this appearance, taking me to be the master of the house nearby, he said, "Have you any cider?" "No sir," was my reply, "but we expect to make some next week; call then and we shall be glad to treat you." This said, we each went his own way.

Commencing my journey at another time, early in the evening, I was accosted by a man of a stern appearance and address, standing on his doorstep. He wished to know whence I came and where I was bound. I told him I had just sailed out of New York, bound to Augustine in Florida, and was driven ashore by an American privateer, a little to the eastward of Sandy Hook, and was making my way down to Huntington, where I belonged. "What," says he, "you belong to an American privateer? I wonder you have not been taken up before." By this it seems he would have apprehended me had he known what I was. He was, no doubt, a Long Island Tory. But I replied, "Sir, you mistake me, I did not say I belonged or had belonged to an American privateer. I meant to say I belonged to an English vessel out of New York, and had been driven ashore by such a privateer." Then without further ceremony I passed on, and he did not attempt to stop me.

Now again I sought rest and concealment, as it grew late in the evening, and again I found it in a barn. I had by exposure contracted a violent cough, and could not suppress it, though deep sunk in a haymow. The owner coming into the barn in the morning heard me, but he offered me no disturbance, and I hoped it would have been my peaceful retreat for the whole day. Some time after the man who visited the barn had left, a number of children came up, placed their hands against the door, and gave it a violent shaking, crying out at the same time, "Come out, you runaway, you thief, you robber," and then retreated with great precipitation. But I did not remove out of my bed, hoping they might not give me another such honorable salute. It was not long before they appeared again, and cried out, "Come out, you old rogue, you runaway, you thief. We know you are here, for Daddy heard you cough," and then retreated as before. And I retreated also, fearing some older children might honor me with a visit and find out in very deed that I was a runaway.

After I had experienced so many narrow escapes and had now

passed, as I supposed and as proved to be the fact, beyond all further danger from foraging parties, scouts, and patrols of a military character—and though the fever was still upon me, yet it seemed rather to abate than to be aggravated by all the exposure, cold, storms, fatigues, fears, anxieties, and privations I endured—I inferred with great confidence that it was the design of Almighty God that I should yet again see home. Entering a wood where no human eye could see me, I fell upon my knees, and looking up to heaven, I attributed to him all my deliverances, and all the understanding, assistance, and strength by which I had been sustained; and besought the continuance of his mercy to extricate me from all remaining danger and sufferings, and to complete my deliverance. I arose, and now went forward more than ever under a sense of the Divine goodness and protection.

LETTER FOUR

I COME NOW to a day in which various and interesting incidents occurred. By this time I ventured to travel in open daylight, and no longer to ask protection from the sable hours of an absent sun. Commencing my journey early in the morning, I came to a large and respectable dwelling house, and thinking it time to seek something to nourish my feeble frame (for appetite I had scarcely any) I entered. Neatness, wealth, and plenty seemed to reside there. Among the inmates a decent woman, who appeared to be the mistress of the family, and a tailor, who was mounted upon a large table and plying his occupation, were all that attracted my notice. To the lady I expressed my wants, telling her at the same time, which was my invariable practice, if she could impart to me a morsel, it must be a mere act of charity. For poverty was a companion of which I could not rid myself. She made no objections, asked no questions, but promptly furnished me with the dish of light food I desired. Expressing my obligations to her, I rose to depart. But going round through another room, she met me in the front entry, placed a hat on my head, put an apple pie in my hand, and said, "You will want this before you get through the woods." I opened my mouth to give vent to the grateful feelings with which my heart was filled. But she would not tarry to hear a word, and instantly vanished out of my sight. The mystery of her conduct, as I suppose, was this. The woman, her family, and her property were under British government. She was, doubtless, well satisfied that I was a prisoner escaping from the hands of the English, and if she granted me any protection or succor, knowing me to be such, it might cost the family the confiscation of all their estate. She did not, therefore, wish to ask me any questions, or hear me explain who I was, within hearing of that tailor. He might turn out to be a dangerous informer. I then departed, but this mark of kindness was more than I could well bear, and as I went on for some rods, the tears flowed copiously. What a melting power there is in human kindness! The recollection of her humanity and pity revives in my breast even now the same feeling of gratitude towards her. Oh, how true are Solomon's words, "A man that hath friends must show himself friendly."

Indeed, there were but two things that could thus dissolve me in my greatest sufferings and dangers, and these were an act of real kindness and compassion from a stranger, and the thought of the pungent grief my misfortunes must occasion to the kindest of mothers. As to my father, his paternal affection and care had been long sleeping in the grave.

By and by I began to recollect and consider what the lady meant by the woods. I supposed it possible there might be a forest, four or five miles in length, through which I must pass; of the real fact I had not the least anticipation. But very soon I came to the woods, and found a narrow road of deep loose sand leading through them. The bushes on both sides grew hard up to the wagon ruts, and there was not a step of a sidewalk of more solid ground. The traveling was hence very laborious, but I pressed on with what strength I had, and after a few miles supposed I was nearly through the wilderness, and began to look ahead for cleared land and human dwellings; but none appeared. After I had with great labor and almost insupportable distress traveled a distance I deemed at least nine miles, I met two men pressing in a direction opposite to my own. They seemed to be in a hurry, and anxious to know how far I had come in these woods.

"About nine miles," said I. "How far have you come in them?"

They replied, "About the same distance," and immediately pushed forward, asking me no other question.

Then said I to myself, "Here I make my grave; farewell,

thoughts of home and all earthly expectations; here I must lie down and die!" My feet were swelled so that the tumefaction hung over the tops of my shoes for three-fourths of an inch, and I was about to seek out a favorable spot to lie down and rise no more. But at this instant something seemed to whisper to me, "Will it not be just as well, if you must die, to die standing up and walking?" I could not say no, and resolved to walk on till I fell down dead. And this whisper has been of great service to me in after life, when I have been ready to sink in discouragement under difficulties and troubles, or opposition and persecution. For I have since found that the old *Jersey* was not the only abode of inhumanity and woe; but the whole world is but one great prisonhouse of guilty, sorrowful, and dying men who live in pride, envy, and malice, "hateful and hating one another."

When I say, "I have been ready to sink under such trials," I have recollected these woods and said, "Will it not be as well to die standing up as lying down?" And thus I have taken courage and gone forward, and the result has been as auspicious. For such was the goodness of God that I was carried through this Long Island wilderness, and a little before sunset I discovered, as it were, land at no great distance.

The first house I came to at the east end of these woods, I entered in quest of humanity and pity. But these virtues appeared not to be at home there. Everything without and within denoted a situation happily above penury, or the trials, vexations, and griefs of poverty. A degree of elegance and neatness appeared. In the kitchen I discovered a number of fish just touched with salt and hung up and dried. My feverish appetite fixed on a piece of one of these fish, as a rasher that might taste well. I besought the lady of the house to give me a very small bit, but my request was not granted. I repeated it again and again. But her denial was irrevocable. Now, thought I, I will try an experiment, and measure the hardness of your heart. So I stated to her my sickly, destitute condition, told her she might judge by my appearance that I was overwhelmed by misfortune and had been very unsuccessful at sea. I wished her to consider how she would be delighted had she a brother, or dear friend, suffering in a strange land, if anyone should stretch out to him the hand of relief, minister to his necessities, wipe away his tears, and console his heart. Indeed,

I suggested every thought and plea of which I was master, that could move a heart not made of steel. And what was it all for? For a piece of dried bluefish not more than two inches square! And did I succeed? No. All my entreaties were vain. So without murmuring or casting on her any reflection I took my leave.

Here, O woman, thou didst for once forget thyself, and forfeit thy character for humanity and pity. After I was gone, I presume thou didst reflect upon thine own insensibility, and reproach thyself, and I most cheerfully forgive thee.

Passing on but a few rods, I entered another human dwelling, and what renders the circumstance that took place the more to be noticed is, it appeared to be a tavern. I expressed my wants to a lady who I had no doubt was the mistress of the house. By the cheerfulness and good nature depicted in her countenance and her first movements, I knew my suit was granted, and I had nothing more to say than to apprise her that I was penniless, and that if she afforded me any relief she must do it hoping for nothing again. Now, behold the contrast! In a few moments she placed on the table a bowl of bread and milk, the whole of one of those fish, roasted, that I had begged for in vain at the other house, and a mug of cider. And, says she, "Sit down and eat." But her mercy came near to cruelty, in its consequences; for although I was aware of the danger, yet I indulged too freely. My fever was soon enraged to violence, and I was filled with alarm.

It was now growing dark and I went but a short distance farther, entered another house, and begged the privilege of lodging by the fire. My request was granted, and I sat down in silence, too sick and distressed to do or say anything. But I could see and hear. There was no one in the house but the man and his wife. They appeared to be plain, openhearted, honest people, who never had their minds elated with pride, nor their taste perverted by false refinement, or that education which just unfits persons to be useful and happy in the common walks of life. They possessed good common sense, which is the best kind of sense. Everything within indicated economy and neatness, order and competence. But what was better than all this, they appeared to be cordial friends to each other. It was indeed one of the few happy matches.

Nor was this all, for I soon perceived they were united by still

higher principles than mere conjugal affection—it was evident
that the fear of God had taken up residence there. Before it became late in the evening the man took his Bible and read a chapter, and that with a tone and air that induced me to think he believed it. He then arose and devoutly offered up his grateful
acknowledgments and supplications to God, through the Media-
tor. By this time I began to think I had got into a safe as well as
a hospitable retreat. They had before made many inquiries, not
impertinent and captious, but such as indicated they felt tenderly
and took an interest in my welfare; but they evidently obtained
no satisfaction from my answers, for I was too weary and distressed to take pains to form or relate anything like a consistent
story. And I was the less careful to do it from my supposed safety,
founded on their evident fear of God and kind feelings. They
seemed as if they could not rest till they had drawn from me the
real truth, though they gave not the least hint that might reproach
me for the want of truth and honesty. At last I resolved I would
treat them so no longer. I would throw off the mask, risk all consequences, and let them into the real secret of my condition.

Accordingly I said, "You have asked me many questions this
evening, and I have told you nothing but falsehoods. Now hear
the truth. I am a prisoner, making my escape from the old *Jersey*,
at New York. Of the horrors of this dreadful prison you may
have been informed. There, after many sufferings, I was brought
to have no prospect before me but certain death. But by a remarkable and unexpected interposition of Providence I got on
shore, and having had many hairbreadth escapes, I have reached
this place, and am now lodged under your hospitable roof. I am
loaded with disease, and am in torment from the thousands of
vermin which are now devouring my flesh. I have dear and kind
friends in Connecticut, and I am now aiming to regain my native
home. The kindest of mothers is now probably weeping for me as
having, ere this, perished in my captivity, never more expecting
to see her child. Thus I have told you the real truth. I have put
my life in your hands. Go and inform against me and I shall be
taken back to the prisonship, and death will be inevitable."

I ceased to speak, and all was profound silence. It took some
time to recover themselves from a flood of tears in which they
were bathed. At last the kind and amiable woman said, "Let us

go and bake his clothes." No sooner said than the man seized a brand of fire and threw it into the oven. The woman provided a clean suit of clothes to supply the place of mine till they were purified by fire. The work done, a clean bed was laid down, on which I was to rest, and rest I did as in a new world; for I had got rid of a swarm of cannibals, who were without mercy eating me up alive!

And what think you were my views and impressions in regard to what had here passed? Never before or since have I seen a more just, practical comment on that religion which many profess but few properly exemplify: "I was anhungered and ye gave me meat; a stranger, and ye took me in; sick, and ye visited me." With wonder and gratitude these words chimed in my very soul. Well might I have said, O Jesus, is this the religion thou hast given to the human family? If it universally prevailed, the woes of man would be relieved, and heaven would come down to earth. This happy couple who are now, in all probability, called away by their gracious Redeemer to fill a mansion in the skies, and are now rejoicing before the throne of him whom they supremely loved, appeared to enjoy a rich reward in the mercy they had shown to a wretched stranger. It was all they asked. It was all performed with such cheerfulness, such tenderness, simplicity, and ease, as must have compelled even the infidel to admire the beauty of true Christianity.

In the morning I took my leave of this dear family, who had enchanted and riveted my soul to them by their kindness, in an esteem and gratitude which have for fifty years suffered no abatement. I learned of them a lesson of humanity I have ever remembered and ever wished to imitate.

The day was clear, and after traveling a short distance I threw myself down on the sunny side of a stunted pitch pine, upon a bed of warm sand. And what a deliverance did I now find I had experienced! My body was no longer food for millions. I rested as on a bed of down.

*   *   *   *

Some time in the latter part of October, 1781, I arrived at home. And near the close of winter I so far regained my health, through the great kindness of the God of love, as to engage in the instruction of a school, in the town where I resided. And since that period almost my whole life has been devoted to the instruction of youth, and preaching the everlasting Gospel. And whether my life has been in any degree useful, or whether it would have been (as to the glory of God and the good of mankind) as well that I should have made my grave in the old *Jersey*, will doubtless be made manifest in the last day. Of one thing I am certain—that it becomes me to say to the God of unchanging love, in review of the whole history of my life,

> "Thy thoughts of love to me surmount,
> The power of numbers to recount."

THE LOYALISTS

Throughout the course of the Revolution one unhappy group of Americans played a difficult role. Some were sincere adherents to the established government, some were timorous citizens fearful of rebellion, who remained loyal to the King. They suffered the hatred of their brethren and the disdain which British gentlemen displayed toward colonials. During the war they were visited by Whig committees, jailed or paroled, restricted in their movements, often forced into exile, to Canada, Jamaica, or England, and stripped of their possessions. The defeat of the British sealed the loss of their homes, and those who sought restitution under the provisions of the peace treaty found little sympathy from hostile courts in the United States.

Although the Tory following embraced many of the well-to-do, Anglican ministers and Crown officials and large landowners, Tory activities fell far below the energy of the patriots. The Whigs organized their committees, convened their Continental Congress, enacted their "test laws" to coerce the sideliners into the open, while the Tories chiefly harangued in the coffeehouses and poured forth billingsgate in their newspapers. Relying confidently on the armed power of their sovereign, they drifted in the wake of the British army, gathering first in Boston when Gage arrived in 1774, then in New York after Howe occupied it in 1776, again in Philadelphia when Howe made his sortie there in 1777, and to Cornwallis's banner in the South in 1780 and 1781. New York, the state with the largest Loyalist element, remained the Tory stronghold from the Battle of Long Island in August, 1776, until the last forlorn ships carried the expatriates off to Nova Scotia in 1783.

In various ways the Tories served the cause of George III more effectively than by entertaining his officers with balls and banquets. Loyalist militia companies in New York, New Jersey, and Pennsylvania made forays on patriot farms; thousands of Loyalists enlisted in the British army; individual Loyalists scouted and spied on the Continental troops. Most of these raiding parties presented only a limited nuisance to the Continental Army, but they served to hold the rebel militia at home, and sometimes in-

tercepted the mails and captured small detachments of regulars.
Because of the British contempt for colonial militia, rebel or
Tory, little effort was made by Howe, Clinton, and Cornwallis
to utilize their services in any systematic fashion.

Two types of Loyalists are represented in the selections given
here. Nicholas Cresswell, a young Englishman who spent only
three harassed years on American shores, typifies the Tory born
abroad (who constituted two-thirds of the Loyalists claiming
damages in 1783) and never thoroughly Americanized. Cresswell
is an extreme case, since he came over just the year before fighting began, but his reactions to the war news and his distresses
in living as a known Tory in Virginia and Maryland give us a
first-rate picture of the civilian Loyalist during the Revolution.
No man of any means or standing could escape declaring his
sentiments, and no supporter of the King could avoid the sur-
veillance of his neighbors and the badgering of committees. Poor
Nicholas took to drink when the rebel position improved. Eventually he made his way to New York where he saw the aftereffects
of the rebel withdrawal, and witnessed a spirited action in Long
Island. In 1777 he luckily obtained a return passage to England,
and spent the remainder of his days on the family estate, in a
much more fortunate condition than the majority of dispossessed
Tories.

On the other hand James Moody belongs to the native-born
Americans who fought actively for the King. A comfortable New
Jersey farmer, he remained outside the pale of war in its first
years until his Whig neighbors began molesting his property and
assaulting his person. With the removal of Howe from Boston
to New York and the establishment of the British in lower New
York following the Battle of Long Island, the war took on
immediacy for him, and Moody developed into a talented spy
and petty raider. His most ambitious schemes—for abducting
the patriot governor of New Jersey and for seizing the entire
Continental Congress—never materialized, but in July, 1780, he
executed a successful coup with the capture of eighteen Whig
committeemen and militia officers. In the resulting state-wide
search for Moody he was captured and thrust into prison, whence
he effected a dramatic escape. Exhausted by his escapades, and
impoverished by the confiscation of his lands, Moody sailed for

England in 1782 to present his claims at Court. These meeting with success, he removed to Nova Scotia for the remainder of his life. In Moody one sees the same dash and determination that characterized the most ardent patriots. Yet his activities in spying on Washington's movements and nipping at his communications and supplies during the years that Washington lay outside New York made small impact on history. There were too few Moodys to overcome the weak liaison among Tories scattered throughout the thirteen colonies, or between the Tories and the British. Those Americans who for self-interest or for principle maintained allegiance to their King during the years of rebellion found little reward for their loyalty in their own or in later generations.

Nicholas Cresswell

Restless young Nicholas Cresswell (1750-1784) decided to leave his sheep-raising duties on his father's estate at Crowden-le-Booth, Edale, in north England, for a taste of American life. He landed in Virginia in May, 1774, took a trip down the Ohio River from February to July, 1775, moped about in Alexandria for the better part of a year, visited New York in September, 1776, in a vain effort to join the British army, returned to Virginia, and finally, in May 1777, managed to secure passage back to England. His father put him to work the day after he returned. Poor hapless Nicholas arrived in America just in time to be badgered by committees of safety, and to his journal he confided his sorrows at being miserably trapped in Virginia and Maryland in the midst of patriots. His sketches reveal the bachelor life of an irresponsible young Englishman of the landed middle class, and cover in amusing fashion a variety of experiences, from tavern bouts to his Western trip down the Ohio with an ill-assorted crew. Cresswell's descendants treasured the silver-mounted bison horn, Indian headdress, snowshoes, and tomahawk he brought back from America, as well as the manuscript journal which eventually saw print a century and a half later.

The Journal of Nicholas Cresswell 1774-1777 was published by Lincoln MacVeagh, The Dial Press, New York, 1924, with a prefatory note by Samuel Thornely and a portrait, and was reprinted in 1928 with an introduction by A. G. Bradley. The following selections are edited from the 1928 edition, pp. 104-106, 173-176, 179-181, 234-236, 240-242, 243-245.

INDIAN HOSPITALITY

Saturday, August 26, 1775. Set out early this morning, traveled very hard till noon, when we passed through the largest plum-tree thicket I ever saw. I believe it was a mile long, nothing but the plum and cherry trees. Killed a rattlesnake. Just as the sun went down we stopped to get our supper on some dewberries (a small berry something like a gooseberry). Mr. Anderson had gone before me and said he would ride on about two miles to a small run where he intended to camp, as soon as I had got sufficient. I mounted my horse and followed him till I came to a place where the road forked. I took the path that I supposed he had gone and

7. NICHOLAS CRESSWELL

rode till it began to be dark, when I imagined myself to be wrong, and there was not a possibility of my finding my way back in the night. Determined to stay where I was till morning, I had no sooner alighted from my horse, but I discovered the glimmering of a fire about four hundred yards from me. This rejoiced me exceedingly, supposing it was Mr. Anderson. When I got there, to my great disappointment and surprise found three Indian women and a little boy. I believe they were as much surprised as I was. None of them could speak English and I could not speak Indian. I alighted, and marked the path I had come and that I had left on the ground with the end of my stick, made a small channel in the earth which I poured full of water, laid some fire by the side of it, and then laid myself down by the side of the fire, repeating the name of Anderson which I soon understood they knew.

The youngest girl immediately unsaddled my horse, unstrapped the belt, hobbled him, and turned him out, then spread my blankets at the fire and made signs for me to sit down. The oldest made me a little hash of dried venison and bear's oil, which eat very well, but neither bread nor salt. After supper they made signs I must go to sleep. Then they held a consultation for some time which made me very uneasy, after which the two eldest women and the boy laid down on the opposite side of the fire and some distance away. The youngest (she had taken so much pains with my horse) came and placed herself very near me. I began to think she had some amorous design upon me. In about half an hour she began to creep nearer me and pulled my blanket. I found what she wanted and lifted it up. She immediately came to me and made me as happy as it was in her power to do. She was young, handsome, and healthy. Fine regular features and fine eyes, had she not painted them with red before she came to bed—and I suppose answers as well as My Lady in the dark.

Sunday, August 27, 1775. This morning my bedfellow went into the woods and caught her horse and mine, saddled them, put my blanket on the saddle, and prepared everything ready, seemingly with a great deal of good nature. Absolutely refused my assistance. The old woman got me some dried venison for breakfast. When I took my leave returned the thanks as well as I could by signs. My bedfellow was my guide and conducted me through the woods, where there were no signs of a road and without my knowing with certainty whither I was going. She often mentioned John Anderson and talked a great deal in Indian. I attempted to speak Indian, which diverted her exceedingly. In about an hour she brought me to Mr. Anderson's camp, who had been very uneasy at my absence and employed an Indian to seek me. I gave my Dulcinea a matchcoat, with which she seemed very well pleased.

DEBAUCHERY

Alexandria, Virginia—Friday, November 29, 1776. Very sick with my last night's debauch, and very sorry for my last night's conduct. My present disagreeable confinement, the loss of three years of the most valuable part of life, the disappointments and misfortunes I have met with since I left my native country, and what is worst of all, the certainty of being reproached with obstinacy and extravagancy on my return—these bitter reflections will intrude themselves involuntarily, and create a lowness of spirit which too often is the cause of me drinking more than is of service. I must and will call my resolution and fortitude to my aid, or I shall insensibly sink into the sot or the drunkard. A character so despicable ought to be avoided with the greatest care. Mr. Kirk and I made up the quarrel this morning. Must not quarrel with him. He confesses that he did everything in his power to intoxicate me, on purpose to raise my spirits. I will not borrow my spirits in that manner for the future. Left Leesburg. Dined at Moss's Ordinary. Got to Alexandria. Spent the evening with Mr. McCrey.

Saturday, November 30, 1776. This morning went to Mrs. Hawkins, expecting to get paid for my coat, supposing that she was not informed that I was forbid to depart the colony, but the d—d jade tells me that I am a Tory and she won't pay me a farthing. This is provoking, but I cannot help myself. Spent the evening with Mr. McCrey.

Leesburg, Loudoun County, Virginia—Sunday December 1, 1776. Left Alexandria. Dined at Moss's. Got to Leesburg at night. News that the English have taken Fort Washington and twenty-five hundred prisoners in it. This is the strongest fortification they had; it is on the north end of New York Island. They have long boasted that all the forces belonging to Great Britain could not take it. What is it that Englishmen cannot do whenever they choose to exert themselves? It is said they have deserted Fort Lee. If this be true I hope the rascals will soon be humbled.

Monday, December 2, 1776. Troubled with the rheumatism in my arms.

Tuesday, December 3, 1776. Abundance of political puffs and lies told to amuse the public. It is a matter of dispute with me whether the Whigs or Tories are the greatest propagators of falsehood.

Wednesday, December 4, 1776. A Dutch mob of about forty horsemen went through the town today on their way to Alexandria to search for salt. If they find any they will take it by force. All of them armed with swords or large clubs. This article is exceedingly scarce; if none comes in the people will revolt. They cannot possibly subsist without a considerable quantity of this article. The people in general live on salt meat in the summer. The excessive heat renders the keeping of fresh meat very difficult, even for one day, and the thinness of inhabitants and markets prevents them killing little else but young hogs and fowls. They likewise give salt to their horses, cattle, hogs, and sheep almost every day in the summer. The cattle are exceedingly fond of it, so much that they will follow you anywhere for a lick of it and it is so essentially necessary that they will not thrive without it.

Thursday, December 5, 1776. Exceedingly unhappy; was it not for the company of a few friends I should be completely miserable.

Friday, December 6, 1776. This day the Dutchmen returned from Alexandria without doing the least mischief; the poor wretches have got about three pints of salt per man. They are told that there will be plenty in a little time. But I hope His Majesty's ships will prevent it coming into the Bay. Spent the evening at Mr. Kirk's in company with Captain McCabe and Mr. George West. T. K. had a scuffle with McCabe. It is true they were both in liquor, but whether Mr. Kirk's anger was bent against Mr. McCabe or not, is a mystery to me. I kept perfectly sober and left them as soon as I could.

Saturday, December 7, 1776. Mr. Kirk is very uneasy concerning his conduct last night. Sobriety is a noble virtue.

Sunday, December 8, 1776. News by private letters (the public papers are stopped) that General Howe was at Woodbridge in the Jerseys. God send him a safe and speedy arrival in Philadelphia. It is said the Sleber* are flying before him.

Monday, December 9, 1776. This morning I was remarkably low-spirited. About three o'clock in the afternoon Mr. Hugh Neilson came and insisted on my spending the evening at The Billet. I have spent it with a vengeance with Flemming, Patterson, Cleone More, Captain Wm. Johnston and H. Neilson. Sent them all to bed drunk and I am now going to bed myself at nine in the morning as drunk as an honest man could wish.

Tuesday, December 10, 1776. Got up at two in the afternoon. Got drunk before ten with the same company I was with yesterday and am now going to bed at two in the morning, most princely drunk indeed. I saw all my companions in bed before I left them, but most damnable drunk. A fine course of life truly, drunk every night, this is tampering with the Devil to it.

Wednesday, December 11, 1776. Much indisposed this morning. I hear my pet companions and brothers in iniquity coming upstairs, but am determined to keep sober today.

Thursday, December 12, 1776. Last night was the worst we have had since we first commenced the trade of drunkards. Mr. Kirk and P. Cavan joined us. We instituted a foolish society by the name of the Black-Eyed Club. I was President and Mr. More Secretary. All of us got most intolerably drunk. This is the first day that I have had any time for reflection this week. Uneasiness of mind first engaged me in this last debauch. Good company induced me to continue it, and now a bitter reflection, an aching head, a sick stomach, a trembling hand, and a number of disagreeable concomitants that are annexed to this detestable vice cause me to quit the pursuit. Drunkenness is certainly one of the most odious vices that mankind can possibly be guilty of, the consequences are so exceedingly pernicious to our health, our hap-

* Cresswell's code for Rebels.

piness and interest. It is astonishing that any being endowed with the faculty of thinking should take such pains to divest himself of reason, that knowingly and willingly he will destroy his constitution and sink himself below the level of a brute. Mr. Kirk came and spent the evening at my lodgings.

Saturday, December 14, 1776. News that General Howe is at Trenton in the Jerseys, from Philadelphia. It is certain the Congress has left Philadelphia and are now at Baltimore. Great numbers of recruiting parties are out to raise men, but can scarcely get a man by any means, though their bounty is twelve pounds. None will enlist that can avoid it. They get some servants and convicts which are purchased from their masters; these will desert the first opportunity. The violent Slebers are much dispirited. The politicians (or rather timid Whigs) give all up for lost. And the Tories begin to exult. The time is out that the Flying Camp was enlisted for, and it is said that they refuse to serve any longer, though they have been solicited in the strongest terms. This will make a great deficiency in their army, the loss of ten thousand men. I am convinced that if General Howe will push to Philadelphia the day is his own. Find it will be best for me to remove out of town for a little while or I may stand a chance of going to jail as I am too often abusing these rascals. Am determined to go into Berkeley.

Sunday, December 15, 1776. Dined with Mr. Kirk. After dinner went to Mr. Neilson's.

Monday, December 16, 1776. Left Mr. Wm. Neilson's in company with Mr. Hugh Neilson, who lent me a horse. Crossed the Shenandoah River and got to Mr. Francis Willis. Spent the evening with Mr. John Cook, Captain Throgmorton, and Doctor Armstrong, son of General Armstrong. All violent Slebers, but a little discouraged.

THE TIDE TURNS

Monday, January 6, 1777. News that Washington had taken 760 Hessian prisoners at Trenton in the Jerseys. Hope it is a lie. This afternoon hear he has likewise taken six pieces of brass cannon.

8. THE BRITISH INVADING NEW YORK AND NEW JERSEY
TO SURPRISE FORT LEE, 1776

A. Cornwallis Landing Troops in New Jersey, Nov. 20
B. The Attack on Fort Washington outside New York City, Nov. 16

Tuesday, January 7, 1777. The news is confirmed. The minds of the people are much altered. A few days ago they had given up the cause for lost. Their late successes have turned the scale and now they are all liberty-mad again. Their recruiting parties could not get a man (except he bought him from his master) no longer since than last week, and now the men are coming in by companies. Confound the turncoat scoundrels and the cowardly Hessians together. This has given them new spirits, got them fresh succors, and will prolong the war, perhaps for two years. They have recovered their panic and it will not be an easy matter to throw them into that confusion again. Volunteer companies are collecting in every county on the continent and in a few months the rascals will be stronger than ever. Even the parsons, some of them, have turned out as volunteers and pulpit drums or thunder, which you please to call it, summoning all to arms in this cursed babble. D— them all.

Wednesday, January 8, 1777. This is a most unhappy country. Every necessary of life is at an extravagant price, some of them indeed not to be had for money. Poor people are almost naked. Congress or Committee of Safety or some of those infernal bodies have issued an order that everyone that is fortunate enough to be possessed of two coats is to give one to their naked soldiers. Grain now begins to bear a good price, owing to such great quantities being distilled and the small proportion that is in the ground. I am persuaded there will be a famine very soon as well as a War.

Saturday, January 11, 1777. Very cold weather for three days. Almost stupid for want of employment.

Sunday, January 12, 1777. News that the Slebers' ships had taken thirty thousand suits of clothes that were intended to clothe our Army for the winter. Believe it is a lie. However, it serves the rascals' purpose to entice the people to enlist.

Tuesday, January 14, 1777. News that Washington had entirely routed our army and the few that had escaped had been obliged to take refuge on board the ships. This must certainly be a lie.

Wednesday, January 15, 1777. I am exceedingly kindly treated here, and am very happy in the company of Mr. Neilson, but the thought of receiving such unmerited kindness from an entire stranger, whom in all probability it will never be in my power to repay, makes me uneasy.

Thursday, January 16, 1777. Intend to go to Leesburg tomorrow. I am unhappy everywhere. The late news has increased my anxiety to be at home that I may have an opportunity to be revenged of these miscreants.

Leesburg, Loudoun County, Virginia—Friday, January 17, 1777. Left Mr. Neilson's. Got to Leesburg to my old lodgings. Dined and spent the evening at Mr. Kirk's, who begs me to make him the model of a machine for driving piles into the river to build wharfs upon. Their late successes have made him believe that they will have a free and open trade to all parts of the world very soon. Such is the instability of human affairs. Six weeks ago this gentleman was lamenting the unhappy situation of the Americans and pitying the wretched condition of their much-loved General, supposing his want of skill and experience in military matters has brought them all to the brink of destruction. In short, all was gone, all was lost. But now the scale is turned and Washington's name is extolled to the clouds. Alexander, Pompey, and Hannibal were but pygmy Generals, in comparison with the magnanimous Washington. Poor General Howe is ridiculed in all companies and all my countrymen abused. I am obliged to hear this daily and dare not speak a word in their favor. It is the damned Hessians that has caused this, curse the scoundrel that first thought of sending them here.

A SOLDIER'S WIDOW IN TRAVAIL

Tuesday, June 17, 1777. Dined with Mr. Furneval on board the *Bell and Mary*. Furneval and I went ashore and spent the evening at the Hull Tavern. In our return to the boat, coming by some houses that were burnt down, we heard the cries of a woman. We searched about and soon, to our great surprise, found a poor woman in labor, and all alone. She told us she was a soldier's widow and begged we would help her to some assistance. We immediately carried her to the house of a saddler in the Broadway, whom we raised from his pillow and told him the poor woman's situation. But he absolutely refused to let her stay in his house, declaring that he would not keep a lying-in hospital for our w——s. However, with threats, promises, and the poor woman declaring that it was impossible for her to be removed, he at length consented that she might lay in a back shop he had. We immediately removed her thither and made her a very poor bed of a bearskin, a pack sheet, and an old blanket. Furneval went with a Negro boy to see for a midwife, while I stayed with the woman, for fear of the saddler turning her out of doors. The poor woman cried out lustily and I was confoundedly afraid of the young one coming before the midwife arrived. The Irish rogue of a saddler nor the unfeeling jade his wife would not come near us, or offer the poor creature the least assistance, though she begged for help in the most pitiful tone I ever heard. I was much afraid that I must have been under the disagreeable necessity of trying my skill in the obstetric way, but in the critical minute Furneval arrived with an old drunken woman he had picked up somewhere or other. She refused to perform the office without we would give her two dollars. Furneval gave her one and I another. She immediately fell to work. I am sure the pains of labor must be violent for the poor woman roared out most horridly. I think I hear the sound yet in my ears. However, in about ten minutes she produced a girl, which was wrapped in the mother's apron, with the addition of Furneval's handkerchief and mine, for she had not one single rag prepared for the occasion. We then got some wine, rum, nutmeg bread, etc., to the amount of two dollars more, and got the good wife a caudle,* which she took without much invitation. In about half an hour she was able to sit up in her miserable bed and returned us her thanks for saving her life, as she said in the most sincere and moving manner. The d——d unnatural b——h of a saddler's wife never came near us all the time, but lay in bed cursing the poor woman with the most horrid imprecations. About twelve o'clock we left her in good spirits considering her situation. When we came away I gave her one dollar and a quarter which is the last and all I have in the world.

The poor woman is heartily welcome to it and I am happy that I had it in my power to relieve such real distress. Furneval gave her two dollars and swears he will stand godfather to the child.

* A warm drink for sick persons.

I have no intention of doing myself that honor, am in hopes it will be dead before morning. We promised to go and see her in the morning, and make her case known to some of the officers. I hope the drunken jade of a midwife don't rob her before morning; I don't like her looks. Captain Park is very merry at our adventure and declares he will be at the christening. He says we must keep the child between us, which part of the ceremony I don't like. This is the first birth I have ever been concerned with, and I hope it will be the last time I shall meet with such a complication of distress. She told us a long story about her virtue and sufferings, but she is an Irishwoman and I don't believe half of it.

I am confoundedly tired with scribbling about the Girl in the Straw, therefore will give over.

A SKIRMISH

Staten Island—Sunday, June 22, 1777. Last night I had most uncomfortable lodgings along with Colonel Reid upon a tent only spread upon the ground in which we wrapped ourselves. Almost bit to death with mosquitoes and poisoned with the stink of some rebels, who have been buried about three weeks in such a slight manner that wagons have cut up parts of the half-corrupted carcasses and made them stink most horribly. By five o'clock this morning all the tents were struck and the army ready to march.

About 8 A.M. the main body of the army came up. At that instant some of the rebels' scouting parties fired upon our sentinels, which brought on a smart skirmish. I happened to see them in the bushes before they fired, but mistook them for some of our rangers. They were about three hundred yards from me. When the engagement began I got upon a little hillock to see the better, but an honest Highlander advised me to retire into a small breastwork just by, without I had a mind to stick up myself as a mark for the rebels to shoot at. I thought proper to take his advice and retired to the place he directed me to, where I had a very good view of their proceedings. I observed a party of our men going through a rye field, I suppose with an intent to get into the rear of the rebels and by that means surround them, but they were met as soon as they got out of the field by about the same number of the rebels. When they were about a hundred yards from each other both parties fired, but I did not observe any fall. They still advanced to the distance of forty yards or less, and fired again; I then saw a good number fall on both sides. Our people then rushed upon them with their bayonets and the others took to their heels. I heard one of them call out "Murder" lustily. This is laughable if the consequence was not serious. A fresh party immediately fired upon our people, but were dispersed and pursued into the woods by a company of the Fifteenth Regiment. A brisk fire then began from six fieldpieces the rebels had secreted in the woods, which did some mischief to our men. The engagement lasted about thirty-five minutes. Our people took the fieldpieces, about 40 prisoners, and killed about 150 of the scoundrels with the loss of 39 killed and 27 wounded.

I went to the place where I saw the two parties fire upon each other first, before the wounded were removed, but I never before saw such a shocking scene: some dead, others dying, death in different shapes; some of the wounded making the most pitiful lamentations, others that were of different parties cursing each other as the author of their misfortunes. One old veteran I observed (that was shot through both legs and not able to walk) very coolly and deliberately loading his piece and cleaning it from blood. I was surprised at the sight and asked him his reasons for it. He, with a look of contempt, said, "To be ready in case any of the Yankees come that way again."

About ten o'clock the whole army was in motion. It is said our army burnt Brunswick when they left, others contradict the report and say it was left without damage, but all the county's houses were in flames as far as we could see. The soldiers are so much enraged they will set them on fire, in spite of all the officers can do to prevent it. They seem to leave the Jerseys with reluctance. The train of artillery and wagons extends about nine miles and is upwards of a thousand in number. Some people say there are twenty thousand men, but I am afraid there is not so many; the real numbers are for very good reasons kept secret.

THE DESTRUCTION OF NEW YORK

Tuesday, June 24, 1777. On board all day. When I see this once flourishing, opulent, and happy city one-third part now in ruins, it brings a sadness and melancholy upon my mind to think that

9. THE GREAT FIRE IN NEW YORK, SEPTEMBER 19, 1776,
with British Soldiers Putting to the Sword Alleged Rebel Incendiaries

a set of people who three years ago were doing everything they could for the mutual assistance of each other, and both parties equally gainers, should now be cutting the throats of each other and destroying their property whenever they have an opportunity—and all this mischief done by a set of designing villains. The reflection is too severe to bear with patience. This city is an unhappy instance of the strange madness and folly that reigns amongst them. When the rebels were driven out of it in September last by the Royal Army, they formed a hellish design, burnt it down to the ground, and then laid the blame upon our troops; they so far succeeded as to burn about one-third, the most beautiful and valuable part of the city.

If one was to judge from appearances, they would suppose the rebels had intended to dispute every inch of ground with our troops. In every street they have made ditches and barricades, every little eminence about the town is fortified, but they basely and cowardly deserted them all as soon as ever our people got ashore. Now all these ditches and fortified places are full of stagnant water, damaged sauerkraut, and filth of every kind. Noisome vapors arise from the mud left in the docks and slips at low water, and unwholesome smells are occasioned by such a number of people being crowded together in so small a compass almost like herrings in a barrel, most of them very dirty and not a small number sick of some disease, the itch, pox, fever, or flux, so that altogether there is a complication of stinks enough to drive a person whose sense of smelling was very delicate and his lungs of the finest contexture into a consumption in the space of twenty-four hours. If any author had an inclination to write a treatise upon stinks and ill smells, he never could meet with more subject matter than in New York; or to anyone who had abilities and inclinations to expose the vicious and unfeeling part of human nature or the various arts, ways, and means that are used to pick up a living in this world, I recommend New York as a proper place to collect his characters. Most of the former inhabitants that possessed this once happy spot are utterly ruined and from opulence reduced to the greatest indigence; some in the rebels' jails by force, others by inclination in their armies.

James Moody

"It has several times happened that an artful and enterprising fellow by the name of Moody, employed by the British in New York, has succeeded in taking our mail from the post rider on the road," noted James Thacher ruefully in his war diary, adding that "he has had some very remarkable escapes." Thacher was referring to the New Jersey Loyalist, James Moody (1744-1809), a peaceable farmer who developed, under the abuses of his Whig neighbors, into the most brazen and intrepid spy of the Revolution. As he himself wrote, only circumstances changed him from a plain contented farmer into a soldier and then into a writer. When associations, committees, and liberty poles had thrown the country into a ferment, "the general cry was, *Join or die!* Mr. Moody relished neither of these alternatives." Accordingly he resolved to fight, to bleed, to die, rather than see the Constitution lost and his countrymen enslaved. "It would be impolitic and dangerous for him to recount, at large, all his various stratagems; it would be barbarous and base to divulge all the means by which he effected his almost miraculous escapes," wrote Moody modestly.

In April, 1777, after a number of armed men had shot at him on his grounds, he set out for the British lines with seventy-three neighbors. In June he joined Colonel Barton's battalion in General Cortlandt Skinner's brigade, known as "Skinner's Greens," and began recruiting Tories in the countryside, contacting the Loyalist forces at Niagara, spying on the movements of Washington and Sullivan, and making small raids. His biggest bag came on June 10, 1779, when he marched from Sandy Hook to Shrewsbury, gained a position known as The Falls, and captured five militia officers and a store of ammunition, which he afterwards sold for five hundred pounds, giving the proceeds to his men. In May, 1780, he attempted first to capture Governor Livingston and then, when the plot leaked out, to blow up a magazine near Morristown. But the Whigs were alert for Moody, and, foiled, he returned to his men in Sussex County. The present selection continues his narrative from this point.

Moody published his experiences in England in 1782, where he had gone to seek compensation for the loss of his property and reward for his activities. He enlarged and reissued it the following year, as *Lieut. James Moody's Narrative of his Exertions and Sufferings in the Cause of Government, since the Year 1776, authenticated by proper certificates.* The second edition, London 1783. Moody's case met with favor, and the Crown awarded him one thousand, three hundred and thirty pounds. He settled in Nova Scotia in 1786, where he spent his remaining years, giving himself the title Colonel Moody and speaking often about his exploits.

The second edition of the *Narrative* was reprinted by Charles I. Bushnell in 1865 and collected with other Revolutionary reprints in his *Crumbs for Antiquarians* (New York, privately printed, 1866), Vol. II, 9-98, with an introduction and notes. Moody wrote with swashbuckling arrogance, and referred to himself majestically in the third person. The present text is edited from the London 1783 edition, pp. 15-34.

RETURNING again into Sussex County, he now heard that several prisoners were confined, on various suspicions and charges of loyalty, in the jail of that county, and that one of them was actually under sentence of death. This poor fellow was one of Burgoyne's soldiers, charged with crimes of a civil nature, of which, however, he was generally believed to be innocent. But when a clergyman of the Church of England interposed with his unrelenting prosecutor, and warmly urged this plea of innocence, he was sharply told that, though he might not perhaps deserve to die for the crime for which he had been committed, there could be no doubt of his deserving to die as an enemy to America.

There was something so piteous, as well as shameful, in the case of this ill-fated victim to republican resentment that it was determined, if possible, to release both him and his fellow-prisoners. For this purpose Mr. Moody took with him six men and, late at night, entered the country town, about seventy miles from New York. The inhabitants of the town were but too generally disaffected. This suggested the necessity of stratagem. Coming to the jail, the keeper called out from the window of an upper room, and demanded what their business was. The Ensign instantly replied he had a prisoner to deliver into his custody. "What! One of Moody's fellows?" said the jailer. "Yes," said the Ensign. On his inquiring what the name of this supposed prisoner was, one of the party, who was well known by the inhabitants of that place to be with Mr. Moody, personated the character of a prisoner, and spoke for himself. The jailer gave him a little ill language, but notwithstanding seemed highly pleased with the idea of his having so notorious a Tory in his custody.

On the Ensign's urging him to come down and take charge of the man, he peremptorily refused, alleging that, in consequence of Moody's being out, he had received strict orders to open his doors to no man after sunset, and that therefore he must wait till morning.

Finding that this tale would not take, the Ensign now changed his note, and in a stern tone told him, "Sirrah, the man who now speaks to you is Moody. I have a strong party with me, and, if you do not this moment deliver up your keys, I will instantly pull down your house about your ears."

The jailer vanished in a moment. On this, Mr. Moody's men, who were well skilled in the Indian war whoop, made the air resound with such a variety of hideous yells as soon left them nothing to fear from the inhabitants of Newton, which, though the county town, consists only of twenty or thirty houses. "The Indians, the Indians are come!" said the panic-struck people, and happy were they who could soonest escape into the woods. While these things were thus going on, the Ensign had made his way through a casement and was met by a prisoner, whom he immediately employed to procure him a light. The vanished jailer was now again produced, and most obsequiously conducted Mr. Moody to the dungeon of the poor wretch under sentence of death.

It may seem incredible, but it is an undoubted fact, that notwithstanding all the horrors and awfulness of his situation, this poor, forlorn, condemned British soldier was found fast asleep, and had slept so sound as to have heard nothing of the uproar or alarm. There is no possibility of describing the agony of this man when, on being thus suddenly aroused, he saw before him a man in arms, attended by persons whom, though they were familiarly known to him, so agitated were his spirits, he was utterly at a loss then to recognize. The first and the only idea that occurred to him was that, as many of the friends of government had been privately executed in prison, the person he saw was his executioner. On Mr. Moody's repeatedly informing him of his mistake, and that he was come to release him in the name of King George, the transition from such an abyss of wretchedness to so extravagant a pitch of joy had well-nigh overcome him.

Never before had the writer been present at so affecting a

scene. The image of the poor soldier, alternately agitated with the extremes of despair and rapture, is at this moment present to his imagination, as strong almost as if the object were still before him; and he has often thought there were few subjects on which a painter of taste and sensibility could more happily employ his pencil. The man looked wild and undoubtedly was wild, and hardly in his senses; and yet he labored, and was big, with some of the noblest sentiments and most powerful passions by which the human mind is ever actuated. In such circumstances, it was with some difficulty that the Ensign got him away. At length, however, his clothes were got on, and he, with all the rest who chose to avail themselves of the opportunity, were conducted into safety, notwithstanding a warm pursuit of several days.

The humane reader, Mr. Moody persuades himself, will not be less affected than he himself was, at the mournful sequel of this poor soldier's tale. In the course of war he was again taken, and again conducted to the dungeon, and afterwards actually executed on the same sentence on which he had been before convicted, though he left the world with the most solemn asseverations of his innocence as to any crime of which he had been accused, excepting only an unshaken allegiance to his sovereign.

A few other particulars respecting this poor man, who, though but a common soldier in a marching regiment, was in all the essential and best parts of the character a hero, the writer cannot excuse himself from the relation of. His situation and circumstances in the rebel country being peculiar, Mr. Moody, not thinking it proper himself to return thither so soon, took the earliest means he could to have him conveyed safe to New York. But no arguments, no entreaties, could prevail with him to leave his deliverer. "To you," said he, "I owe my life; to you, and in your service, let me devote it. You have found me in circumstances of ignominy; I wish for an opportunity to convince you that you have not been mistaken in thinking me innocent. I am, and you shall find me, a good soldier." It was to this fatal but fixed determination that he soon afterward owed the loss of his life.

When he was brought to the place of execution, the persons who had charge of him told him they had authority to promise him a reprieve; and they did most solemnly promise it to him, on condition only that he would tell them who the Loyalists in the

country were that had assisted Moody. His reply was most manly
and noble, and proves that real nobility and dignity of sentiment
are appropriated to no particular rank or condition of life. "I
love life," he said, "and there is nothing which a man would not
do to save it; but I cannot pay this price for it. The men you wish
me to betray must be good men, because they have assisted a good
man in a good cause. Innocent as I am, I feel this an awful moment; how far it becomes you to tempt me to make it terrible, by
overwhelming me in the basest guilt, yourselves must judge. My
life is in your power; my conscience, I thank God, is still my
own."

Another extraordinary circumstance is said to have befallen
him, which, as well as the preceding, Mr. Moody relates on the
testimony of an eyewitness yet living. Though he was a small and
light man, yet the rope with which he was suspended broke. Even
still this poor man's admirable presence of mind and dignity of
conscious innocence did not forsake him. He instantly addressed
himself to the surrounding multitude, in the following words:
"Gentlemen, I cannot but hope that this very extraordinary event
will convince you of what I again solemnly protest to you, that
I am innocent of the crime for which you have adjudged me to
die." But he still protested in vain.

The supposed crime for which he suffered was the plundering
and robbing the house of a certain furious and powerful rebel.
But it would be unjust to his memory not to certify, as Mr.
Moody does, that he has since learned, from the voluntary confession of a less conscientious Loyalist, that this honest man was
charged wrongfully; inasmuch as he himself, without the knowledge of the other, on the principles of retaliation and revenge,
had committed the crime. The name of the above-mentioned
honest soldier and martyr was Robert Maxwell, a Scotsman, who
had had a good education.

*   *   *   *

Not long after, obtaining information of the British army's
moving towards Springfield, Mr. Moody concluded that the campaign was open. There appeared no way in which, with his small
party of seven men, he could be more useful than by securing as

many as he could of the rebel militia. Accordingly, it was not long before he contrived to take prisoners a Major, a Captain, two Lieutenants, and sundry committee men, in all to the amount of eighteen. Some requested to be paroled, and the Ensign complied with their request, because it was not only reasonable and humane, but because also it left him at liberty to pursue fresh objects. Some requested to take the oath of neutrality, and it was not less willingly administered to them.

The rebel part of the country was now again in an alarm; and the Ensign was again pursued and sought, according to the strong expression of the Scripture, "as a partridge in the mountains." But "wandering in deserts, and in mountains, and in dens and caves of the earth," by the blessing of God he still eluded all their researches. At length, however, being under a necessity of returning to New York, he collected a few more of Burgoyne's men, and having now augmented his party to thirteen, he set out for that capital. But his former good fortune now forsook him, and he himself was soon doomed to feel all those bitter calamities from which it had been the object of his exertions to extricate others.

On the twenty-first of July, 1780, it was his ill hap to fall in with an army which the rebel General Wayne was conducting to the siege of the blockhouse, commanded by Captain Ward. Resistance was vain, and retreat impracticable. Mr. Moody and the greater part of his men were now obliged to submit to captivity.

He and two of his men were immediately sent to a place called the Slote, where they were confined with their hands tied behind their backs. On the twenty-second they were removed to Stony Point, and on the twenty-third to Colonel Robertson's house at West Point. The rebel General Howe, who commanded at this post, treated Mr. Moody with great civility, and permitted his servant to attend him. From thence he was sent to Fishkill, to the rebel Commissary of Prisoners, who passed him on to Esopus. At Esopus he remained till the second of August, when, in the night, he was put into a strong room, guarded by four soldiers, two within the door and two without. The Sergeant, in the hearing of the Ensign, gave orders to the sentinels who were in the room with him to insist on his lying down on a bed, and instantly to shoot him if he attempted to rise from it. On this he requested

and insisted to see the Commissary. The Commissary came, and
was asked if these orders were from him. His answer was, "The
Sergeant had done his duty, and he hoped the men would obey
their orders." Mr. Moody remonstrated, and urged that it was
no uncommon thing with him to rise from his bed in his sleep;
he requested therefore only that, if he should happen now to be
overtaken with such an infirmity, the men might be ordered to
call him by his name, and at least to awake him before they fired.
All the answer he could obtain from this tyrant-minion of tyrant-
masters was a cool and most cutting repetition of his former
words.

After having twice more changed the place of his confinement,
on the tenth of August he was carried back to West Point. And
here his sufferings seemed to be but beginning, for the cruelties
he experienced under the immediate eye of General Arnold, who
then commanded there, infinitely exceeded all that he has ever
met with before or since.

Nothing can be further from Mr. Moody's wishes than to become any man's accuser, but no man should be afraid either to
hear or to tell the truth, which is of no party, and should be observed by all. Humanity, moreover, is so lovely and necessary a
virtue, and especially in times of civil war, that Mr. Moody owns
he is proud, and loves to acknowledge and to praise it, even in
an enemy; of course, he must lament and reprobate the want of
it, though in his best friend. Under new masters, it is hoped,
General Arnold has learned new maxims. Compelled by truth,
however, Mr. Moody must bear him testimony, that he was *then*
faithful to his employers, and abated not an iota in fulfilling both
the letter and the spirit of their general orders and instructions.

Mr. Moody feels this to be an unpleasant part of his narrative.
It is with pain he pursues it. May it be permitted him then to
give the subsequent part of it in the words of an affidavit, taken
in the Judge Advocate's office at New York, from the mouth of
William Buirtis, who was confined for his loyalty in the same
prison with Mr. Moody.

"JUDGE ADVOCATE'S OFFICE
New York, May 11, 1782
This day personally appeared William Buirtis, a refugee from

the county of Westchester, in the province of New York, but now residing on York Island, in the province aforesaid; and, being duly sworn on the Holy Evangelists of Almighty God, deposeth and saith;

'That some time in the month of August, 1780, he (the deponent) was confined in a dungeon at West Point Fort, under sentence of death, having been charged with giving certain intelligence and information to General Mathew, one of His Britannic Majesty's Generals serving at that time in America; that, about the middle of the month of August aforesaid, Lieutenant James Moody, of Brigadier General Skinner's First Battalion, was brought under guard, and confined in the same dungeon with him (the deponent); that, the day following, he (Lieutenant Moody) was put in irons and handcuffed; that the handcuffs were of a particular sort and construction, *ragged on the inside* next the wrist, which raggedness caused his wrists to be much cut and scarified; that soon after he (Lieutenant Moody) was ironed and handcuffed, an officer came and demanded his money, saying, *"he was ordered to take what money he had, and should obey his orders punctually"*; that the money was not delivered, as he (Lieutenant Moody) was resolute in refusing, and determined not to give it up. He (Lieutenant Moody) then petitioned General Benedict Arnold, at that time in the rebel service, and Commanding Officer at West Point, to grant him relief; in which petition he set forth the miserable situation he was in, as also the torment he suffered, occasioned by the handcuffs; to which petition he received no answer, though he was told, by two officers in the rebel service, his petition had been delivered to General Arnold.

'That about a week after his first petition had been sent, he petitioned a second time for relief from his suffering, requesting moreover to be brought up to a trial, observing that if he should be found guilty of death he should desire to suffer, as death was much preferable to torment and being murdered by inches. Some little time after the delivery of the second petition, one of General Arnold's aides-de-camp, whose name he (the deponent) cannot recollect, came to the dungeon; and on seeing him (Lieutenant Moody) asked if that was the Moody whose name was a terror to every good man? On his replying that his name was Moody, he (the aide-de-camp) replied in a scoffing manner, *"You have got yourself into a pretty situation.*" On his (Lieutenant Moody's) saying the situation was disagreeable but he hoped it would not be of long continuance, he answered, he believed not, as he would soon meet with justice (pointing at the same time to a gallows that was erected in the light and view of the dungeon), and also added, *there* is the gallows ready erected, which he (meaning Moody) had long merited.

'Lieutenant Moody answered, he made no doubt he (the aide-de-camp) wished to see every loyal subject hanged, but he thanked God the power was not in *him;* but if he (Lieutenant Moody) was hanged, it could be for no other reason than being a loyal subject to one of the best of Kings, and under one of the best of governments; and added, if he had *ten* lives to lose, he would sooner forfeit the ten as a loyal subject than *one* as a rebel; and also said, he hoped to live to see him (the aide-de-camp) and a thousand such other villains hanged for being rebels.

'The officer then said he was sent to examine his irons, as he (Lieutenant Moody) had been frequently troubling General Arnold with his petitions. On examining the irons, he said *they were too bad* and asked, who put them on, saying, "*Irons were intended for security, not for torment; but if anyone merited such irons, he* (Lieutenant Moody) *did in his opinion.*"

'Lieutenant Moody, however, was not relieved at that time from his irons; but, about a week or ten days afterwards, an officer came from General Washington, ordered the irons to be taken off, and Lieutenant Moody to be better treated. In consequence of General Washington's order, he was better used. He (the deponent) knows nothing further that happened, as he (Lieutenant Moody), in a few days afterwards, was removed from that place.

WILLIAM BUIRTIS'

Sworn before me at the time and place above mentioned,

RICHARD PORTER
As. Dy. Judge Advocate"

The above-mentioned dungeon was dug out of a rock, and covered with a platform of planks badly jointed, without any roof to it; and all the rain which fell upon it immediately passed through and lodged in the bottom of this dismal mansion. It had no floor but the natural rock, and the water, with the mud and filth collected, was commonly ankle-deep in every part of it. Mr. Moody's bed was an old door, supported by four stones, so as just to raise it above the surface of the water. Here he continued near four weeks; and during most of the time, while he was tormented with irons in the manner mentioned above, no food was allowed him but stinking beef and rotten flour, made up into balls or dumplings, which were thrown into a kettle and boiled with the meat, and then brought to him in a wooden bowl which was never washed, and which contracted a thick crust of dough, grease, and dirt. It is a wonder that such air, and such food, to say nothing of the wounds upon his legs and wrists, were not fatal to him, especially as the clothes on his back were seldom dry, and at one time were continually wet for more than a week together. After Mr. Washington interfered he was served with wholesome provisions, and he was allowed to purchase for himself some milk and vegetables.

The ways of Providence are often mysterious, frequently bringing about its ends by the most unlikely means. To this inhuman treatment in General Arnold's camp, Mr. Moody owed his future safety. On the first of September he was carried to Washington's camp, and there continued near their liberty pole. Colonel Scammel, the Adjutant General, came to see him put in irons. When they had handcuffed him he remonstrated with the Colonel, desiring that his legs, which were indeed in a worse situation than even his wrists, might be examined, further adding only that death would be infinitely preferable to a repetition of the torments he had just undergone. The Colonel did examine his legs, and on seeing them he also acknowledged that his treatment had indeed been too bad, and asked if General Arnold had been made acquainted with his situation. Mr. Moody feels a sincere pleasure in thus publicly acknowledging his obligations and his gratitude to Colonel Scammel, who humanely gave orders to the Provost Marshal to take good care of him, and by no means to suffer any irons to be put on his legs, till they were likely to prove less distressing.

Mr. Moody attended the rebel army in its march over the New Bridge, and had an opportunity of observing their whole line and counting their artillery. Everything seemed smooth and fair, and he felt himself much at ease, in the prospect of being soon exchanged, when, very unexpectedly, he was visited by an old acquaintance, one of their Colonels, who informed him that he was in two days' time to be brought to trial; that Livingston was to be his prosecutor, and that the court-martial was *carefully picked* for the purpose. He subjoined that he would do well to prepare for eternity, since, from the evidence which he knew would be produced, there was but one issue of the business to be expected. Mr. Moody requested to be informed what it was the purpose of this evidence to prove. It was, his well-wisher told him, that he had assassinated a Captain Shaddock and a Lieutenant Hendrickson. These were the two officers who had fallen fairly in battle near Black Point, as has been already related. The Ensign replied that he felt himself much at ease on that account, as it could be sufficiently cleared up by their own people who had been in and had survived the action, as well as by some of their officers, who were at that time prisoners to him and spectators of the whole affair.

"All this," said his friend, "will be of little avail: you are so obnoxious; you have been, and are likely to be, so *mischievous* to us that, be assured, we are resolved to get rid of you at any rate. Besides, you cannot deny, and it can be proved by incontestable evidence, that you have enlisted men, in this *state,* for the King's service, and this, by our laws, is *death.*"

Ensign Moody affected an air of unconcern at this information, but it was too serious and important to him to be really disregarded. He resolved, therefore, from that moment, to effect his escape or perish in the attempt.

Every precaution had been taken to secure the place in which he was confined. It was nearly in the center of the rebel camp. A sentinel was placed within the door of his prison, and another without, besides four others close round and within a few yards of the place. The time now came on when he must either make his attempt or lose the opportunity forever. On the night, therefore, of the seventeenth of September, busy in ruminating on his project, he had, on the pretense of being cold, got a watch coat thrown across his shoulders, that he might better conceal from his unpleasant companion the operations which he meditated against his handcuffs. While he was racking his invention to find some possible means of extricating himself from his fetters, he providentially cast his eye on a post fastened in the ground, through which a hole had been bored with an auger; and it occurred to him that it might be possible, with the aid of this hole, to break the bolt of his handcuffs. Watching the opportunity, therefore, from time to time, of the sentinel's looking another way, he thrust the point of the bolt into the above-mentioned hole, and by cautiously exerting his strength and gradually bending the iron backwards and forwards, he at length broke it. Let the reader imagine what his sensations were when he found the manacles drop from his hands! He sprung instantly past the interior sentinel, and rushing on the next, with one hand he seized his musket and with the other struck him to the ground. The sentinel within, and the four others who were placed by the fence surrounding the place of his confinement, immediately gave the alarm, and in a moment the cry was general—"Moody is escaped from the Provost!"

It is impossible to describe the uproar which now took place throughout the whole camp. In a few minutes every man was in a bustle; every man was looking for Moody, and multitudes passed him on all sides—little suspecting that a man whom they saw deliberately marching along, with a musket on his shoulder, could be the fugitive they were in quest of. The darkness of the night, which was also blustering and drizzly, prevented any discrimination of his person, and was indeed the great circumstance that rendered his escape possible.

But no small difficulty still remained to be surmounted. To prevent desertion, which at that time was very frequent, Washington had surrounded his camp with a chain of sentinels, posted at about forty or fifty yards' distance from each other. He was unacquainted with their stations; to pass them undiscovered was next to impossible, and to be discovered would certainly be fatal. In this dilemma Providence again befriended him. He had gained their station without knowing it, when luckily he heard the watchword passed from one to another—"Look sharp to the chain—Moody is escaped from the Provost." From the sound of the voices he ascertained the respective situations of these sentinels, and, throwing himself on his hands and knees, he was happy enough to crawl through the vacant space between two of

10. LIEUTENANT MOODY RESCUING A BRITISH SOLDIER FROM JAIL.

them, unseen by either. Judging that their line of pursuit would naturally be towards the British Army, he made a detour into the woods on the opposite side. Through these woods he made as much speed as the darkness of the night would permit, steering his course, after the Indian manner, by occasionally groping and feeling the white oak. On the south side the bark of this tree is rough and unpleasant to the touch, but on the north side it is smooth, hence it serves the sagacious traverser of the desert by night as well as by day for his compass. Through the most dismal woods and swamps he continued to wander till the night of the twenty-first, a space of more than fifty-six hours, during which time he had no other sustenance than a few beech leaves (which, of all that the woods afforded, were the least unpleasant to the taste and least pernicious to health), which he chewed and swallowed, to abate the intolerable cravings of his hunger.

In every inhabited district he knew there were friends of government, and he had now learned also where and how to find them out, without endangering *their* safety, which was always the first object of his concern. From some of these good men he received minute information how the pursuit after him was directed, and where every guard was posted. Thus assisted, he eluded their keenest vigilance and at length, by God's blessing, to his unspeakable joy he arrived safe at Paulus Hook.

WAR AT SEA

The rebelling States could create a Continental Army much more easily than a Continental Navy. A navy involved a considerable capital outlay, and it must build from nothing in a match against the giant of the seas. Members of the Continental Congress nevertheless felt the value of naval forces and legislated promptly for their establishment. George Wythe of Virginia asked, "Why should not America have a navy? No maritime power near the seacoast can be safe without it. It is no chimera. The Romans suddenly built one in their Carthaginian war. Why may not we lay a foundation for it? We abound with firs, iron ore, tar, pitch, turpentine; we have all the materials for the construction of a navy." Accordingly the Congress appropriated funds for the building of thirteen frigates, and appointed Esek Hopkins Commander-in-Chief on November 5, 1775. Hopkins set sail with a motley squadron in January, 1776, first for Chesapeake Bay and then to Nassau, New Providence, in the Bahamas. After failing to seize the stores he was after, Hopkins encountered a single British ship of the line on the way home, and let it get away from his whole fleet. This was the first enterprise of the American navy, and it prophetically illustrated the ineffectuality of fleet action by the patriots during the war.

War at sea involved a continuous variety of major actions, small engagements, and individual raids and cruises. Besides the Continental Navy, American ships of war included the navies of eleven states, fleets operated by the army, privateers licensed by the Congress or the states, and some freebooters. Sometimes these forces combined on a single objective, but more often they competed for the services of seamen and pursued separate courses. American naval activity included operations on Lake Champlain and the Mississippi River, on the high seas, along the coastal shores of the Atlantic seaboard and the British Isles, and around the islands of the Caribbean Sea.

The big guns that flashed on the ocean waters belonged, however, not to American ships of the line but to the French and Eng-

*lish squadrons that strove mightily for dominance from 1778 to
1782. The first French fleet under the Comte d'Estaing threatened Clinton at Philadelphia and caused his withdrawal to New
York; another fleet under De Grasse shook off the enemy long
enough to pin Cornwallis at Yorktown. Three times French
armadas massed on the Channel to strike at English homes. And
in reverse, Arbuthnot confined De Ternay for most of the winter
of 1780-1781 at Newport, and Admiral Rodney defeated De
Grasse in the West Indies and took him prisoner at the Battle
of the Saints in 1782. In these major stratagems the Americans
took no part. When an all-American navy of twenty sail manned
by two thousand seamen and accompanying twenty transports of
state militia attacked an enemy base on the Penobscot River, in
August, 1779, it melted like the dew at the sight of a smaller English fleet. The American sailors fled up the river, beached and
burned their ships, and walked home to Massachusetts and New
Hampshire, leaving a bill of nearly two million pounds as their
sole souvenir. When the French navy took French leave from
the Atlantic coast, British gunboats enabled Benedict Arnold to
ravage Virginia early in 1781, and Rodney mercilessly strangled
the Philadelphia and New Jersey privateers in the last year of the
war.*

*Nevertheless a goodly measure of glory on the seas fell to Ameri-
can sailors. In privateering lay the marine success of audacious
Yankees, whose speedy schooners made sport of the heavy English
frigates. At first Lord Howe, supplying his brother the general
at the siege of Boston, allowed the privateers to commit their
depredations under his very nose, in his policy of seeking to woo
the common folk from their rebel leaders. In the Seven Years'
War the colonists had already practiced the technique of taking
prizes, and they leaped at their new opportunities with a zeal both
patriotic and mercenary. The privateersman at sea matched the
frontiersman on land, a daredevil on the prowl. Free-lance raiders
struck at rich merchantmen laden with West India sugar and
rum, or English woolens and Irish linens bound for the continent,
or furs and stores from Quebec and Hudson Bay. They inter-
cepted British transports and relayed their supplies to the needy
Continental troops. Twenty thousand Americans sailed on privateers, and took two thousand prizes and sixteen thousand British*

11. **THE FRENCH FLEET ARRIVES IN AMERICAN WATERS, 1778**

A. French Ships of the Line Blockading the English Fleet
outside New York Harbor, July 2

B. The French Fleet in Boston Harbor, September

prisoners. John Paul Jones struck at English and Scottish ports like a wolf in the night, and terrorized the British waters in his cruises of 1778 and 1779. British insurance rates soared; British mercantile houses went bankrupt; the Admiralty was compelled to divert its sorely needed ships for convoy and patrol duty; British prestige and morale sank.

French aid alone made possible these Yankee exploits. Unneutral France sent her merchant ships in droves to the States, either directly or via the West Indies, and she also opened her ports to the privateers. At Lorient and Brest and Bordeaux they outfitted, secured their crews, often mainly Frenchmen, and sailed out to harry the British coastal waters. To the same ports they scurried when in trouble, or brought their prizes and offered them for sale. When France officially entered the war, in the summer of 1778, the Americans lost her invaluable neutral cloak. After the alliance French and American naval action merged to the point that American captains took commissions in the French navy.

Privateering harmed as well as helped the rebel cause. It drew farmers and laborers and soldiers into its magnetic grip, and drained the army and navy of their manpower. Greed rather than ardor inspired the backers and the crews, and in their lust for booty the raiders scooped up neutral merchant ships, and even those of their French ally. Privateering and profiteering proceeded hand in hand, and stirred up the evils of inflation and speculation. As an independent weapon, unsupported by the French and Spanish navies to fend off the English, the fast-flying schooners could not survive, and left to themselves when the French withdrew in the summer of 1782 they withered before a fully mounted blockade by regular ships of the line.

The career of a particularly intrepid privateersman appears in the autobiography of Nathaniel Fanning. Fanning sailed under John Paul Jones during his cruises on the Ranger *and the* Bonhomme Richard, *and later he attained his own command and darted from French ports to prey on convoys and slip past lumbering British frigates with all the deviltry of his master. Fanning's narrative demonstrates in vivid detail how the patriots fought at sea.*

Nathaniel Fanning

Born in Stonington, Connecticut, where his Irish forebears had settled
five generations before, in 1653, Nathaniel Fanning (1755-1805) and
his seven younger brothers all followed the sea from early youth. Two
were captured by the English during the Revolution and confined in
the *Jersey*, where one died, and the other avoided death only through
the intervention of a prominent Tory uncle, Edmund Fanning, who
eventually became a general in the British Army. Another brother, also
named Edmund, achieved prominence as an explorer of the South Seas
and promoter of the China trade. Nathaniel himself became something
of a naval hero during the war, and was offered a commission by the
French government; his whole narrative reveals how closely American
seamen and the French navy collaborated to harry the English home
waters. He left France for the United States at the war's end, and was
commissioned a Lieutenant in the United States Navy in 1804, but
died of yellow fever within a year, while commanding the naval station
at Charleston, South Carolina.

The year following his death his lengthy manuscript was published
anonymously, under the title *Narrative of the Adventures of an American Navy Officer who served during part of the American Revolution
under the Command of Captain John Paul Jones, Esq.*, and two years
later (1808) a reissue carried his name, *Memoirs of the Life of Captain
Nathaniel Fanning*. Both editions are extremely rare, and a modern
editor, John S. Barnes, believes that Edmund, who was then seeking
support for his South Seas exploring expeditions, suppressed the editions for fear of discredit to the family. Nathaniel spoke candidly about
the tyrannies of John Paul Jones, a popular idol, while his forthright
language might be regarded as coarse. Still it is difficult to see why
Edmund would first print and then withdraw the two editions (or two
issues of the same edition), or what in the narrative would seem so very
indelicate. The Naval History Society reprinted the book in an edition
of three hundred copies in 1912 as *Fanning's Narrative, being the
Memoirs of Nathaniel Fanning, an Officer of the Revolutionary Navy
1778-1783*, edited and annotated by John S. Barnes, late Lt.-Commander
U. S. N. (New York, the DeVinne Press). It also reappeared in the
Magazine of History, Extra Number 21 (1913), pp. 1-229. The narrative
was written in 1801, but Fanning drew upon a contemporary diary and
ships' logs for his dates and precise facts.

A biographical sketch with a portrait appears in W. F. Brooks, *History of the Fanning Family* (2 vols., 1905), I, 249; II, 715-738. These ex-
tracts are edited from the 1912 edition, pp. 1-7, 32-55, 197-204, 211-221.

PREFACE

THE AUTHOR of the following pages, at the time they were first written, never intended that they should appear before the public eye. But through the earnest solicitation of a number of friends, who having read his journal, from which the following sheets have been compiled, he has been induced (together with a view of opposing the zeal with which certain characters in this country have strove lately to debase the American name, by branding it with the epithet of coward, poltroon, *"not so brave as an Englishman,"* and the like; which has often sounded in the ears of the author), to change his intentions, and to commit the whole to the press. He pledges himself that he has, in the compilation, kept truth on his side. That the perusal will meet with the entire approbation of everyone is not to be expected, but it is hoped that the reader will forbear censuring the author too much, as he does not pretend to be a scholar (in regard of style or orthography), never having had but barely a common education; having followed the seas for a livelihood from his early youth upwards to the present time. However the manner of writing, or the style, may suit the reader, as coming from the pen of an experienced sailor, he flatters himself that the public will condescend to give it a kind and favorable reception. In the meantime, he has the honor to be

The public's most obedient servant,
THE AUTHOR

1. CAPTURED

HAVING BEEN born in 1755, in the state of Connecticut, in the early part of the American Revolution for independence, I imbibed the idea that the struggles between Great Britain and her American colonies would eventually prove to the advantage of the latter. In full belief of the same, I took an active and decided part in favor of my country.

After having made two successful cruises against the English, I embarked on a third at Boston, on the twenty-sixth day of May, 1778, on board the brig *Angelica*, William Dennis commander, a new vessel mounting sixteen carriage guns and carrying ninety-

12. NATHANIEL FANNING

eight men and boys, on a six months' cruise against the enemies of my country. We sailed from Boston on the same day on which I embarked. (It may be well perhaps to observe that I was only a prize master on board said privateer.) We saw nothing but a privateer belonging to Salem, which we spoke, till the thirty-first of May at noon, when we discovered a sail bearing S.S.E. of us, the wind then being about N. by E. Orders were immediately given by the Captain to make sail for her; in a short time after we could perceive with our glasses that she was a ship standing by the wind to the eastward; at 1 P.M. saw that she was a long frigate-built ship.

All hands were now ordered to quarters and to prepare for action. At 4 P.M. we were near enough to distinguish the chase from a Jamaica merchantman, which we at first view supposed it to be. In consequence of our being convinced that she was an English ship of war we jibbed ship and hauled on a wind to the westward, but too late, as the ship immediately hove in stays, run out her guns, and gave us chase in her turn, and in about three-quarters of an hour more she came alongside of us and obliged us to haul down our Yankee colors. She proved to be the *Andromeda* frigate of twenty-eight guns, five days from Philadelphia, and had on board as a passenger the celebrated General Howe, of Bunker Hill memory, and was bound to Portsmouth, in England.

The enemy soon obliged us to abandon the poor *Angelica,* and conducted us on board the *Andromeda,* where we were all paraded on the quarter-deck in presence of their great and mighty General, who asked us a number of insignificant questions; among which was, "If we were willing to engage in His Majesty's service?" We having answered pretty unanimously in the negative, he then upbraided us with these words: "You are a set of rebels, and it is more than probable that you will all be hanged on our arrival at Portsmouth." The master-at-arms was then ordered on the ship's quarter deck, who soon made his appearance, and under the pretense of searching our baggage for concealed knives he, with some of his comrades, very dexterously conveyed our said baggage out of sight, so that we saw nothing of it, or any part thereof, afterwards. This was the more astonishing as it was done under the General's eye, who ordered us all to be confined in the ship's hold.

We soon began our march for this young hell upon the seas, and on our way we were ordered by some of the Jack tars to halt, who began to strip us, saying, or rather accosting us with these words: "D—n my eyes, shipmate, but you have got a d—d fine coat there—fine hat—fine shoe buckles—fine jacket—fine breeches," etc., but taking care to lard these expressions with an oath. In short everything that we then had was fine to them; and after saying, "Come, come, shipmates, these fine things will only be a plague to you, as the climate is very hot where you are bound" (meaning the ship's hold), they then without any further ceremony fell to work and stripped us of our clothes.

There happened at this juncture to pass by a midshipman, who said, "That is right, lads, strip the d—d rebels, and give each of them a frock and trousers, those will be good enough for them to be hanged in!" We were, according to his orders, stripped, and after being furnished with frocks and trousers, we continued our march till we were shoved headlong into the aforesaid hell upon the seas. Two sentinels were then placed at the mouth thereof to prevent our running away. Here they kept us fasting during twenty hours, and then sent us our small pittance of provisions, which was no more per man per day than two-thirds of the allowance of a prisoner of war. However, it was in vain we petitioned for redress to the Captain of the ship, and to General Howe; they were deaf to our complaints, and answered that we were treated with too much lenity, being considered as rebels, whose crimes were of such an aggravated kind that we should be shown no mercy. The enemy at about nine at night set the *Angelica* on fire, and she soon after blew up, and the ship continued on her course for England.

The next day after being confined in the frigate's hold, a plan was set on foot by our surgeon to make ourselves masters of her. His plan met with the approbation of all, to appearance, and we agreed to put it in execution on the third of June, at half-past eleven at night, or to die in the attempt. In the meantime the surgeon had frequent conversations with the forecastle men and sentinels, who agreed all as one to join us. We had by this time pretty severely felt the effects of the heat in our confinement in the ship's lower hold upon the orlop deck (a temporary one laying over the water punchions, ballast, etc.) as we were obliged from the excessive heat to go stark-naked, save when we had occasion to go upon deck, which we were allowed to do only one at a time, and once in twenty-four hours. I have often, while confined in this young hell, being almost suffocated, crawled into the wings of the ship and got my nose to the air holes before I could fetch breath. In fine, we all suffered so much here we were willing to be all cut to pieces in our intended attempt, rather than suffer in this dismal place any longer. The most of the ship's crew at this time were so much affected with the scurvy that we had no reason to expect any great opposition to obstruct us in our intended design, as we had some arms, cutlasses, etc., secretly conveyed down to us by persons who were in league with our surgeon.

Our plan was now ripe for execution. The surgeon having been upon deck the two preceding nights, by consent of those who kept sentinel over us, they being in the plot, he had observed that the greater part of the watch were almost all the time fast asleep, so that it was very probable that we should not meet with a very warm reception. But an unforeseen casualty entirely frustrated our plan. About nine at night, on the third of June, when we were all prepared and in high spirits, having as we thought arrived almost to the height of our wishes, as we saw nothing then to hinder our taking possession of the frigate, one Spencer, Captain Dennis' clerk, stole upon deck and made known to the General our plot. Presently after the marines and sailors were all armed, and so great was the panic among both officers and crew that they were almost ready to believe that we were masters of their ship. However, the lower hatches were immediately thrown on and barred down; and now it was that we began to think seriously that we should very soon die in a heap, as the heat became intolerable. To complete our sufferings, orders were given by this great and mighty General to give us only as much provisions as would serve to keep us alive and to deal out to us no more water than half a pint per man per day; this was British humanity to a witness!

Luckily, as we were lodged upon the water casks, over which was laid a temporary deck, we with a kind of proof glass got a sufficiency; but as to provisions it was next to none. However, as there was nothing but a partition of plank between us and the General's storeroom, we fell upon an expediment to augment our stores. We had frequently beheld the Captain's steward and General's servants from between the shifting boards abaft the pump-well, drawing off wines and other liquors, and only securing the bungs of each cask with their fingers; getting white biscuit out of one keg, neat's tongues out of another, raisins out of another, hams out of a cask they were stowed in, mess beef out of tierces; in fine, this storeroom contained almost everything agreeable to the taste, and in great plenty. On the evening of the fifth of June, at ten at night, one Howard, a native of Rhode Island, a bold and enterprising fellow, declared he would not that night close his eyes until he drank some Madeira wine, and that he would be the person who would run the hazard of losing his life in order to serve us all, if we could make a breach so that he could get into the said storeroom.

Accordingly we went to work, and soon found that one of the shifting boards abaft the pump-well was loose, and that we could ship and unship it as we pleased. When it was unshipped there was just room enough for a man to crawl into the storeroom already mentioned, which Howard no sooner saw than he improved the precious occasion, and in he went, and presently after desired one to hand him a mug or can, with our proof glass. A few minutes after he handed me back the same full, saying at the same time, "My friends, as good Madeira wine as ever was drunk at the table of an Emperor." I took it from his hands, and being very dry, I drank about one-third of it, which was I judge about half a pint, and then gave it to my fellow-sufferers. The can thus went round merrily till we were all but Howard what may be called decently drunk; and Howard, after having secured us some eatables of several kinds, and likewise putting the shifting boards in their place, retired to the general rendezvous upon the orlop deck.

Thus we lived like hearty fellows, taking care every night to secure provisions, dried fruit, and wines for the day following, until the frigate came to anchor in Portsmouth, and all in pretty large quantities, without being beholden to our enemies' bounty, and without their knowledge. However, that they might not suspect this conduct of ours, we used to snatch at the small pittance of provisions allowed us when they dealt it out to us as if we were half starved, and at the water they allowed us the same.

On our way to England the frigate lost part of her crew with the scurvy, but as for us the General, as well as the Captain and his officers, were astonished on the score of our being all brave and hearty. The former even expressed himself in this manner: "What, are none of them d—d Yankees sick!" Somebody made answer, "Not one." "D—n them," says he, "there is nothing but thunder and lightning will kill them." This was reported to us by the Captain's steward and one of the General's servants.

2. THE *BONHOMME RICHARD* AND THE *SERAPIS*

[After a confinement in Forton Prison, near Portsmouth, Fanning was freed on exchange and sent to Nantes, in France. From there he made his way to Lorient, where he signed with John Paul Jones as midshipman, intending to return to America after a short cruise in the English Channel. The *Bonhomme Richard* left Lorient August 14, 1779, on what was to prove an historic voyage.]

WE NOW shaped our course for Scarborough, a seaport town in Yorkshire situated on the German Ocean, and soon arrived off this port. We cruised here several days without meeting anything but small English coasters and pilot boats, the latter sloops rigged and decked, burthen about fifteen tons. One of these we converted into a small tender; she served us for a decoy, and likewise to land in, when we had occasion for fresh water and fresh provisions. On the twenty-second day of September, 1779, at 4 P.M., we discovered a fleet in the S.E. quarter, standing for Scarborough. At 5 P.M. we could plainly discover that this fleet were convoyed by two English sloops of war, the largest of which, taking us to be an enemy, made the signal for the fleet to disperse and save themselves. The two sloops of war then made sail from us, as did also the merchantmen, although they had by this time got pretty near us. Our commodore also made the signal for our little squadron to chase the enemy's fleet by crowding all the sail we could set. Soon after the *Alliance* brought two of them to, who struck their colors.

We had just put the Second Lieutenant of our ship on board of the small tender, with about twenty men well armed, in order to take possession of these merchant vessels that were the nearest to us, when a fleet was discovered in the eastern board. The weather clearing off a little about the same time, we could count thirty-seven sail of vessels in that quarter, all apparently standing in for the land. As soon as Jones had taken a peep or two at them with his spyglass, he expressed himself to his officers, then standing by him upon the quarter-deck, in this manner: "That is the very fleet which I have been so long cruising for." He immediately ordered a signal to be made for the squadron to abandon the small fleet, which we were then almost in the possession of, consisting of thirteen sail of vessels, some of which was said to be very valuable. Another signal was made for the squadron to crowd all sail after the fleet in the eastern board, and without waiting for the tender, which had on board one of his best officers and twenty of our best men. He appeared to be impatient, till all the sail we could set on board of our ship, the wind then being between the south and west, was spread; and now came on a general chase for the enemy.

At half-past six o'clock we were near enough to distinguish two of this fleet to be ships of war; one of them had the appearance of a frigate, and the other a sloop of war. These two ships perceiving that we were enemies, and that by our maneuvering our intentions were to attack them, hove in stays, and stood off the land with a view, as afterwards appeared, of engaging us, while the merchant ships kept hovering in with the land, but could not make a harbor as there was none nearer than Scarborough. At seven P.M. we made a signal to speak the *Alliance* and *Pallais;* in a quarter of an hour thereafter we spoke the *Alliance,* when Captain Jones ordered her Captain to engage the largest of the two ships of war, in conjunction with the *Good Man Richard;* and that as soon as he had fired his broadsides, if a favorable opportunity then presented, to board her; and for that purpose to have his men in readiness. He answered that the Commodore should be obeyed; this was succeeded by three cheers from the officers and crew of the *Alliance.* Captain Jones also ordered the Captain of the *Pallais* to engage the smallest ship of the enemy, who was now pretty near us. We then had a breeze from the S.S.W. of perhaps six knots.

They soon after hove to, and hauled up their courses, and showed St. George's colors. Our little squadron, drawn up in order of battle, showed them the thirteen stripes, the colors which we fought under. Soon after the largest of the enemy's ships made a signal in consequence of which her consort, in the twinkling of an eye, set all the sail she could, and endeavored to make her escape by running to the leeward. The *Pallais,* agreeable to orders, made sail after her. The *Alliance* too, disobeying orders, quit her station and ran to the leeward, making all the sail she could crowd, so that we were now left alone (the *Vengeance* being then astern, and never come into the action) to contend with a ship far superior to ours, as will be seen hereafter.

The command of the maintop having been given to me some time before, I was ordered down on the quarter deck, as were the captains of the fore- and mizzentops, both midshipmen and very young, neither of them exceeding seventeen years of age. There we received our orders from Captain Jones in person, which were, in substance, that at first and until the enemy's tops were silenced, to direct the fire from our tops into the enemy's tops of the musketry, blunderbusses, cowhorns, and swivels, always taking care to fire into the enemy's top nearest the one we occupied in our own ship, in order, he said, that we might, after silencing the enemy's tops, have the fairer opportunity of clearing their decks. The captains of the tops, having received their orders how to proceed during the action, then, within a few minutes of commencing, mounted to their stations and drew up into the tops a double allowance of grog for their men. By this time we were near our antagonist, when she hauled down St. George's colors and hoisted the red flag, with the union on the upper corner of it, which the Captain with his own hands nailed to the flagstaff. This was told us by some of his officers after the battle, and which fact the Captain did not deny, after he was made a prisoner.

Before I proceed to give the reader a relation of the action, it may be well to state the force of the two ships, with the number of men, etc., with the arrangements made on board of our ship before the battle. The reader, I hope, will not be displeased when he will here see at one view the correct force of each ship, which will enable him, let him be of what country he may, to form a tolerable judgment which had the advantage in this long and bloody battle, the American or the English. Besides, the *Good*

Man Richard had since she sailed from Lorient lost some of her officers and men by desertion, others by manning prizes, and one Lieutenant and about twenty men who were on board the small tender and did not come alongside the *Bonhomme Richard* till after the action was over.

I begin first with the *Good Man Richard* of 40 guns; viz.

6 eighteen-pounders upon her lower gun deck;
14 twelve   ”   ”   ”   middle ”
14 nine   ”   ”   ”   ”   ”
2 six   ”   ”   ”   quarter ”
2 ”   ”   ”   spar or upper ”   viz.
1 in each gangway; and lastly,
2 six-pounders upon the forecastle.

N.B. Several men out of the vessels which we had captured, entered on board of our ship, and others of the same class who would not enter, chose to fight, which they did like brave fellows. These last, however, did not exceed seven or eight, so that the whole number of officers, men and boys, on board of the *Good Man Richard,* at the commencement of the action, did not exceed 380. The greater part of these were Americans, I think to the number of 300. The rest were English, French, Scotch, Irish, Portuguese, and Maltese, in fact, a perfect medley of different nations.

The *Serapis,* commanded by Captain Pearson, our antagonist, was rated a 44, but had mounted at the beginning of the battle 50 guns: viz.

20 eighteen-pounders upon her lower gun deck;
20 nine   ”   ”   ”   upper ”
6 six   ”   ”   ”   quarter ”
4 ”   ”   ”   ”   forecastle; carrying in all 305 men, including the officers, and about 15 Lascars (East Indians).

Disposition made on board of our ship before the battle began: There were stationed—

In the maintop, myself, fifteen marines, and four sailors, 20
In the foretop, one midshipman, ten marines, and three sailors, 14

In the mizzentop, one midshipman, six marines, and two sailors, 9

On the poop, a French Colonel, a volunteer, with twenty marines (French)

On the quarter deck, the Commodore, a Lieutenant-Colonel (Irish volunteer), three midshipmen as aides-de-camp to the Commodore, the purser, and a number of sailors and marines.

The sailing master was occasionally on the quarter deck, the ship's gangways, forecastle, and poop.

One of the master's mates had charge of the 6 eighteen-pounders upon the lower gun deck, where there were also stationed ten men to each of these guns.

The First Lieutenant, Richard Dale, was stationed upon the second or middle gun deck, with the gunner and the other master's mate; these two last acted as lieutenants as occasion required, as we had at this time but one lieutenant on board, as the reader will recollect. The First Lieutenant had a sufficient number of men stationed with him, for managing the guns, etc.

The boatswain's station was upon the forecastle, and he had the command of the guns mounted there, and also the forecastle men.

The carpenter had no particular part of the ship assigned to him, but he was merely told to do his duty.

The rest of the petty officers and crew were placed in different parts of the ship.

I shall now proceed to give a circumstantial account of this famous battle, fought on the night of the twenty-second day of September, 1779, between the *Good Man Richard,* an American ship of war commanded by John Paul Jones, and the *Serapis,* an English ship of war, commanded by Captain Pearson, off Flamborough Head, upon the German Ocean.

To proceed then with the thread of my journal, from where the two ships were nearly within hail of each other, when Captain Jones ordered the yards slung with chains and our courses hauled up. By this time the *Serapis* had tacked ship, and bore down to engage us. At quarter past eight, just as the moon was rising with majestic appearance, the weather being clear, the surface of the great deep perfectly smooth, even as in a millpond, the enemy hailed thus: "What ship is that?" (in truly bombastic English style, it being hoarse and hardly intelligible).

The answer from our ship was, "Come a little nearer, and I will tell you."

The next question by the enemy came in a contemptuous manner, "What are you laden with?"

The answer returned was, if my recollection does not deceive me, "Round, grape, and double-headed shot."

And instantly the *Serapis* poured her range of upper- and quarter-deck guns into us; she did not show her lower-deck guns till about ten minutes after the action commenced. The reason of this I could not learn but suppose they intended to have taken us without the aid of their lower-deck guns. We returned the enemy's fire, and thus the battle began.

At this first fire, three of our starboard lower-deck guns burst, and killed the most of the men stationed at them. As soon as Captain Jones heard of this circumstance, he gave orders not to fire the other three eighteen-pounders mounted upon that deck, and that the men stationed to them should abandon them. Soon after this we perceived the enemy, by their lanterns, busy in running out their guns between decks, which convinced us the *Serapis* was a two-decker, and more than our match. She had by this time got under our stern, which we could not prevent. And now she raked us with whole broadsides and showers of musketry. Several of her eighteen-pound shot went through and through our ship, making a dreadful havoc among our crew. The wind was now very light and our ship not under proper command, and the *Serapis* outsailing us by two feet to one; which advantage the enemy discovered, and improved it by keeping under our stern and raking us fore and aft, till at length the poor French Colonel, who was stationed upon the poop, finding almost all his men slain, quit that station with his surviving men and retired upon the quarter deck. All this time our tops kept up an incessant and well-directed fire into the enemy's tops, which did great execution. The *Serapis* continued to take a position either under our stern or athwart our bow, and galled us in such a manner that our men fell in all parts of the ship by scores.

At this juncture it became necessary on the part of our commander to give some orders to extricate us from this scene of bloody carnage; for had it lasted one-half an hour longer, in all human probability the enemy would have slain nearly all our officers and men, and compelled us to strike our colors and yield to superior force. Accordingly, Captain Jones ordered the sailing master, a true-blooded Yankee whose name was Stacy, to lay the enemy's ship on board; and as the *Serapis* soon after passed across our fore foot, our helm was put hard aweather, the main and mizzen topsails, then braced aback, were filled away, a fresh flaw of wind swelling them at that instant, which shot our ship quick ahead, and she ran her jib boom between the enemy's starboard mizzen shroud and mizzen vang. Jones at the same time cried out, "Well done, my brave lads, we have got her now; throw on board the grappling-irons, and stand by for boarding." This was done, but the enemy soon cut away the chains which were affixed to the grappling-irons; more were thrown on board, and this often repeated. And as we now hauled the enemy's ship snug alongside of ours with the tailings to our grappling-irons, her jib-stay was cut away aloft and fell upon our ship's poop, where Jones was at the time, and where he assisted Mr. Stacy in making fast the end of the enemy's jib-stay to our mizzenmast. The former here checked the latter for swearing, by saying, "Mr. Stacy, it is no time for swearing now, you may by the next moment be in eternity; but let us do our duty."

A strong current was now setting in towards Scarborough, the wind ceased to blow, and the sea became as smooth as glass. By this time the enemy, finding that they could not easily extricate themselves from us, let go one of their anchors, expecting that if they could cut us adrift the current would set us away out of their reach, at least for some time. The action had now lasted about forty minutes, and the fire from our tops had been kept up without intermission, with musketry, blunderbusses, cowhorns, swivels, and pistols directed into their tops, till these last at this time became silent, except one man in her foretop, who would once in a while peep out from behind the head of the enemy's foremast and fire into our tops. As soon as I perceived this fellow, I ordered the marines in the maintop to reserve their next fire, and the moment they got sight of him to level their pieces at him

**13. THE FIGHT BETWEEN THE "BONHOMME RICHARD"
AND THE "SERAPIS," SEPT. 23, 1779**

and fire; which they did, and we soon saw this skulking tar, or marine, fall out of the top upon the enemy's forecastle.

Our ensign-staff was shot away, and both that and the thirteen stripes fell into the sea at the beginning of the action. This ought to have been mentioned before, but I had so many other circumstances to relate of more importance, and the succession of them was so quick, one close upon the heels of another, that I hope the reader will take this for an excuse.

Both ships were now lying head and stern, and so near together that our heaviest cannon amidships, as well as those of the enemy, could not be of any use, as they could neither be sponged nor loaded. In this situation the enemy, to prevent (as they told us afterwards) our boarding them, leaped on board of our ship, and some of them actually got upon the fore part of our quarter-deck. Several were there killed and the rest driven back on board of their own ship, whither some of our men followed them, but were most of them killed. Several other attempts to board were made by both parties in quick succession, in consequence of which many were slain upon the two ships' gangways, on both sides.

We were now something more than a league E. by S. from a point of land called Flamborough Head, and in about ten or twelve fathoms of water (and the reader may rest assured, as the *Serapis's* anchor was at the bottom, and her crew not having any leisure time to weigh it, we remained here until the battle was at an end). At this time the enemy's fleet was discernible by moonlight in shore of us, but we could not perceive any of our squadron except the brig *Vengeance* and the small tender, which lay about half a league astern of us, neither of whom dared to come to our assistance. It had now got to be about forty-eight minutes since the action began, as near as I can judge, for we had not time to keep glasses running, or to look at our watches. The enemy's tops being entirely silenced, the men in ours had nothing to do but to direct their whole fire down upon the enemy's decks and forecastle; this we did, and with so much success that in about twenty-five minutes more we had cleared her decks so that not a man on board the *Serapis* was to be seen. However, they still kept up a constant fire, with four of their foremost bow guns on the starboard side, viz., two eighteen-pounders upon the lower gun deck, and two nine-pounders upon her upper gun deck; these last were mounted upon her forecastle, under cover from our fire from our tops. Her cannon upon the larboard side, on the quarter deck and forecastle, from the position of both ships were rendered altogether useless; her four guns which she could manage annoyed us very much and did our ship considerable damage.

About this time the enemy's light sails, which were filled onto the *Serapis's* cranes over her quarter-deck sails, caught fire. This communicated itself to her rigging and from thence to ours; thus were both ships on fire at one and the same time. Therefore the firing on both sides ceased till it was extinguished by the contending parties, after which the action was renewed again. By this time the topmen in our tops had taken possession of the enemy's tops, which was done by reason of the *Serapis's* yards being locked together with ours, so that we could with ease go from our maintop into the enemy's foretop, and so on from our foretop into the *Serapis's* maintop. Having knowledge of this, we transported from our own into the enemy's tops stinkpots, flasks, hand grenadoes, etc., which we threw in among the enemy whenever they made their appearance. The battle had now continued about three hours, and as we in fact had possession of the *Serapis's* top, which commanded his quarter deck, upper gun deck, and forecastle, we were well assured that the enemy could not hold out much longer, and were momently expecting that they would strike to us, when the following farcical piece was acted on board our ship.

It seems that a report was at this time circulated among our crew between decks, and was credited among them, that Captain Jones and all his principal officers were slain; that the gunners were now the commanders of our ship; and that the ship had four or five feet of water in her hold, and was then sinking. They therefore advised the gunner to go upon deck, together with the carpenter and master-at-arms, and beg of the enemy quarters, in order, as they said, to save their lives. These three men being thus delegated mounted the quarter deck and bawled out as loud as they could, "Quarters, quarters, for God's sake, quarters! Our ship is a sinking!" and immediately got upon the ship's poop with a view of hauling down our colors. Hearing this in the top, I told my men that the enemy had struck and was crying out for quarters, for I actually thought that the voices of these men sounded as if on board of the enemy; but in this I was soon undeceived. The three poltroons, finding the ensign and ensign-staff gone, proceeded upon the quarter deck and were in the act of hauling down our pendant, still bawling for "Quarters!," when I heard our Commodore say in a loud voice, "What d—d rascals are them? Shoot them—kill them!" He was upon the forecastle when these fellows first made their appearance upon the quarter deck where he had just discharged his pistols at some of the enemy. The carpenter and the master-at-arms, hearing Jones's voice, skulked below, and the gunner was attempting to do the same, when Jones threw both of his pistols at his head, one of which struck him in the head, fractured his skull, and knocked him down at the foot of the gangway ladder, where he lay till the battle was over.

Both ships now took fire again, and on board of our ship it communicated to and set our maintop on fire, which threw us into the greatest consternation imaginable for some time, and it was not without some exertions and difficulty that it was overcome. The water which we had in a tub in the fore part of the top was expended without extinguishing the fire. We next had recourse to our clothes, by pulling off our coats and jackets and then throwing them upon the fire, and stamping upon them, which in a short time smothered it. Both crews were also now, as before, busily employed in stopping the progress of the flames, and the firing on both sides ceased. The enemy now demanded of us if we had struck, as they had heard the three poltroons halloo for quarters.

"If you have," said they, "why don't you haul down your pendant?" as they saw our ensign was gone.

"Ay, ay," said Jones, "we'll do that when we can fight no longer, but we shall see yours come down the first; for you must know that Yankees do not haul down their colors till they are fairly beaten."

The combat now recommenced again with more fury if possible than before on the part of both, and continued for a few minutes, when the cry of fire was again heard on board of both ships. The firing ceased, and both crews were once more employed in extinguishing it, which was soon effected; then the battle was renewed again with redoubled vigor, with what cannon we could manage, hand grenadoes, stinkpots, etc., but principally, towards the closing scene, with lances and boarding pikes. With these the combatants killed each other through the ships' portholes, which were pretty large; the guns that had been run out at them, becoming useless, as before observed, had been removed out of the way.

At three-quarters past eleven P.M. the *Alliance* frigate hove in sight, approached within pistol shot of our stern, and began a heavy and well-directed fire into us, as well as the enemy, which made some of our officers as well as men believe that she was an English man of war. (The moon at this time, as though ashamed to behold this bloody scene any longer, retired behind a dark cloud.) It was in vain that some of our officers hailed her and desired them not to fire any more; it was in vain they were told that they were firing into the wrong ship; it was in vain that they were told that they had slain a number of our men; it was in vain also that they were told that the enemy was fairly beaten, and that she must strike her colors in a few minutes. The *Alliance*, I say, notwithstanding all this, kept a position either ahead of us or under our stern and made a great deal of havoc and confusion on board of our ship; and she did not cease firing entirely till the signal of recognizance was displayed in full view on board of our ship, which was three lighted lanterns ranged in a horizontal line about fifteen feet high, upon the fore, main, and mizzen shrouds, upon the larboard side. This was done in order to undeceive the *Alliance*, and had the desired effect; the firing from her ceased.

At thirty-five minutes past twelve at night, a single hand grenado was thrown by one of our men out of the maintop of the enemy, designing it to go among the English who were huddled together between her gun decks. On its way it struck on one side of the combings of her upper hatchway and, rebounding from that, took a direction and fell between their decks, where it communicated to a quantity of loose powder scattered about the enemy's cannon; and the hand grenado, bursting at the same time, made a dreadful explosion and blew up about twenty of the enemy. This closed the scene, and the enemy now in their turn (notwithstanding the gasconading of Captain Pearson) bawled out, "Quarters, quarters, quarters, for God's sake!" It was, however, some time before the enemy's colors were struck.

The Captain of the *Serapis* gave repeated orders for one of his crew to ascend the quarter deck and haul down the English flag, but no one would stir to do it. They told the Captain they were afraid of our riflemen, believing that all our men who were seen with muskets were of that description. The Captain of the *Serapis* himself therefore ascended the quarter-deck and hauled down the very flag which he had nailed to the flagstaff a little before the commencement of the battle, and which flag he had at that time, in the presence of his principal officers, sworn he never would strike to that infamous pirate J. P. Jones.

The enemy's flag being struck, Captain Jones ordered Richard Dale, his First Lieutenant, to select out of our crew a number of men and take possession of the prize, which was immediately put in execution. Several of our men (I believe three) were killed by the English on board of the *Serapis* after she had struck to us, for which they afterwards apologized by saying that the men who were guilty of this breach of honor did not know at the time that their own ship had struck her colors. Thus ended this ever-memorable battle, after a continuance of a few minutes more than four hours. The officers, headed by the Captain of the *Serapis,* now came on board of our ship; the latter (Captain Pearson) inquired for Captain Jones, to whom he was introduced by Mr. Mase, our purser.

They met, and the former accosted the latter, in presenting his sword, in this manner: "It is with the greatest reluctance that I am now obliged to resign you this, for it is painful to me, more particularly at this time, when compelled to deliver up my sword to a man who may be said to fight with a halter around his neck!"

Jones, after receiving his sword, made this reply: "Sir, you have fought like a hero, and I make no doubt but your sovereign will reward you in a most ample manner for it."

Captain Pearson then asked Jones what countrymen his crew principally consisted of. The latter said, "Americans." "Very well," said the former, "it has been 'diamond cut diamond' with us."

Captain Pearson's officers had, previous to coming on board our ship, delivered their side arms to Lieutenant Dale. Captain Pearson in his conversation with Captain Jones owned that the Americans were equally as brave as the English. The two Cap-

14. **JOHN PAUL JONES SHOOTING A COWARDLY SAILOR
DURING THE ENGAGEMENT WITH THE "SERAPIS"**

tains now withdrew into the cabin, and there drank a glass or two of wine together.

Both ships were now separated from each other, and were mere wrecks. The *Serapis's* three masts, having nothing to support them, fell overboard with all the sails, tops, yards, rigging, etc., belonging to them, making a hideous noise in the water; they had been shot off by our guns in the early part of the action: the mainmast about one foot above the ship's gangway and quarter deck, the foremast just below the foretop, and the mizzenmast about ten feet above her quarter deck. Several eighteen-pound shot had gone through our mainmast and most of the shrouds belonging to it were cut away, so that nothing kept it standing but the stoppers put on them by the quartermasters where the shrouds had been shot away. We that were stationed on the main-top found it, during a part of the action, a very ticklish situation, from which we were ordered down upon the quarter-deck as soon as the English had struck.

We were now much alarmed on board of our ship in consequence of having two more enemies to encounter with, almost as formidable as those we had but just conquered, viz., fire and water. Our pumps had been kept going without any intermission for about two hours, and still the water in the ship's hold increased fast. The ship had received several shot in her bottom so low, or so far under water, that it was impossible to find means to stop them up, so that it was reduced to a certainty that she must sink in a short time. The fire had communicated itself to several parts of our ship made up with rotten wood, pitch, tar, and oakum. This being the case, the more water thrown on the fire, the more furiously it would burn; in fact, the effect was the same as throwing water upon and over a pot or kettle of pitch, tar, or turpentine when on fire. The fire had now penetrated to within the thickness of a pine board to the bulkhead of the magazine of powder. It was therefore found to be impracticable to extinguish the fire, or to free the ship of water, for we well knew that one of two things must happen: either the ship would burn down to the water's edge and then sink, or she would sink first. In this dilemma Jones ordered the signal of distress to be hung out, which the *Alliance, Pallais,* and *Vengeance* observing, sent their boats to our assistance. He now further ordered that the powder be removed from our magazine, and that no man should quit the *Good Man Richard* till every cask of powder was safe on board of the boats then alongside. The English officers were much frightened at this, as was the case with many of us, as the fire was at that moment in and about the powder room, and we expected every moment to be blown into the air. The English officers therefore assisted us in getting up the powder, and Captain Jones encouraged them by telling them that he would not abandon his own ship till every cask of powder was out of her. This piece of service was accomplished in a few minutes, after which Jones and the English officers embarked in the boats and went on board of the *Serapis*, first leaving orders with his officers to abandon the *Good Man Richard* after we had got all the wounded men and English prisoners out of her and put them on board of the squadron.

One circumstance relative to the First Lieutenant, by the name of Stanhope, is so singular that I am induced to relate the fact. It was this. Early in the action he hung himself down by one of the *Serapis's* stern ladders into the water, so that his body was immersed; in this situation he hung with only his head above water during the remainder of the action. It was noticed by one of our officers when Stanhope surrendered among his brother officers and came on our quarter deck that he appeared to be entirely wet, and the question was put to him how his clothes came to be so wet. He said he had, just before the *Serapis* struck, attempted to sound her pump-well to see how much water she had in her, and fell into it. But the petty officers of the *Serapis* declared to us that the fact was above stated, and this was also confirmed by several of the English sailors.

The *Pallais* had captured the consort to the *Serapis*, an English ship of war mounting twenty-two guns and called the *Countess of Scarborough*, after a brisk action which lasted about half an hour; these two ships now joined the squadron. The *Serapis*, having been pierced with several shot during the action, between wind and water was thought to be sinking; consequently, the assistance of the crews of the different ships composing the squadron was demanded on board of the *Serapis*. Her chain pumps were kept constantly going, and the cranks attached to them were double manned, and were often relieved. Two chain pumps, the number the *Serapis* then had, if kept at work as fast as possible, are allowed to deliver about a ton of water in a minute; the reader may therefore, according to this computation, form some judgment how much water must have been pumped out of the *Serapis* in four hours, the time taken with the pumps constantly going for sucking her out. The carpenters at this time were employed in stopping shot holes, etc.

But to return to the *Good Man Richard*. We were busily employed in getting out the wounded and embarking them on board of the boats belonging to the squadron, when the alarm was given that the English prisoners, to the number of about fifty, who had been let out of confinement after the battle, had taken possession of our ship and were running her on shore. They were at this time absolutely masters of the quarter deck, spar deck, and forecastle, and had got the ship before the wind and her yards squared by the braces, steering directly in for the land, the wind being about east. In consequence of this another battle ensued, but we, having in our possession the greater part of the arms suitable for a close fight, although they outnumbered us, soon overpowered them, and again became masters of the ship; not, however, until we had killed two of them, and wounded and driven overboard several others. These last, about thirteen in number, took possession of one of the boats lying alongside of our ship and made their escape to land. After this, the rest of these desperate Englishmen were ordered into the boats and transported on board the *Pallais*.

I now took a full view of the mangled carcasses of the slain on board of our ship, especially between decks, where the bloody scene was enough to appall the stoutest heart. To see the dead lying in heaps—to hear the groans of the wounded and dying—the entrails of the dead scattered promiscuously around, the blood (American too) over one's shoes, was enough to move pity from the most hardened and callous breast. And although my spirit was somewhat dampened at this shocking sight, yet when I came to reflect that we were conquerors, and over those who wished to bind America in chains of everlasting slavery, my spirits revived, and I thought perhaps that some faithful historian would at some future period enroll me among the heroes and deliverers of my country. Pardon me, gentle reader, for this involuntary digression, and let this be my excuse that I felt the spirit which infused courage into my breast on the night of and during the battle which I have just given you a faithful relation of, even while my pen was tracing the dreadful conflict.

The two prizes were King's ships, and before their capture they were convoying a fleet from the Baltic to Scarborough, in England, consisting of thirty odd sail. Not one of them was taken by any one of our squadron, although they were in sight during the battle, and were to be seen by us the morning after near the land, but no orders were given nor any attempts made by either of our squadron to take possession of any of them. The reason was that the then wrecked situation of the *Serapis* required the utmost exertions of all who belonged to the squadron to save this valuable ship.

However, it is certain that had the Captain of the *Alliance* frigate obeyed the orders given to him before the commencement of the action by the commander-in-chief, which the reader no doubt remembers, the whole of the enemy's fleet must have fallen into our hands; this the English commander acknowledged after the fight. But after this long and hard-fought battle was over, it was not thought advisable, for reasons before given, to dispatch either of the squadron to capture any of the English merchant ships.

Having now executed the orders left us by Captain Jones, we thought of leaving the *Good Man Richard* to the mercy of the winds and waves. The wind now blowing a fresh gale at N.E. I went down into the gunroom with some others, to see the Lieutenants' and other officers' trunks taken out from thence and put into the boats. But, good God! What havoc! Not a piece of them could be found as large as a continental dollar! 'Tis true we found several shirts, coats, etc., but so shockingly were they pierced with the enemy's shot, round and grape, that they were of no value. In fact, such a large breach was made through and through our ship's quarter and gunroom that, provided the ship could have been placed upon the land in a position so as to have buried her in it to her lower gun deck, one might have drove in with a coach and six at one side of the breach and out the other. The splinters and pieces of our ship that were here scattered about upon the deck lay in heaps, and perhaps twenty carpenters at work upon wood and timber would not have caused as many in five days' constant labor. Upon the whole, I think this battle, every circumstance attending it minutely considered, may be ranked with propriety the most bloody, the hardest fought, and the greatest scene of carnage on both sides ever fought between two ships of war of any nation under heaven.

3. YANKEE TRICKS ON THE HIGH SEAS

[After breaking with Jones, whose highhanded conduct caused much bad feeling among his officers and men, Fanning sailed on a French privateer as second in command, was again captured by the English and freed on exchange, and continued his sallies from French ports, in a manner reminiscent of Jones himself. In May, 1782, he received command of the cutter *Eclipse,* a privateer, and the following August finds him again in British waters.]

ON THE MORNING of the eleventh we fell in with the *Jupiter,* a fifty-gun ship and one of the fastest sailers in the British navy, and two frigates. They bore from us when we first discovered them about W. by S., distance nearly five leagues, the wind then blowing a fresh gale at W.S.W. We bore away before the wind, and packed all sail upon the privateer. The three ships gave chase to us, and spread all their canvas which would draw. We soon after saw a large cutter directly ahead of us with English colors set. The largest ship astern now hove out a signal and the cutter hove to, to obstruct our passing her. All hands were now called to quarters on board of our privateer. We approached the English cutter fast, and perceived that she mounted fourteen guns, and that she had hauled up the tack of her mainsail, and was prepared to give us a warm reception. The ships in chase of me were now in such a position that in order to avoid them I was obliged to run within pistol shot of the cutter. We passed her, in doing which we exchanged broadsides. She did us no injury. We then rounded to, and gave her our other broadside, which carried away her topmast, jib tack, and peak tye. In this crippled situation we left her, and continued our course before the wind without taking in a rag of sail, as the ships were then close to our heels. One of the ships in chase, having got up with the cutter, hove to, to her assistance. The cutter very soon disappeared as we thought, and we concluded that she had sunk, but after this we saw the other ship take her in tow and stretch in towards the land.

At 3 P.M. we had so far outsailed them that we had lost sight of all but the fifty-gun ship, which was now about three leagues' distance of us, but about the same time we discovered ahead of us the English Channel Fleet of men of war, extending in a line from abreast of the east end of the Isle of Wight towards the southward about nine miles. There appeared to be no alternative left us now but to run directly through this line. In order to succeed in this hazardous and Don Quixote attempt, I ordered the French colors hauled down, and an English ensign and pendant hoisted. Soon after we could distinctly count in this fleet twenty-eight ships of the line, several of which were three-deckers, besides a number of frigates, sloops of war, and cutters. Several signals were displayed on board of the ship astern of us. The grand fleet also made several signals. I certainly at this time had faith to believe that the deception which I contemplated would succeed. Our cutter, having been built in England, was now painted exactly like the King's cutters, and the most of my officers and crew spoke English and were dressed like Englishmen; this being the case, the deception was the more easy. I ordered all those on board who could speak no English to go below, and then approached the English fleet with boldness, entered the center of their line, and passed through between two three-deckers. From on board of both (we being then within pistol shot of them) they hailed us in these words, "What cutter is that?" The answer was "His Majesty's cutter Surprize." We dropped our peak and doused our colors, passing these wooden castles, but did not take in a rag of sail.

We had nearly got without hail when they hallooed us to bring to. We answered, "Ay, ay," but notwithstanding kept on our course. We had now given them the slip, and meant to show them a Yankee trick by giving them leg bail. The ships of the line in the center fired several cannon at us, the shot of which flew considerably beyond us, passing over our heads. Finding that we did not bring to, three frigates, a sloop of war, and a cutter separated from the fleet and gave us chase. The fifty-gun ship at the same time passed through the grand fleet and continued to chase us. The cutter appeared to outsail either of them, and she in fact sailed faster than we did. Perceiving this, I ordered the man at the helm from time to time to give our privateer a rank sheer, and ordered the drag overboard to retard her way through the water. The English cutter came up within musket shot and began firing into us. We gave her two broadsides and cut away some of her rigging (which she hove to to repair, as we supposed). But after this she did not attempt even to follow us. This was done just in the dusk of the evening; and at the same time the other ships, except the *Jupiter,* gave over chasing us, and hauled upon a wind, which increased, and the last-mentioned ship appeared to gain upon us; however, night shut in, and we could not see her with our naked eyes, but could perceive her quite plain with our night-glass.

Being by this time much fatigued, after having gone through so many different scenes in the course of the day, and anhungered withal, I stepped below to get some refreshment, not apprehending that we should be taken at this time by any of those ships which had been chasing us, excepting perhaps the *Jupiter.* I had no sooner got below than the fellow at the helm broached to the cutter and carried away our topmast just above the uppermost withe. The steering sail, ringtail, and water sail halyards gave way and parted at the same instant, which threw us into some confusion. I ordered the ringtail and water sail cut clear, and took the helm. My gunner in attempting to execute my orders fell off the main boom, there being a bad sea running. We strove to save him but did not succeed; the poor fellow was drowned. Having got the cutter before the wind again and the light sails secured on board, all hands were employed with as much expedition as possible in order to get a spare topmast on end; but before we succeeded in this, the fifty-gun ship came up with us, ran under our stern, luffed up under our lee, and accosted us in this manner, "Strike, you d—d Irish rascal; drop the peak of your mainsail, and haul down your jib sheet to the windward; hoist out your boat, and come on board of His Majesty's ship." I answered that my boat was so full of holes that she could not swim. It was now about four o'clock in the morning and nearly three hours before day would break, no moon, and pretty dark. They replied that they would hoist out their own boat, and ordered me to hoist a lighted lantern at the peak; which was complied with. She had her light sails taken in, her courses hauled up, ready for action, with her head to the southward, ours at the same time being in the opposite direction.

My officers were now in readiness to surrender as prisoners of war to the enemy, having dressed themselves in their best clothes and two shirts apiece. I suggested to them the idea and probability there was at present of making our escape from the enemy. A majority of them was for attempting this truly hazardous business, and I told them I would risk myself at the helm till we should get out of reach of the enemy's shot. The plan thus being concerted, we proceeded to carry it into effect. The enemy was at this state of the business busily employed in hoisting out their boat, which we knew by the boatswain's call. I ordered some men to sway up the peak and let draw the jib sheets; this done, I directed every man and boy to lie flat upon the deck, and our privateer just began to gather headway when the enemy's boat left the ship in order to board us. I desired everyone to obey my orders and we should quickly get away from the enemy (and they paid implicit obedience), but I must confess I had not much faith at the same time in getting away.

The *Jupiter* perceiving our intentions, their boat returned on board, and she instantly began a most tremendous fire upon us from all parts of the ship; she had the appearance for a few minutes of a luminous body of fire. She was at this time within musket shot of us. They by this time finding that we were trying to make our escape in good earnest, wore ship, and got aboard their fore and main tacks, set their topgallant sails, and in fact crowded all the sail which they could set by the wind after us. She, however, continued to fire her bow chasers at us. We now hove in stays, and were obliged in stretching by her to expose ourselves to another broadside, as well as her musketry. I knew this to be the pinch of the game, and therefore once more cautioned everybody upon deck to lie as close as possible. She blazed away at us from every part of her as we passed each other.

At this moment I received a flesh wound in the leg and another in the forehead by a splinter, which knocked me down and stunned me upon deck, where I lay some time motionless. Several of my officers and men were wounded at the same time and some of them cried out, "For God's sake, let us strike." Having now recovered myself and got hold of the helm, I answered these men that in ten or fifteen minutes more we should be out of gunshot of the enemy. We were now gaining away from the enemy very fast. We tacked again, and in passing her this time she could but just reach us with her shot. We found it best to tack often, as we were then plying to windward, and since we could manage our privateer with more ease and expedition than the enemy, we could ply to the windward much faster than they could. Accordingly, the next time we passed the ship, though she fired her broadside at us, yet her shot did not reach us. At daylight in the morning the enemy were at least four leagues to leeward of us, and she soon after gave up the chase and bore away from us. It is my opinion that the enemy expended more powder and shot in firing at us than she would have done in an engagement with an enemy's ship of equal force for two hours. So much for the Irish rascal—as they called me—but the bird had flown. And now, Messieurs Braggadocio Englishmen, you may return home and tell your royal master "that you catched an Irishman and lost him."

In this running fight we did not fire a single gun. We had enough else to do, to maneuver our privateer and keep out of reach as much as possible of the shot of the enemy. We had on this occasion thirteen men slightly wounded, but none killed. Our waist and boat (stowed in the chocks) were pierced through and through with eighteen- and nine-pound shot. Our sails also were full of shot holes; not less than seven hundred and fifty of these last could be counted (after we had got clear of the *Jupiter*) in our mainsail alone; but during the whole of her firing upon and into our privateer, she did not cut away a single piece of rope or rigging of any kind whatsoever. We now had some leisure time to dress our wounded men, and to take some refreshment, there not being any vessels in sight except the *Jupiter,* and she was so far to leeward that we could but just discern her.

4. SNATCHING PRIZES

[The *Eclipse* being no longer seaworthy, Fanning accepted command of a new brig. While waiting for its masts to arrive, however, he purchased part of a small forty-ton cutter, the *Ranger,* an

English-built vessel lightly armed but with full boarding equipment, and fretful at inaction he put to sea as her captain.]

I SET SAIL from Dunkirk in said privateer [the *Ranger*] with a fair wind for the English coast on the evening of the twenty-third of October, and shaped our course for the Downs. At daylight next morning we found ourselves amidst an English fleet of sixty odd sail of ships and other vessels, not far from Dover, all of which appeared to be bound to the westward; we had at that time a light breeze of wind from the eastward. The first thing we did in this perilous situation was to cover our guns with light sails, unship our swivels and stow them away (our guns having been housed), and hoist English colors. We steered along the same course which they did. I also ordered all my men below, except the one at the helm and two others, and disguised our privateer as much as possible, so as to make her appear like a coasting vessel.

As soon as it was broad daylight I reconnoitered the fleet, and could not discover but one frigate of thirty-two guns among them, and she appeared to be the commodore, by her broad pendant. There were, however, several letters of marque among them, mounting from four to sixteen carriage guns, besides two large sixteen-gun cutters. At meridian the wind shifted to the westward, but was very light, and the current ahead. The commodore made a signal for the fleet to bring to and come to anchor. This being done, I had the mortification to see several boats passing and repassing from one ship to another, and was momentarily in expectation of their paying me a visit. If they had, they must have discovered who we were, in all human probability. However, our alarms on this score subsided when we saw the vessels who had got out their boats to visit each other hoist them on board.

At 5 P.M. the signal was made for the fleet to get under way. We did the same, and steered along with them. My Lieutenant and myself now cracked some jokes on the subject of being made prisoners again. We spoke two ships and a brig towards night, and passed within pistol shot of them, and besides had a long conversation with the people on board of one of the ships, the wind being light and the sea smooth. On the first night we agreed not to separate from the fleet until we had captured some of them. (Whereas we might have possibly sneaked away, and got clear of them this very night, without its being attended with any great risk, had we made the attempt.) But the fact was, we could not reconcile it to ourselves, to be forced to quit so many valuable vessels as we expected there were in the fleet, without making the trial agreed on. We found by conversing, as before mentioned, with some of those who were in one of these vessels, that the whole fleet was bound for Portsmouth. In fine, we kept company with this fleet (without, I believe, being suspected by the English of being an enemy) three days and two nights, during which the winds were ahead and very light; and on the third night—the two preceding nights having been too light to attack either of the fleet—we made the attempt, and succeeded in the following manner.

Before dark, the sun having set in or behind a dark cloud, and the weather having at the same time an appearance of becoming squally, the commodore made a signal by firing three guns, and hoisting several flags. This we understood afterwards by some of the prisoners was for the fleet to disperse and seek shelter in the nearest port, which was Rye, then not far distant to the northward and eastward of us. At 9 P.M. we ran under the lee of a large ship (having our men ready for boarding), hailed them, and asked them if they were acquainted with going into that port. They answered in the negative. I then demanded of them if we should put a pilot on board of them, to which they replied, "Ay, ay."

It was then very dark and nearly all the ship's crew were upon the yards, reefing her topsails. I ran under her lee quarter and ordered the Lieutenant who had the command of the men for boarding to leap on board with his party, which he did instantly. The Captain of the ship with his men upon deck made but a faint resistance, and after a short skirmish the English yielded and were made prisoners, as were those also who were upon her yards, as they came down. Not a single cannon or musket was discharged by either party during the conflict, and but three or four pistols. The enemy had several slightly wounded. The Lieutenant, the first man who mounted on board of the ship, and three others of his party were also wounded, but very slightly. She proved to be the *Maria*, letter of marque, mounting eight double fortified six-pound cannon, mounted upon carriages between decks, and was calculated to fight then in close quarters, as nearly all her rigging was led between decks, in such a manner as to maneuver the ship without exposing her men to the fire of an enemy. Her crew, including the Captain and his officers, consisted of thirty-five picked men, besides three gentleman passengers. She was bound from the Downs to Portsmouth, laden with sundry articles for the navy, and was one of the fleet aforesaid. As soon as we had got all the prisoners secured in irons in the privateer's hold, I ordered the First Lieutenant to take charge of the ship, put ten men on board to assist in working her, gave him a copy of my commission, and directed him to steer across the Channel and make the first French port in his power, and to crowd as much sail upon the prize as she could carry.

Several of the lights of the fleet were now plainly seen, notwithstanding the darkness of the night; however, no alarm guns were as yet fired by any of them. We next ran alongside of a large brigantine, and boarded and took her, no resistance being made by her crew. She was one of the fleet, mounted four carriage guns, was manned with fifteen men and boys, including the Captain and mate, and laden with sheathing copper for the navy; she was called the *Speedwell*. Put a prize master and six men on board of her, took out the prisoners and secured them in our hold, and ordered the prize master to make all sail and crowd over to the French shore as fast as possible, and get into the first port he could.

The next thing which I did was to board a large sloop, and capture her. We ran a great risk, in laying alongside of her (as the wind blew fresh at W.S.W. and the sea ran pretty high), of going to the bottom. The prisoners who were confined in our hold made a dreadful noise, hallooing that we were sinking, and that water came in where they were confined very fast. However, all this ado did not induce me to quit this last prize without manning her for France, and taking out the prisoners, both of which were completed in a few minutes. I put the boatswain and gunner on board of this prize (neither of whom understood navigating a vessel) and one seaman; gave the boatswain a copy of my commission, and gave him the same orders as I had given the other two prize masters. This last prize had in a few bales of dry goods; the rest of her lading was pigs of lead, and sea coal. She was from the river Thames, bound for Portsmouth, was one of the fleet, and called the *Dolphin*.

Taking these prizes, securing the prisoners, and manning them spun away the greater part of the night, and I began to think seriously of skulking off as fast as possible. I had now only left on board with me two Irish lads (although I shipped them at Dunkirk for American seamen), neither of whom could steer. This placed me in a very awkward situation, as I knew it would not be safe to let any of the prisoners out of the hold to assist in working our privateer. However, I made shift to set some sail and left the fleet, and at daybreak we could distinctly hear alarm guns fired. We were now several leagues from them. At 6 A.M. I had overtaken two of my prizes, to wit, the brigantine and the sloop, and at the same time saw a large cutter bearing down upon us, which appeared to have come from the fleet. We were then abreast of the port of Dieppe, a small seaport upon the French coast. I spoke my prizes and ordered those who had command of them to endeavor to gain that port, not thinking it prudent to remain with them, as in that case I might make my escape with the privateer, but my prizes would certainly be retaken (provided the cutter in question was an English one). I then hauled upon a wind to the northward and eastward, the wind being about N.N.W. The large cutter at the same time stood nearly across our fore foot, and when we had got nearly out of sight of our prizes I bore away nearly before the wind; the enemy's cutter did the same. I could not set any more sail, being obliged to keep the helm myself, for the reason before given; the two lads that were left on board of my original crew did not know how to set even the square sail and topsail.

I could not perceive that the cutter in chase of me gained upon us very fast, but at 2 P.M. she came up with and captured me. She mounted fourteen carriage guns, was in the King's service, and commanded by a Lieutenant in the Royal Navy by the name of Laines. We found, after the *Ranger* was taken, that she would sail faster than the cutter which took us, when she came to be managed right, and a sufficiency of sail set upon her. The commander of the King's cutter I was acquainted with, having seen him in Ostend some time before, where we lodged both together in that place. He used me with friendship and indulgence while on board of his vessel. Both cutters now steered for Dover. The Captain of the large prize which I had taken in the night out of the English fleet (who had been liberated from irons, as had also all the English, after they had been retaken) made several attempts to kill himself, on account of his having been boarded and captured by such a small picaroon privateer, and which his own countrymen upbraided him with. Only the night before he was taken he had bragged that he could take a French privateer of sixteen guns. They were obliged to confine him to his bed and to put a sentinel over him to prevent his committing suicide.

At ten o'clock on the second day after I was captured we arrived at Dover, and came to anchor nearly abreast of the town, which was soon in an uproar when they found that the person who went by the name of "John Dyon, commander of His Majesty's Cutter the *Surprize*," was taken a prisoner, and that he was then on board of a cutter lying off the town. The next morning the cutter's boat was ordered to be manned and carry me on shore with my baggage, and the two lads taken with me. Accordingly we embarked on board of the boat, and the Second Lieutenant with us, and the boat's crew rowed towards the shore. As they approached we saw the quay covered with women, appearing to amount to about two hundred, who had heard of my being captured, and who, it seemed by their conduct, were determined to execute the old Levitical law upon me by stoning me to death. They threw stones at me as we drew near the quay, which flew so thick and in such showers that it was impossible for me to escape being hurt. And it surprised me very much to hear the heroines cry out, "Welcome, welcome, Captain Dyon." These expressions were followed instantly by showers of stones, which pelted me so much, and were so often repeated, as occasioned my head to swell to double its ordinary size, and caused it to be very painful. As good luck would have it, I had on at the time a glazed hat (otherwise I should have been in the greatest hazard of losing my life) which I pulled over my face to prevent losing my eyes. And such oaths, imprecations, and threats as these heroines uttered at me, I never before heard proceed from the mouth of any human being.

At length a guard consisting of upwards of one hundred officers and soldiers were sent express to disperse the mob. A part of them, after I landed, conducted me and the two lads taken with me to the fort. There we were examined by a young man about seventeen years of age, Commissary for Prisoners of War, and a one-eyed, surly-looking fellow who had been First Lieutenant on board of the *Rose* sloop of war, commanded by that noted plunderer J. Wallace, and for a long time stationed at or near Newport in the first part of the American Revolution.

This Lieutenant boasted of his great knowledge of the American coast from New Hampshire to Georgia, and said that he knew the way in and out of every seaport within those two extremities, and that he knew the bearings and distances from one cape or headland to another all along that extent of seacoast. And I was afterwards fully convinced that he did know something of what he boasted, from the questions he put to me. His station here at present was that of Regulating Captain at this port; he held his office under the King and was appointed to examine all the prisoners brought here or into the ports nearby by His Majesty's cruisers of all descriptions. His universal knowledge of the American coast was (as I was told) the reason of his appointment under the Crown in this place.

The two lads were examined first, before the Commissary and the Regulating Captain, and were by these last found to be Irish boys, in consequence of which they were sent on board of the guard ship lying off Dover, and were afterwards hanged, for being taken under an enemy's flag and proved to be British subjects.

I was then conducted into the presence of these two King's officers. At my first entrance into the room, the Regulating Captain swore that I was an Englishman, and the Commissary, after asking me a few questions, declared that I was an Irishman. The interrogatories which they intended to put on me were already written down and lying on a table before the King's officers. The first question which they put to me was: "Where were you born?" When I had answered it, they made a great deal of diversion to themselves, and the Regulating Captain told several Yankee stories, relative to the town and the people where I said I was born. They afterwards put a great number of other questions to me, such as, "Is there a lighthouse at the mouth of New London Harbor? Upon which hand do you leave it, in going into the same? How far is it from the lighthouse to the west end of Fisher's Island, and what course and distance? How far is it from the mouth of New London Harbor to the mouth of the Connecticut River? Who was His Majesty's collector in New London, before the rebel war broke out in America?" etc., etc.

To all of these questions I gave such kind of answers as appeared to convince these officers that I was really an American by birth. After this the Commissary told me that I might be admitted upon my parole, if I chose it, but at the same time advised me not to be paroled, giving this as a reason—that if I was committed to close confinement I should be so much the sooner set at liberty, by being exchanged. However, he told me I might choose which I pleased. I chose to be close confined; and the Commissary assured me that I should have a small apartment in prison by myself, and should have the liberty of the yard during every day I remained a prisoner. He besides pledged his word and honor that I should go over to France in the first cartel vessel which should be dispatched from that quarter, and which he thought would probably go to Calais in the course of eight or ten days with prisoners. I also knew that if I had accepted of my parole and remained in Dover, it was likely that my boarding and lodging would have in a short time amounted to a considerable sum of money, as I had, after I first landed, paid at an inn half a guinea for my breakfast only, which consisted of a dish or two of coffee, a wheaten toast, and some dried beef, shredded up very thin.

When I had gone through with my examination, I was dismissed from the guardhouse, and was conducted from thence by a corporal and four soldiers to Deal, a small town situated at or near the mouth of the river Thames, about eleven miles from Dover. At the first of these places I remained a prisoner (but with every indulgence, as had been promised me by the Commissary) only ten days. I was then exchanged, and arrived in Dunkirk on the seventeenth day after sailing on my cruise, where I found all my prizes safe.

THE CRUCIAL WINTER OF 1777-1778

After evacuating Boston Sir William Howe had sailed for New York and conquered that city by September, 1776. In the months that followed he extended his position along the Hudson, and in the summer of 1777 the Colonial Secretary, Lord Germain, made plans to finish off the rebels. Conceding that the American resistance was not despicable, he financed a crack new army that Major-General John Burgoyne would lead from Canada down the Lake Champlain–Lake George route to connect with Howe at Albany. The rebellious states would be split asunder, New England and her nests of privateers would be isolated, and only mopping-up operations would remain. Instead of co-ordinating with Burgoyne, however, Howe decided to march for Philadelphia, and by invading Pennsylvania force Washington to do battle to protect the country's vital center. Such a battle would result in the erasure of the Continental Army and an equally certain end to the war. Howe believed that Burgoyne could easily take care of himself, and the ease with which Gentleman Johnny captured Fort Ticonderoga on the first leg of his march, by simply training his cannon on the fort from a nearby bluff, seemed amply to confirm that opinion. Not one but two mortal threats were thus posed at the American forces in the autumn months of 1777.

With Ticonderoga recaptured and General Schuyler sick in Albany while his demoralized troops took to their heels before Burgoyne, the English General apparently had little to do but walk to Albany. Then one by one new factors came into play. Gates replaced Schuyler as commander of the Northern army, and New England militia rallied to their champion. Washington detached Colonel Morgan's riflemen to aid Gates, and so strengthened him with the keenest marksmen in America. Burgoyne blundered in continuing through the woods with his swollen baggage trains, instead of retracing his steps long enough to embark on Lake George. Before the scorched-earth policy of the Yankees, his difficulties of supply increased each foot he advanced. His

Indian scouts, already unhappy at Burgoyne's restraints on their mayhem, deserted in the face of Morgan's dead shots. His Canadian allies decided they could return to Canada much more speedily than they could progress to New York. Five hundred German mercenaries whom Burgoyne in sore necessity dispatched to Bennington to procure supplies fell easy prey to the superior woodcraft of John Stark and the Green Mountain Boys. A diversionary expedition under St. Leger coming down the Mohawk Valley ran into stiff resistance at Fort Stanwix and turned back. Gates established himself in strongly prepared positions laid out by the Polish engineer Kosciusko, and at the Battle of Freeman's Farm on September 19, Morgan's riflemen slithering through the trees raked the redcoats with a murderous fire, and although they quit the field when fresh German troops arrived, the Yankees had drawn lifeblood. They gave the coup de grâce *a month later, October 17, at the Battle of Saratoga.*

Just too late General Clinton, left behind by Howe at New York, moved up the Hudson, reduced the two forts blocking him, and saw a clear road to his beleaguered partner. But Burgoyne had surrendered, and Clinton turned back. Clinton's tardy success suggests what Howe might have done had he moved north instead of west. But in July Howe had placed his troops aboard his brother's ships and cleared for an unknown destination. He stopped at Delaware Bay, but decided to land farther south at the Chesapeake, as an easier route to the capital and one more deceptive to Washington. With that decision passed all chance of a coalition between the two British armies.

Howe reached and entered Philadelphia, without crushing the Continental Army. He met Washington at Brandywine and Germantown, and demonstrated his superior power in the heavy fighting, but an army still remained in existence to bay him in his winter quarters. First in Boston, then in New York, now in Philadelphia, British officers had passed the winter months in the lavish homes of Loyalist hosts, while the scraggly troops of Washington hung grimly outside the gates. The question was, could the harassed commander keep his army in being throughout another winter? Washington took up quarters at Valley Forge, twenty miles outside the city on the banks of the Schuylkill, and waited. Inflation squeezed empty the purse of his quartermaster and kept his army ill fed and half naked while the Pennsylvania German farmers stocked high the British larder, in return for the King's gold. Morale declined, as his men compared their plight with the situation of war-wealthy profiteers and turncoat Loyalists, and drifted home. The Loyalists and British officers reveled in Philadelphia, and feted Howe with a grand ball when that worthy relinquished his command to Clinton and sailed wearily home.

Meanwhile the leaven of the Saratoga victory was working through the layers of diplomatic discussion, and mighty France signed a military alliance with the infant nation in February. Clinton received orders to quit Philadelphia, and sailed away on the eighteenth of June, 1778, to avoid being bottled by a French fleet heading for Delaware Bay. A seasoned, tough, and confident American army dogged him back to New York. The crucial winter had ended with the British back where they had started from, but minus one army and facing a reinvigorated foe now teamed with the foremost Continental power in Europe.

The disastrous campaign of Burgoyne can be followed with intimate detail in the journal of the Baroness von Riedesel, wife of a Brunswick general employed by George III. Life in the camp at Valley Forge is described by Dr. Albigence Waldo, a surgeon attached to the Continental Army. For a close-up of American officers traveling to and from Washington's headquarters, the diary of young Sally Wister, living fifteen miles outside Philadelphia, provides an unusual record of war's frivolous asides.

Baroness von Riedesel

ON MAY 14, 1776, a spirited and attractive young mother set out with her three tiny daughters from Wolfenbüttel in the duchy of Brunswick to join her husband in Canada. Her friends remonstrated with the Baroness Friederike Charlotte Luise von Massow Riedesel (1746-1808) at this foolhardy venture. "They represented to me not only the perils of the sea, but told me, also, that we were in danger of being eaten by the savages, and that the people in America lived upon horseflesh and cats. Yet all this frightened me less than the thought of going into a country where I could not understand the language." One must admire the intrepidity of the sheltered noblewoman, born the daughter of Count Massow, a governing president of the allied army commissioned by Frederick II, and wife of Major General Friedrich von Riedesel, who commanded the Brunswick regiments in Burgoyne's army. She experienced undreamt-of difficulties in traveling across the Continental post roads, seeking passage in London, Bristol, and Portsmouth (where the mob called her a "French whore" for wearing a calico dress trimmed with green taffeta), crossing the ocean, and accompanying her husband on the ill-fated expedition that set out from Canada June 3, 1777. After the surrender of Burgoyne's army, Madame von Riedesel ("Red-Hazel" the English cockneys called her) and her children were ordered successively to Boston and Cambridge, Virginia and New York, where her husband was exchanged. She sailed from Quebec in August, 1783, and reached Germany before the year's end.

The Baroness recorded the events of her American experience in a richly detailed and perceptive journal. Her influential contacts lend her account added interest; Lord Germain and General Howe gave her advice in London; she met Washington and Schuyler, and speaks candidly of Burgoyne, whom she personally reproved for neglecting his officers. She had no love for Burgoyne, who treated her husband shabbily, never imparting to him the plans for the New York campaign or entrusting him with independent command.

The journal was first printed privately, with other letters and papers of the General and the Baroness, in Berlin in 1800, under the title *Auszüge aus den Briefen und Papieren des Generals Freyherrn von Riedesel und seiner Gemahlin*. It was published for general circulation the same year with the title *Die Berufsreise nach America*. A Dutch translation appeared in 1802, and an English edition in 1827, titled *Letters and Memoirs relating to the War of American Independence, and the Capture of the German Troops at Saratoga. By Madame de Riedesel.*

New York, published by G. and C. Carvill. The anonymous translator took it on himself to purge the journal of its indelicate expressions, and omitted nearly forty pages of the German text. A complete and more faithful translation was rendered by William L. Stone in 1867, as *Letters and Journals relating to the War of the American Revolution, and the Capture of the German troops at Saratoga. By Mrs. General Riedesel. Albany, Joel Munsell.* The following selection is edited from pages 113-135 of the Stone translation, and commences at the point when Burgoyne advanced to Freeman's Farm and there met the army of General Gates.

THE DISASTER AT SARATOGA

WHEN THE ARMY again moved, on the eleventh of September, 1777, it was at first intended to leave me behind; but upon my urgent entreaties, and as other ladies were to follow the army, I received, finally, the same permission. We made only small day's marches, and were very often sick, yet were always contented at being allowed to follow. I had still the satisfaction of daily seeing my husband. A great part of my baggage I had sent back, and had kept only a small summer wardrobe. In the beginning all went well. We cherished the sweet hope of a sure victory, and of coming into the "promised land"; and when we passed the Hudson River and General Burgoyne said, "The English never lose ground," our spirits were greatly exhilarated.

But that which displeased me was, that the wives of all the officers belonging to the expedition knew beforehand everything that was to happen. And this seemed the more singular to me as I had observed, when in the armies of the Duke Ferdinand, during the Seven Years' War, with how much secrecy everything was conducted. But here, on the contrary, the Americans were apprised beforehand of all our intentions, so that at every place where we came they already awaited us; a circumstance which hurt us exceedingly. On the nineteenth of September there was an affair between the two armies which, it is true, ended to our advantage, although we were, nevertheless, obliged to make a halt at a place called Freeman's Farm. I was an eyewitness of the whole affair, and as I knew that my husband was in the midst of it, I was full of care and anguish, and shivered at every shot, for I could hear everything. I saw a great number of wounded, and what was still more harrowing, they even brought three of them into the house where I was. One of these was Major Harnage, the husband of a lady of our company; another, a lieutenant, whose wife, also, was of our acquaintance; and the third, a young English officer of the name of Young. Major Harnage, with his wife, lived in a room next to mine. He had received a shot through the lower part of the bowels, from which he suffered exceedingly.

A few days after our arrival I heard plaintive moans in another room near me, and learned that they came from Young, the young English officer just mentioned, who was lying very low. I was the more interested in him, since a family of that name had shown me much courtesy during my sojourn in England. I tendered him my services, and sent him provisions and refreshments. He expressed a great desire to see his benefactress, as he called me. I went to him, and found him lying on a little straw, for he had lost his camp equipage. He was a young man, probably eighteen or nineteen years old, and actually the own nephew of the Mr. Young whom I had known, and the only son of his parents. It was only for this reason that he grieved; on account of his own sufferings he uttered no complaint. He had bled considerably, and they wished to take off his leg, but he could not bring his mind to it, and now mortification had set in. I sent him pillows and coverings, and my women servants a mattress. I redoubled my care of him, and visited him every day, for which I received from the sufferer a thousand blessings. Finally, they attempted the amputation of the limb, but it was too late, and he died a few days afterward. As he occupied an apartment close to mine, and the walls were very thin, I could hear his last groans through the partition of my room.

I lived in a pretty, well-built house, in which I had a large room. The doors and the wainscot were of solid cedar, a wood that is very common in this vicinity. They burn it frequently, especially when there are many midges around, as these insects cannot stand the odor of it. It is said, however, that its smoke is very injurious to the nerves, so much so, indeed, as to cause women with child to bring forth prematurely. As we were to march farther, I had a large calash made for me, in which I, my children, and both my women servants had seats; and in this manner I followed the army, in the midst of the soldiers, who were merry, singing songs, and burning with a desire for victory. We passed through boundless forests and magnificent tracts of country, which, however, were abandoned by all the inhabitants, who fled before us and reinforced the army of the American General, Gates. In the sequel this cost us dearly, for every one of them was a soldier by nature, and could shoot very well; besides, the thought of fighting for their fatherland and their freedom inspired them with still greater courage.

During this time, my husband was obliged to encamp with the main body of the army. I remained about an hour's march behind the army, and visited my husband every morning in the camp. Very often I took my noon meal with him, but most of the time he came over to my quarters and ate with me. The army were engaged daily in small skirmishes, but all of them of little consequence. My poor husband, however, during the whole time could not get a chance either to go to bed or undress. As the season had now become more inclement, a Colonel Williams of the artillery, observing that our mutual visits were very fatiguing, offered to have a house built for me, with a chimney, that should not cost more than five or six guineas, and which I could steadily occupy. I took him up, and the house, which was twenty feet square, and had a good fireplace, was begun. They called it the blockhouse. For such a structure, large trees of equal thickness are selected, which are joined together, making it very durable and warm, especially if covered with clay. I was to remove into it the following day, and was the more rejoiced at it as the nights were already damp and cold, and my husband could live in it with me, as he would then be very near his camp.

Suddenly, however, on the seventh of October, my husband, with the whole General Staff, decamped. Our misfortunes may be said to date from this moment. I had just sat down with my husband at his quarters to breakfast. General Frazer and, I believe, Generals Burgoyne and Phillips also were to have dined with me on that same day. I observed considerable movement among the troops. My husband thereupon informed me that there was to be a reconnaissance, which, however, did not surprise me, as this often happened. On my way homeward I met many savages in their war-dress, armed with guns. To my question where they were going, they cried out to me, "War! war!" which meant that they were going to fight. This completely overwhelmed me, and I had scarcely got back to my quarters when I heard skirmishing and firing, which by degrees became constantly heavier, until finally the noises became frightful. It was a terrible cannonade, and I was more dead than alive.

About three o'clock in the afternoon, in place of the guests who were to have dined with me, they brought in to me, upon a litter, poor General Frazer (one of my expected guests), mortally wounded. Our dining table, which was already spread, was taken away, and in its place they fixed up a bed for the General. I sat in a corner of the room trembling and quaking. The noises grew continually louder. The thought that they might bring in my husband in the same manner was to me dreadful, and tormented me incessantly. The general said to the surgeon, "Do not conceal anything from me. Must I die?" The ball had gone through his bowels, precisely as in the case of Major Harnage. Unfortunately, however, the General had eaten a hearty breakfast, by reason of which the intestines were distended, and the ball, so the surgeon said, had not gone, as in the case of Major Harnage, between the intestines, but through them. I heard him often, amidst his groans, exclaim, "Oh, fatal ambition! Poor General Burgoyne! My poor wife!" Prayers were read to him. He then sent a message to General Burgoyne, begging that he would have him buried the following day at six o'clock in the evening, on the top of a hill, which was a sort of a redoubt.

I knew no longer which way to turn. The whole entry and the other rooms were filled with the sick, who were suffering with the camp sickness, a kind of dysentery. Finally, toward evening, I saw my husband coming, upon which I forgot all my sufferings, and thanked God that he had spared him to me. He ate in great haste with me and his adjutant, behind the house. We had been told that we had gained an advantage over the enemy, but the sorrowful and downcast faces which I beheld bore witness to the contrary, and before my husband again went away, he drew me to one side and told me that everything might go very badly, and that I must keep myself in constant readiness for departure, but by no means to give anyone the least inkling of what I was doing.

I therefore pretended that I wished to move into my new house the next morning, and I had everything packed up.

My Lady Ackland occupied a tent not far from our house. In this she slept, but during the day was in the camp. Suddenly one came to tell her that her husband was mortally wounded, and had been taken prisoner. At this she became very wretched. We comforted her by saying that it was only a slight wound, but as no one could nurse him as well as herself, we counseled her to go at once to him, to do which she could certainly obtain permission. She loved him very much, although he was a plain, rough man, and was almost daily intoxicated; with this exception, however, he was an excellent officer. She was the loveliest of women. I spent the night in this manner—at one time comforting her, and at another looking after my children, whom I had put to bed. As for myself, I could not go to sleep, as I had General Frazer and all the other gentlemen in my room, and was constantly afraid that my children would wake up and cry, and thus disturb the poor dying man, who often sent to beg my pardon for making me so much trouble.

About three o'clock in the morning, they told me that he could not last much longer. I had desired to be apprised of the approach of this moment. I accordingly wrapped up the children in the bed coverings, and went with them into the entry. Early in the morning, at eight o'clock, he expired. After they had washed the corpse, they wrapped it in a sheet and laid it on a bedstead. We then again came into the room, and had this sad sight before us the whole day. At every instant, also, wounded officers of my acquaintance arrived, and the cannonade again began. A retreat was spoken of, but there was not the least movement made toward it. About four o'clock in the afternoon, I saw the new house which had been built for me, in flames; the enemy, therefore, were not far from us. We learned that General Burgoyne intended to fulfill the last wish of General Frazer, and to have him buried at six o'clock, in the place designated by him. This occasioned an unnecessary delay, to which a part of the misfortunes of the army was owing. Precisely at six o'clock the corpse was brought out, and we saw the entire body of generals with their retinues on the hill assisting at the obsequies. The English chaplain, Mr. Brudenel, performed the funeral services. The cannon balls flew continually around and over the party. The American General, Gates, afterward said that if he had known that it was a burial he would not have allowed any firing in that direction. Many cannon balls also flew not far from me, but I had my eyes fixed upon the hill, where I distinctly saw my husband in the midst of the enemy's fire, and therefore I could not think of my own danger.

The order had gone forth that the army should break up after the burial, and the horses were already harnessed to our calashes. I did not wish to set out before the troops. The wounded Major Harnage, although he was so ill, dragged himself out of bed, that he might not remain in the hospital, which was left behind protected by a flag of truce. As soon as he observed me in the midst of the danger, he had my children and maidservants put into the calashes, and intimated to me that I must immediately depart. As I still begged to be allowed to remain, he said to me, "Well, then your children at least must go, that I may save them from the slightest danger." He understood how to take advantage of my weak side. I gave it up, seated myself inside with them, and we drove off at eight o'clock in the evening.

The greatest silence had been enjoined. Fires had been kindled in every direction, and many tents left standing, to make the enemy believe that the camp was still there. We traveled continually the whole night. Little Frederica was afraid, and would often begin to cry. I was therefore obliged to hold a pocket handkerchief over her mouth, lest our whereabouts should be discovered.

At six o'clock in the morning a halt was made, at which everyone wondered. General Burgoyne had all the cannon ranged and counted, which worried all of us, as a few more good marches would have placed us in security. My husband was completely exhausted, and seated himself during this delay in my calash, where my maidservants were obliged to make room for him, and where he slept nearly three hours with his head upon my shoulder. In the meantime, Captain Willoe brought me his pocketbook containing bank bills, and Captain Geismar his beautiful watch, a ring, and a well-filled purse, and begged me to keep all these for them. I promised them to do my utmost. At last, the army again began its march, but scarcely had we proceeded an hour on the way when a fresh halt was made, in consequence of the enemy being in sight. They were about two hundred men who came to reconnoiter, and who might easily have been taken prisoners by our troops had not General Burgoyne lost his head. It rained in torrents. My Lady Ackland had her tent set up. I advised her once more to betake herself to her husband, as she could be so useful to him in his present situation. Finally, she yielded to my solicitations, and sent a message to General Burgoyne through his adjutant, my Lord Patterson, begging permission to leave the camp. I told her that she should insist on it, which she did, and finally obtained his consent. The English chaplain, Mr. Brudenel, accompanied her and, bearing a flag of truce, they went together in a boat over to the enemy. There is a familiar and beautiful engraving of this event in existence. I saw her again afterward in Albany, at which time her husband was almost entirely recovered, and both thanked me heartily for my advice.

On the ninth, we spent the whole day in a pouring rain, ready to march at a moment's warning. The savages had lost their courage, and they were seen in all directions going home. The slightest reverse of fortune discouraged them, especially if there was nothing to plunder. My chambermaid did nothing, cursed her situation, and tore out her hair. I entreated her to compose herself, or else she would be taken for a savage. Upon this she became still more frantic and asked "whether that would trouble me." And when I answered "Yes," she tore her bonnet off her head, letting her hair hang down over her face, and said, "You talk well! You have your husband! But we have nothing to look forward to, except dying miserably on the one hand, or losing all we possess on the other!" Respecting this last complaint, I promised, in order to quiet her, that I would make good all the losses of herself and the other maid. The latter, my good Lena, although also very much frightened, said nothing.

Toward evening we at last came to Saratoga, which was only half an hour's march from the place where we had spent the whole day. I was wet through and through by the frequent rains, and was obliged to remain in this condition the entire night, as I had no place whatever where I could change my linen. I therefore seated myself before a good fire and undressed my children, after which we laid ourselves down together upon some straw. I asked

General Phillips, who came up to where we were, why we did not continue our retreat while there was yet time, as my husband had pledged himself to cover it and bring the army through?

"Poor woman," answered he, "I am amazed at you! Completely wet through, have you still the courage to wish to go further in this weather! Would that you were only our commanding General! He halts because he is tired, and intends to spend the night here and give us a supper."

In this latter achievement especially, General Burgoyne was very fond of indulging. He spent half the nights in singing and drinking and amusing himself with the wife of a commissary, who was his mistress, and who loved champagne as well as he.

On the tenth, at seven o'clock in the morning, I drank some tea by way of refreshment; and we now hoped from one moment to another that at last we would again get under way. General Burgoyne, in order to cover our retreat, caused the beautiful houses and mills at Saratoga, belonging to General Schuyler, to be burned. An English officer brought some excellent broth, which he shared with me, as I was not able to refuse his urgent entreaties. Thereupon we set out upon our march, but only as far as another place not far from where we had started. The greatest misery and the utmost disorder prevailed in the army. The commissaries had forgotten to distribute provisions among the troops. There were cattle enough, but not one had been killed. More than thirty officers came to me who could endure hunger no longer. I had coffee and tea made for them, and divided among them all the provisions with which my carriage was constantly filled; for we had a cook who, although an arrant knave, was fruitful in all expedients, and often in the night crossed small rivers in order to steal sheep, poultry, and pigs from the country people. He would then charge us a high price for them—a circumstance, however, that we only learned a long time afterward.

At last my provisions were exhausted, and in despair at not being able to be of any further help, I called to me Adjutant General Patterson, who happened at that moment to be passing by, and said to him passionately: "Come and see for yourself these officers, who have been wounded in the common cause, and who are in want of everything, because they do not receive that which is due them. It is, therefore, your duty to make a representation of this to the General." At this he was deeply moved, and the result was that a quarter of an hour afterward, General Burgoyne came to me himself and thanked me very pathetically for having reminded him of his duty. He added, moreover, that a General was much to be pitied when he was not properly served nor his commands obeyed. I replied that I begged his pardon for having meddled with things which, I well knew, a woman had no business with, but that it was impossible to keep silent when I saw so many brave men in want of everything, and had nothing more to give them. Thereupon he thanked me once more (although I believe that in his heart he has never forgiven me this lashing), and went from me to the officers, and said to them that he was very sorry for what had happened, but he had now through an order remedied everything, but why had they not come to him as his cook stood always at their service? They answered that English officers were not accustomed to visit the kitchen of their General, and that they had received any morsel from me with pleasure, as they were convinced I had given it to them directly from my heart. He then gave the most express orders that the provisions should be properly distributed. This only hindered us anew, besides not in the least bettering our situation. The General seated himself at table, and the horses were harnessed to our calashes ready for departure.

The whole army clamored for a retreat, and my husband promised to make it possible, provided only that no time was lost. But General Burgoyne, to whom an order had been promised if he brought about a junction with the army of General Howe, could not determine upon this course, and lost everything by his loitering. About two o'clock in the afternoon, the firing of cannon and small arms was again heard, and all was alarm and confusion. My husband sent me a message telling me to betake myself forthwith into a house which was not far from there. I seated myself in the calash with my children, and had scarcely driven up to the house when I saw, on the opposite side of the Hudson River, five or six men with guns aimed at us. Almost involuntarily I threw the children on the bottom of the calash and myself over them. At the same instant the churls fired, and shattered the arm of a poor English soldier behind us, who was already wounded, and was also on the point of retreating into the house. Immediately after our

arrival a frightful cannonade began, principally directed against
the house in which we had sought shelter, probably because the
enemy believed, from seeing so many people flocking around it,
that all the generals made it their headquarters. Alas! It harbored
none but wounded soldiers or women! We were finally obliged to
take refuge in a cellar, in which I laid myself down in a corner
not far from the door. My children laid down on the earth with
their heads upon my lap, and in this manner we passed the entire
night. A horrible stench, the cries of the children, and yet more
than all this, my own anguish, prevented me from closing my
eyes.

On the following morning the cannonade again began, but
from a different side. I advised all to go out of the cellar for a
little while, during which time I would have it cleaned, as otherwise we would all be sick. They followed my suggestion, and I at
once set many hands to work, which was in the highest degree
necessary; for the women and children, being afraid to venture
forth, had soiled the whole cellar. After they had all gone out and
left me alone, I for the first time surveyed our place of refuge. It
consisted of three beautiful cellars, splendidly arched. I proposed
that the most dangerously wounded of the officers should be
brought into one of them; that the women should remain in another; and that all the rest should stay in the third, which was
nearest the entrance. I had just given the cellars a good sweeping,
and had fumigated them by sprinkling vinegar on burning coals,
and each one had found his place prepared for him—when a fresh
and terrible cannonade threw us all once more into alarm. Many
persons, who had no right to come in, threw themselves against
the door. My children were already under the cellar steps, and we
would all have been crushed if God had not given me strength to
place myself before the door and with extended arms prevent all
from coming in; otherwise every one of us would have been
severely injured. Eleven cannon balls went through the house,
and we could plainly hear them rolling over our heads. One poor
soldier, whose leg they were about to amputate, having been laid
upon a table for this purpose, had the other leg taken off by another cannon ball, in the very middle of the operation. His comrades all ran off, and when they again came back they found him
in one corner of the room, where he had rolled in his anguish,

scarcely breathing. I was more dead than alive, though not so much on account of our own danger as for that which enveloped my husband, who, however, frequently sent to see how I was getting along, and to tell me that he was still safe.

The wife of Major Harnage, a Madame Reynels, the wife of the good Lieutenant who the day previous had so kindly shared his broth with me, the wife of the commissary, and myself were the only ladies who were with the army. We sat together bewailing our fate, when one came in, upon which they all began whispering, looking at the same time exceedingly sad. I noticed this, and also that they cast silent glances toward me. This awakened in my mind the dreadful thought that my husband had been killed. I shrieked aloud, but they assured me that it was the Lieutenant—the husband of our companion—who had met with misfortune. A moment after she was called out. Her husband was not yet dead, but a cannon ball had taken off his arm close to the shoulder. During the whole night we heard his moans, which resounded fearfully through the vaulted cellars. The poor man died toward morning.

We spent the remainder of this night in the same way as the former ones. In the meantime my husband came to visit me, which lightened my anxiety and gave me fresh courage. On the following morning, however, we got things better regulated. Major Harnage, his wife, and Mrs. Reynels made a little room in a corner, by hanging curtains from the ceiling. They wished to fix up for me another corner in the same manner, but I preferred to remain near the door, so that in case of fire I could rush out from the room. I had some straw brought in and laid my bed upon it, where I slept with my children—my maids sleeping not far from us. Directly opposite us three English officers were quartered—wounded, it is true, but nevertheless resolved not to be left behind in case of a retreat. One of these was a Captain Green, aide-de-camp of General Phillips, a very valuable and agreeable man. All three assured me, upon their oaths, that in case of a hasty retreat they would not leave me, but would each take one of my children upon his horse. For myself, one of my husband's horses constantly stood saddled and in readiness. Often my husband wished to withdraw me from danger by sending me to the Americans; but I remonstrated with him on the ground that to be with people whom I would be obliged to treat with courtesy while, perhaps, my husband was being killed by them, would be even yet more painful than all I was now forced to suffer. He promised me, therefore, that I should henceforward follow the army. Nevertheless, I was often in the night filled with anxiety lest he should march away. At such times, I have crept out of my cellar to reassure myself, and if I saw the troops lying around the fires (for the nights were already cold), I would return and sleep quietly.

The articles which had been entrusted to me caused me much uneasiness. I had fastened them inside of my corsets, as I was in constant terror lest I should lose some of them, and I resolved in future never to undertake such a commission again. On the third day, I found an opportunity for the first time to change my linen, as my companions had the courtesy to give up to me a little corner—the three wounded officers, meanwhile, standing guard not far off. One of these gentlemen could imitate very naturally the bellowing of a cow and the bleating of a calf, and if my little daughter Frederica cried during the night, he would mimic these animals, and she would at once become still, at which we all laughed heartily.

Our cook saw to our meals, but we were in want of water, and in order to quench thirst I was often obliged to drink wine, and give it also to the children. It was, moreover, the only thing that my husband could take, which fact so worked upon our faithful Rockel that he said to me one day, "I fear that the General drinks so much wine, because he dreads falling into captivity, and is therefore weary of life." As the great scarcity of water continued, we at last found a soldier's wife who had the courage to bring water from the river, for no one else would undertake it, as the enemy shot at the head of every man who approached the river. This woman, however, they never molested; and they told us afterward that they spared her on account of her sex.

The continual danger in which my husband was encompassed was a constant source of anxiety to me. I was the only one of all the women whose husband had not been killed or wounded, and I often said to myself—especially since my husband was placed in such great danger day and night—"Shall I be the only fortunate one?" He never came into the tent at night, but lay outside by the watch fires. This alone was sufficient to have caused his death, as the nights were damp and cold.

I endeavored to divert my mind from my troubles by constantly busying myself with the wounded. I made them tea and coffee, and received in return a thousand benedictions. Often, also, I shared my noonday meal with them. One day a Canadian officer came into our cellar who could scarcely stand up. We at last got it out of him that he was almost dead with hunger. I considered myself very fortunate to have it in my power to offer him my mess. This gave him renewed strength, and gained for me his friendship. Afterward, upon our return to Canada, I learned to know his family.

One of our greatest annoyances was the stench of the wounds when they began to suppurate. One day I undertook the care of Major Plumpfield, adjutant of General Phillips, through both of whose cheeks a small musket ball had passed, shattering his teeth and grazing his tongue. He could hold nothing whatever in his mouth. The matter from the wound almost choked him, and he was unable to take any other nourishment except a little broth, or something liquid. As we had some Rhine wine, I gave him a bottle of it, in hopes that the acidity of the wine would cleanse his wound. He kept some continually in his mouth, and that alone acted so beneficially that he became cured, and I again acquired one more friend. Thus, in the midst of my hours of care and suffering, I derived a joyful satisfaction, which made me very happy.

On one of these sorrowful days General Phillips, having expressed a desire to visit me, accompanied my husband, who at the risk of his own life came once or twice daily to see me. He saw our situation, and heard me earnestly beg my husband not to leave me behind in case of a hasty retreat. Then, as he marked my great reluctance to fall into the hands of the Americans, he spoke in my behalf, and as he was going away he said to my husband, "No! Not for ten thousand guineas would I come here again, for my heart is entirely, entirely broken!"

Not all of those, however, who were with us deserved our compassion. There were, also, poltroons in our little company, who ought not to have remained in the cellar, and who afterwards, when we became prisoners, took their places in the ranks and could parade perfectly well.

In this horrible situation we remained six days. Finally, they spoke of capitulating, as by temporizing for so long a time our retreat had been cut off. A cessation of hostilities took place, and my husband, who was thoroughly worn out, was able, for the first time in a long while, to lie down upon a bed. In order that his rest might not be in the least disturbed, I had a good bed made up for him in a little room, while I, with my children and both my maids, lay down in a little parlor close by. But about one o'clock in the night, someone came and asked to speak to him. It was with the greatest reluctance that I found myself obliged to awaken him. I observed that the message did not please him, as he immediately sent the man back to headquarters, and laid himself down again considerably out of humor. Soon after this, General Burgoyne requested the presence of all the generals and staff officers at a council-of-war, which was to be held early the next morning, in which he proposed to break the capitulation, already made with the enemy, in consequence of some false information just received. It was, however, finally decided that this was neither practicable nor advisable; and this was fortunate for us, as the Americans said to us afterwards, for had the capitulation been broken we all would have been massacred, which they could have done the more easily as we were not over four or five thousand men strong, and had given them time to bring together more than twenty thousand.

On the morning of the sixteenth of October, my husband was again obliged to go to his post, and I once more into my cellar. On this day, a large amount of fresh meat was distributed among the officers, who up to this time had received only salted provisions, which had exceedingly aggravated the wounds of the men. The good woman who constantly supplied us with water made us capital soup from the fresh meat. I had lost all appetite, and had the whole time taken nothing but crusts of bread dipped in wine. The wounded officers, my companions in misfortune, cut off the best piece of the beef and presented it to me, with a plate of soup. I said to them that I was not able to eat anything, but as they saw that it was absolutely necessary I should take some nourishment, they declared that they themselves would

15. BURGOYNE INVADING NEW YORK FROM CANADA, 1777

A. Burgoyne's Army Encamped on the Hudson, Sept. 20,
(*Showing General Frazer's Funeral*)

B. Burgoyne Surrenders to Gates at Saratoga, Oct. 17

not touch a morsel until I had given them the satisfaction of taking some. I could not longer withstand their friendly entreaties, upon which they assured me that it made them very happy to be able to offer me the first good thing which they themselves enjoyed.

On the seventeenth of October the capitulation was consummated. The generals waited upon the American General-in-Chief, Gates, and the troops laid down their arms and surrendered themselves prisoners of war. Now the good woman who had brought us water at the risk of her life received the reward of her services. Everyone threw a whole handful of money into her apron, and she received altogether over twenty guineas. At such a moment, the heart seems to be specially susceptible to feelings of gratitude.

At last, my husband sent to me a groom with a message that I should come to him with our children. I therefore again seated myself in my dear calash, and in the passage through the American camp I observed, with great satisfaction, that no one cast at us scornful glances. On the contrary they all greeted me, even showing compassion on their countenances at seeing a mother with her little children in such a situation. I confess that I feared to come into the enemy's camp, as the thing was so entirely new to me. When I approached the tents, a noble-looking man came toward me, took the children out of the wagon, embraced and kissed them, and then with tears in his eyes helped me also to alight.

"You tremble," said he to me. "Fear nothing."

"No," replied I, "for you are so kind, and have been so tender toward my children, that it has inspired me with courage."

He then led me to the tent of General Gates, with whom I found Generals Burgoyne and Phillips, who were upon an extremely friendly footing with him.

Burgoyne said to me, "You may now dismiss all your apprehensions, for your sufferings are at an end." I answered him that I should certainly be acting very wrongly to have any more anxiety, when our chief had none, and especially when I saw him on such a friendly footing with General Gates.

All the generals remained to dine with General Gates. The man who had received me so kindly came up and said to me,

"It may be embarrassing to you to dine with all these gentlemen; come now with your children into my tent, where I will give you, it is true, a·frugal meal, but one that will be accompanied by the best of wishes." "You are certainly," answered I, "a husband and a father, since you show me so much kindness." I then learned that he was the American General Schuyler. He entertained me with excellent smoked tongue, beefsteaks, potatoes, good butter, and bread. Never have I eaten a better meal. I was content. I saw that all around me were so likewise; but that which rejoiced me more than everything else was that my husband was out of all danger.

Albigence Waldo

In the valuable capacity of surgeon Dr. Albigence Waldo (1750-1794) served his country faithfully from July 6, 1775, until October 1, 1779. Ill health, and news of his family's economic distress, caused him to resign. Born in Pomfret, Connecticut, Waldo apprenticed to Dr. John Spaulding of Canterbury, was attached to Connecticut regiments during the war, and practiced in Windham County in later life. In helping to inoculate the army against smallpox at Valley Forge he rendered an important service. The evidence from a surviving daybook he kept during the 1780's indicates that Waldo possessed outstanding surgical ability for his time. He was known for his charity, and gave so much to the poor that he left nothing for his family. His fellow medical diarist, James Thacher, describes him as "fond of music, painting, and drawing," and an accomplished orator who pronounced "an elegant eulogy at the grave of the late Major General Putnam," his neighbor and close friend.

Waldo's diary, from which the following abridgment is edited, was published in the *Pennsylvania Magazine of History and Biography,* Vol. XXI (1897), pp. 299-323, with a biographical foreword. See also Herbert Thoms, "Albigence Waldo, Surgeon. His Diary Written at Valley Forge," *Annals of Medical History* Vol. X, No. 4, pp. 486-497.

VALLEY FORGE

December 11, 1777. I am prodigious sick and cannot get anything comfortable. What in the name of providence am I to do with a fit of sickness in this place where nothing appears pleasing to the sickened eye and nauseating stomach? But I doubt not Providence will find out a way for my relief. But I cannot eat beef if I starve, for my stomach positively refuses to entertain such company, and how can I help that?

December 12. A bridge of wagons made across the Schuylkill last night consisting of thirty-six wagons, with a bridge of rails between each. Some skirmishing over the river. Militia and dragoons brought into camp several prisoners.

Sunset. We were ordered to march over the river. It snows—I'm sick—eat nothing—no whiskey—no forage—Lord—Lord—Lord. The army were till sunrise crossing the river—some at the wagon bridge and some at the raft bridge below. Cold and uncomfortable.

December 13. The army marched three miles from the west side of the river and encamped near a place called the Gulf and not an improper name either, for this Gulf seems well adapted by its situation to keep us from the pleasures and enjoyments of this world, or being conversant with anybody in it. It is an excellent place to raise the ideas of a philosopher beyond the glutted thoughts and reflections of an Epicurean. His reflections will be as different from the common reflections of mankind as if he were unconnected with the world, and only conversant with immaterial beings. It cannot be that our superiors are about to hold consultations with spirits infinitely beneath their order, by bringing us into these utmost regions of the terraqueous sphere. No, it is upon consideration for many good purposes, since we are to winter here. First, there is plenty of wood and water. Secondly, there are but few families for the soldiery to steal from —though far be it from a soldier to steal. Fourthly, there are warm sides of hills to erect huts on. Fifthly, they will be heavenly minded like Jonah when in the belly of a great fish. Sixthly, they will not become homesick as is sometimes the case when men live in the open world—since the reflections which will naturally arise from their present habitation will lead them to the more noble thoughts of employing their leisure hours in filling their knapsacks with such materials as may be necessary on the journey to another home.

December 14. Prisoners and deserters are continually coming in. The army, which has been surprisingly healthy hitherto, now begins to grow sickly from the continued fatigues they have suffered this campaign. Yet they still show a spirit of alacrity and contentment not to be expected from so young troops. I am sick, discontented, and out of humor. Poor food—hard lodging—cold weather—fatigue—nasty clothes—nasty cookery—vomit half my time—smoked out of my senses—the Devil's in't—I can't endure it —why are we sent here to starve and freeze—what sweet felicities have I left at home! A charming wife—pretty children—good beds—good food—good cookery—all agreeable—all harmonious. Here all confusion—smoke and cold—hunger and filthiness—a pox on my bad luck. There comes a bowl of beef soup—full of burnt leaves and dirt, enough such to make a Hector spew—away with it, boys—I'll live like the chameleon upon air.

"Poh! Poh!" cries Patience within me, "you talk like a fool. Your being sick covers your mind with a melancholic gloom, which makes everything about you appear gloomy. See the poor soldier: when in health, with what cheerfulness he meets his foes and encounters every hardship; if barefoot, he labors through mud and cold with a song in his mouth extolling War and Washington; if his food be bad, he eats it notwithstanding with seeming content—blesses God for a good stomach and whistles it into digestion."

"But harkee, Patience, a moment. There comes a soldier, his bare feet seen through his worn-out shoes, his legs nearly naked from the tatter'd remains of an only pair of stockings, his breeches not sufficient to cover his nakedness, his shirt hanging in strings, his hair disheveled, his face meager; his whole appearance pictures a person forsaken and discouraged. He comes, and cries with an air of wretchedness and despair, I am sick, my feet lame, my legs are sore, my body covered with this tormenting itch—my clothes are worn out, my constitution is broken, my former activity is exhausted by fatigue, hunger, and cold, I fail fast, I shall soon be no more! And all the reward I shall get will be: Poor Will is dead!"

People who live at home in luxury and ease, quietly possessing their habitations, enjoying their wives and families in peace, have but a very faint idea of the unpleasing sensations and continual anxiety the man endures who is in a camp, and is the husband and parent of an agreeable family. These same people are willing we should suffer everything for their benefit and advantage, and yet are the first to condemn us for not doing more!

December 18. Rank and precedence make a good deal of disturbance and confusion in the American army. The army are poorly supplied with provisions, occasioned it is said by the neglect of the Commissary of Purchases. Much talk among officers about discharges. Money has become of too little consequence. The Congress have not made their commissions valuable enough. Heaven avert the bad consequences of these things!

Our brethren who are unfortunately prisoners in Philadelphia meet with the most savage and inhumane treatments that barbarians are capable of inflicting. Our enemies do not knock them in the head or burn them with torches to death, or flay them alive, or gradually dismember them till they die, which is customary among savages and barbarians. No, they are worse by far. They suffer them to starve, to linger out their lives in extreme hunger. One of these poor unhappy men, driven to the last extreme by the rage of hunger, ate his own fingers up to the first joint from the hand, before he died. Others ate the clay, the lime, the stones of the prison walls. Several who died in the yard had pieces of bark, wood, clay, and stones in their mouths, which the ravings of hunger had caused them to take in for food in the last agonies of life! "These are thy mercies, O Britain!"

December 21. (Valley Forge.) Preparations made for huts. Provisions scarce. Mr. Ellis went homeward—sent a letter to my wife. Heartily wish myself at home, my skin and eyes are almost spoiled with continual smoke. A general cry through the camp this evenning among the soldiers, "No meat! No meat!" The distant vales echoed back the melancholy sound, "No meat! No meat!" Imitating the noise of crows and owls also made a part of the confused music.

> "What have you for your dinners, boys?"
> "Nothing but fire cakes and water, sir."
> At night, "Gentlemen, the supper is ready."
> "What is your supper, lads?"
> "Fire cake and water, sir."

Very poor beef has been drawn in our camp the greater part of this season. A butcher bringing a quarter of this kind of beef into camp one day who had white buttons on the knees of his breeches, a soldier cries out, "There, there, Tom, is some more of your fat beef, by my soul I can see the butcher's breeches' buttons through it."

December 22. Lay excessive cold and uncomfortable last night—my eyes are started out from their orbits like a rabbit's eyes, occasioned by a great cold and smoke.

> "What have you got for breakfast, lads?"
> "Fire cake and water, sir."

The Lord send that our Commissaries of Purchases may iive on fire cake and water, till their glutted guts are turned to pasteboard.

Our division are under marching orders this morning. I am ashamed to say it, but I am tempted to steal fowls if I could find them, or even a whole hog, for I feel as if I could eat one. But the impoverished country about us affords but little matter to employ a thief, or keep a clever fellow in good humor. But why do I talk of hunger and hard usage, when so many in the world have not even fire cake and water to eat?

December 24. Huts go on slowly—cold and smoke make us fret. But mankind are always fretting, even if they have more than their proportion of the blessings of life. We are never easy, always repining at the providence of an all-wise and benevolent Being, blaming our country or faulting our friends. But I don't know of anything that vexes a man's soul more than hot smoke continually blowing into his eyes and, when he attempts to avoid it, being met by a cold and piercing wind.

December 25—Christmas. We are still in tents when we ought to be in huts. The poor sick suffer much in tents this cold weather. But we now treat them differently from what they used to be at home, under the inspection of old women and Doctor Bolus Linctus. We give them mutton and grog and a capital medicine once in a while, to start the disease from its foundations at once. We avoid piddling pills, powders, Bolus's Linctus's cordials and all such insignificant matters whose powders are only rendered important by causing the patient to vomit up his money instead of his disease. But very few of the sick men die.

December 26. The enemy have been some days west of the Schuylkill from opposite the city to Derby. Their intentions not yet known. The city is at present pretty clear of them. Why don't His Excellency rush in and retake the city, in which he will doubtless find much plunder? Because he knows better than to leave his post and be caught like a d—d fool cooped up in the city. He has always acted wisely hitherto. His conduct when closely scrutinized is uncensurable. Were his inferior Generals as skillful as himself, we should have the grandest choir of officers ever God made. Many country gentlemen in the interior parts of the states who get wrong information of the affairs and state of our camp are very much surprised at General Washington's delay to drive off the enemy, being falsely informed that his army consists of double the number of the enemy's. Such wrong information serves not to keep up the spirit of the people, as they must be by and by undeceived, to their no small disappointment. It brings blame on His Excellency, who is deserving of the greatest encomium; it brings disgrace on the Continental troops, who have never evidenced the least backwardness in doing their duty, but on the contrary have cheerfully endured a long and very fatiguing campaign. 'Tis true they have fought but little this campaign, which is not owing to any unwillingness in officers or soldiers, but for want of convenient opportunities, which have not offered themselves this season.

Though this may be contradicted by many, impartial truth in future history will clear up these points, and reflect lasting honor on the wisdom and prudence of General Washington. The greatest number of Continental troops that have been with His Excellency this campaign never consisted of more than 11,000 and the greatest number of militia in the field at once were not more than 2,000. Yet these accounts are exaggerated to 50 or 60,000. Howe by the best and most authentic accounts has never had less than 10,000. Thus General Washington, by opposing little more than an equal number of young troops to old veterans, has kept his ground in general, cooped them up in the city, prevented their making any considerable inroads upon him, killed and wounded a very considerable number of them in different skirmishes, and made many proselytes to the shrine of Liberty by these little successes, and by the prudence, calmness, sedateness, and wisdom with which he facilitates all his operations. This being the case, and his not having wantonly thrown away the lives of his soldiers, but reserved them for another campaign (if another should open in the spring) which is of the utmost consequence, ours cannot be called an inglorious campaign. If he had risked a general battle and should have proved unsuccessful, what in the name of Heaven would have been our case this day? Troops are raised with great difficulty in the Southern states; many regiments from these states do not consist of one hundred men. What then was the grand Southern army before the New England troops joined them? And if this army is cut off where should we get another as good? General Washington has doubtless considered these matters and his conduct this campaign has certainly demonstrated his prudence and wisdom.

December 28. Yesterday upwards of fifty officers in General Greene's division resigned their commissions—six or seven of our regiment are doing the like today. All this is occasioned by officers' families' being so much neglected at home on account of provisions. Their wages will not, by considerable, purchase a few trifling comfortables here in camp, and maintain their families at home, while such extravagant prices are demanded for the common necessaries of life. What then have they to purchase clothes and other necessaries with? It is a melancholy reflection that what is of the most universal importance is most universally neglected—I mean keeping up the credit of money.

The present circumstances of the soldier are better by far than the officer's. For the family of the soldier is provided for at the public expense if the articles they want are above the common price, but the officer's family are obliged not only to beg in the most humble manner for the necessaries of life, but also to pay for them afterwards at the most exorbitant rates. And even in this manner, many of them who depend entirely on their money cannot procure half the material comforts that are wanted in a family. This produces continual letters of complaint from home. When the officer has been fatigued through wet and cold and returns to his tent he finds a letter directed to him from his wife, filled with the most heartaching tender complaints a woman is capable of writing: acquainting him with the incredible difficulty with which she procures a little bread for herself and children— and finally concluding with expressions bordering on despair, of procuring a sufficiency of food to keep soul and body together through the winter—that her money is of very little consequence to her—that she begs of him to consider that charity begins at home, and not suffer his family to perish with want in the midst of plenty. When such, I say, are the tidings they constantly hear from their families, what man is there, who has the least regard for his family, whose soul would not shrink within him? Who

would not be disheartened from persevering in the best of causes
—the cause of his country—when such discouragements as these
lie in his way, which his country might remedy if she would?

December 29. So much talk about discharges among the officers,
and so many are discharged, His Excellency lately expressed his
fears of being left alone with the soldiers only. Strange that our
country will not exert themselves for his support, and save so
good, so great a man from entertaining the least anxious doubt
of their virtue and perseverance in supporting a cause of such
unparalleled importance!

All Hell couldn't prevail against us, if Heaven continues no
more than its formal blessings, and if we keep up the credit of
our money, which has now become of the last consequence. If its
credit sinks but a few degrees more, we shall then repent when
'tis too late—and cry out for help when no one will appear to deliver. We who are in camp, and depend on our money entirely to
procure the comforts of life, feel the importance of this matter.
He who is hoarding it up in his chest thinks little more of it than
how he shall procure more.

Valley Forge, December 31, 1777

Doctor Waldo, Surgeon of Col. Prentice's Reg't, is recom-
mended for a furlough.

J. HUNTINGTON, B. General.

Applied with the above for a furlough to Doctor Cochran, who
replied, "I am willing to oblige every gentleman of the faculty,
but some of the Boston surgeons have by taking an underhand
method of getting furloughs occasioned a complaint to be lodged
with His Excellency, who has positively forbid my giving any
furloughs at present. We shall soon have regimental hospitals
erected, and general ones to receive the superabundant sick from
them. If you will tarry till such regulations are made you will
have an honorable furlough, and even now I will, if you desire it,
recommend you to His Excellency for one—but desire you would
stay a little while longer. And in the meantime, recommend to
me some young surgeon for a regiment, and I will immediately
appoint him to a chief surgeoncy from your recommendation. I
shall remember the rascals who have used me ill."

I concluded to stay, and immediately set about fixing accommodations for the sick, etc., etc.

We got some spirits and finished the year with a good drink and thankful hearts in our new hut, which stands on an eminence that overlooks the brigade, and in sight of the front line. In the evening I joyfully received a letter from my good and loving wife.

1778. January 1—New Year. I am alive. I am well. Huts go on briskly, and our camp begins to appear like a spacious city.

January 5. Applied for a furlough, Surgeon General not at home —came back mumping and sulky.

January 6. Applied again—was denied by reason of inoculations being set on foot, and because the Boston surgeons had too many of them gone—one of whom is to be broke for his lying and deceiving in order to get a furlough, and I wish his cursed tongue were pulled out for thus giving an example of scandal to the New England surgeons (though the Connecticut ones are well enough respected at present). Came home sulky and cross— stormed at the boys, and swore round like a piper and a fool till 'most night, when I bought me a bearskin, dressed with the hair on; this will answer me to lie on.

January 8. Unexpectedly got a furlough. Set out for home. The very worst of riding—mud and mire.

Sally Wister

When the British occupied Philadelphia in September, 1777, while Washington and the Continental Army prepared to dig in for the winter at Valley Forge twenty miles away, young Sarah Wister (1761-1804) had just left town with her family. They had sought refuge in the farmhouse of Hannah Foulke on the Wissahickon River, some fifteen miles outside the city, unlike their Tory friends who had stayed to greet the redcoats. On the day that Sir William Howe reached Germantown (September 25, 1777), Sally began keeping a journal, and maintained a lively account of the doings at the Foulke house until the English quitted the city (June 20, 1778). She addressed her entries to a friend in town, Deborah Norris, with whom she had attended Anthony Benezet's fashionable Quaker school, in company with other well-reared young ladies of the Philadelphia aristocracy. To a cloistered but gay-hearted girl suddenly thrust into a male society of gallant officers, who passed and repassed through the Foulke home, life had taken on exciting hues, and with charming naïveté Sally set down her personal impressions and emotional tingles in a private copybook. Eminent personalities entered the drawing room, including three future governors, and grave military talk blends with coquettish asides in her jottings. The sound of cannon can be heard, and speculations are rife as to the actions of Howe and Washington.

Sally Wister descended on her father's side from Pennsylvania Germans originally from the Palatinate, and on her mother's from Welsh Joneses, settled in Merion and Haverford for five generations. Her paternal grandfather became a successful wine merchant and large landowner in the New World, and built a spacious summer home, "Grumblethorpe," in Germantown, where Sally spent many of her later years. She grew into a religious lady, deeply attached to her mother, something of a poetess, and nothing of the coquette that her journal seems to prophesy—she died a spinster.

The journal reached Debby Norris only in her old age, after the death of its author. It was published in the *Pennsylvania Magazine of History and Biography*, Vol. IX (1885), 318-333, 463-478, IX (1886), 51-60, and in 1902 was skillfully edited in book form by Albert Cook Myers, with a valuable introduction (*Sally Wister's Journal, a True Narrative*, Ferris & Leach, Philadelphia). The present text is edited from the Myers edition, pp. 65-137, 152-167, 184-185.

OUTSIDE PHILADELPHIA

To Deborah Norris:

Though I have not the least shadow of an opportunity to send a letter, if I do write I will keep a sort of journal of the time that may expire before I see thee. The perusal of it may some time hence give pleasure in a solitary hour to thee and our Sally Jones.

Yesterday, which was the twenty-fourth of September [1777], two Virginia officers called at our house, and informed us that the British Army had crossed the Schuylkill. Presently after, another person stopped and confirmed what they had said, and that General Washington and army were near Pottsgrove. Well, thee may be sure we were sufficiently scared; however, the road was very still till evening.

About seven o'clock we heard a great noise. To the door we all went. A large number of wagons, with about three hundred of the Philadelphia militia. They begged for drink, and several pushed into the house. One of those that entered was a little tipsy, and had a mind to be saucy.

I then thought it time for me to retreat; so figure me (mightily scared, as not having presence of mind enough to face so many of the military), running in at one door and out another, all in a shake with fear; but after a while, seeing the officers appear gentlemanly, and the soldiers civil, I called reason to my aid. My fears were in some measure dispelled, though my teeth rattled and my hand shook like an aspen leaf. They did not offer to take their quarters with us; so, with many blessings, and as many adieus, they marched off.

I have given thee the most material occurrences of yesterday faithfully.

Fourth Day, September 25th

This day, till twelve o'clock, the road was mighty quiet, when Hobson Jones came riding along. About that time he made a stop at our door, and said the British were at Skippack Road; that we should soon see their light horse, and that a party of Hessians had actually turned into our lane. My Dadda and Mama gave it the credit it deserved, for he does not keep strictly to the truth in all respects; but the delicate, chickenhearted Liddy and I were wretchedly scared. We could say nothing but "Oh! What shall we do? What will become of us?" These questions only augmented the terror we were in.

Well, the fright went off. We saw no light horse or Hessians. O. Foulke came here in the evening, and told us that General Washington had come down as far as the Trappe, and that General McDougal's brigade was stationed at Montgomery, consisting of about sixteen hundred men. This he had from Dr. Edwards, Lord Stirling's aide-de-camp; so we expected to be in the midst of one army or t'other.

Fourth Day Night

We were not alarmed.

Fifth Day, September 26th

We were unusually silent all the morning; no passengers came by the house, except to the mill, and we don't place much dependence on mill news.

About twelve o'clock Cousin Jesse heard that General Howe's army had moved down towards Philadelphia. Then, my dear, our hopes and fears were engaged for you. However, my advice is, summon up all your resolution, call fortitude to your aid, and don't suffer your spirits to sink, my dear; there's nothing like courage; 'tis what I stand in need of myself, but unfortunately have little of it in my composition.

I was standing in the kitchen about twelve, when somebody came to me in a hurry, screaming "Sally, Sally, here are the light horse!" This was by far the greatest fright I had endured; fear tacked wings to my feet; I was at the house in a moment; at the porch I stopped, and it really was the light horse.

I ran immediately to the western door, where the family were assembled, anxiously waiting for the event. They rode up to the door and halted, and one inquired if we had horses to sell; he was answered negatively.

"Have not you, sir" (to my father) "two black horses?"

"Yes, but have no mind to dispose of them."

My terror had by this time nearly subsided. The officer and men behaved perfectly civil; the first drank two glasses of wine, rode away, bidding his men follow, which after adieus in number they did. The officer was Lieutenant Lindsay, of Bland's regiment, Lee's troop. The men to our great joy were Americans, and but four in all. What made us imagine them British was they wore blue and red, which with us is not common.

It has rained all this afternoon, and to present appearances will all night. In all probability the English will take possession of the city tomorrow or next day. What a change will it be! May the Almighty take you under His protection, for without His divine aid all human assistance is vain.

> May heaven's guardian arm protect my absent friends,
> From danger guard them, and from want defend.

Forgive, my dear, the repetition of these lines, but they just darted into my mind.

Nothing worth relating has occurred this afternoon. Now for trifles. I have set a stocking on the needles, and intend to be mighty industrious. This evening some of our folks heard a very heavy cannon. We supposed it to be fired by the English. The report seemed to come from Philadelphia. We hear the American army will be within five miles of us tonight.

The uncertainty of our position engrosses me quite. Perhaps to be in the midst of war, and ruin, and the clang of arms. But we must hope the best.

Here, my dear, passes an interval of several weeks, in which nothing happened worth the time and paper it would take to write it. The English, however, in the interim had taken possession of the city.

Second Day, October 19, 1777

Now for new and uncommon scenes. As I was lying in bed, and ruminating on past and present events, and thinking how happy I should be if I could see you, Liddy came running into the room and said there was the greatest drumming, fifing, and rattling of wagons that ever she had heard. What to make of this we were at a loss. We dressed and downstairs in a hurry. Our wonder ceased.

The British had left Germantown, and our army was marching to take possession. It was the general opinion that they would evacuate the capital. Sister Betsy and myself and G. E. went about half a mile from home, where we could see the army pass. Thee will stare at my going, but no impropriety in my opine, or I would not have gone. We made no great stay, but returned with excellent appetites for our breakfast.

Several officers called to get some refreshment, but none of consequence till the afternoon. Cousin Prissa and myself were sitting at the door; I in a green skirt, dark short gown, etc. Two genteel men of the military order rode up to the door: "Your servant, ladies," etc.; asked if they could have quarters for General Smallwood. Aunt Foulke thought she could accommodate them as well as most of her neighbors said they could. One of the officers dismounted, and wrote

SMALLWOOD'S QUARTERS

over the door, which secured us from straggling soldiers. After this he mounted his steed and rode away.

When we were alone our dress and lips were put in order for conquest, and the hopes of adventures gave brightness to each before passive countenance.

Thee must be told of a Dr. Gould, who by accident had made an acquaintance with my father—a sensible, conversable man, a Carolinian—and had come to bid us adieu on his going to that state. Daddy had prevailed upon him to stay a day or two with us.

In the evening his Generalship came with six attendants, which composed his family, a large guard of soldiers, a number of horses and baggage wagons. The yard and house were in confusion and glittered with military equipments.

Gould was intimate with Smallwood, and had gone into Jesse's to see him. While he was there, there was great running up and downstairs, so I had an opportunity of seeing and being seen, the former the most agreeable, to be sure. One person in particular attracted my notice. He appeared cross and reserved; but thee shall see how agreeably disappointed I was.

Dr. Gould ushered the gentlemen into our parlor and introduced them: "General Smallwood, Captain Furnival, Major Stoddard, Mr. Prig, Captain Finley, and Mr. Clagan, Colonel Wood, and Colonel Line." These last two did not come with the General. They are Virginians, and both indisposed. The General and suite are Marylanders.

Be assured I did not stay long with so many men, but secured a good retreat, heart-safe so far. Some supped with us, others at Jesse's. They retired about ten, in good order.

How new is our situation! I feel in good spirits, though surrounded by an army, the house full of officers, the yard alive with soldiers—very peaceable sort of men, though. They eat like other folks, talk like them, and behave themselves with elegance; so I will not be afraid of them, that I won't.

Adieu. I am going to my chamber to dream, I suppose, of bayonets and swords, sashes, guns, and epaulets.

Third Day Morn, October 20th

I dare say thee is impatient to know my sentiments of the officers; so while Somnus embraces them, and the house is still, take their characters according to their rank.

The General is tall, portly, well made. A truly martial air, the behavior and manner of a gentleman, a good understanding, and great humanity of disposition constitute the character of Smallwood.

Colonel Wood, from what we hear of him and what we see, is one of the most amiable of men; tall and genteel, an agreeable countenance and deportment. These following lines will more fully characterize him:

> How skill'd he is in each obliging art,
> The mildest manners with the bravest heart.

The cause he is fighting for alone tears him from the society of an amiable wife and engaging daughter; with tears in his eyes he often mentions the sweets of domestic life.

Colonel Line is not married, so let me not be too warm in his praise, lest you suspect. He is monstrous tall and brown, but has a certain something in his face and conversation very agreeable; he entertains the highest notions of honor, is sensible and humane, and a brave officer; he is only seven and twenty years old but, by a long indisposition and constant fatigue, looks vastly older, and almost worn to a skeleton, but very lively and talkative.

Captain Furnival—I need not say more of him than that he has, excepting one or two, the handsomest face I ever saw, a very fine person; fine light hair, and a great deal of it, adds to the beauty of his face.

Engraved for BARNARD's New Complete & Authentic HISTORY of ENGLAND.

Portrait & Uniform of An
AMERICAN GENERAL.

A real representation of the Dress of An
AMERICAN RIFLE-MAN.

16. A. PHILADELPHIA AT THE TIME OF HOWE'S OCCUPATION,
NOV. 28, 1777

B. UNIFORMS OF A GENERAL AND A RIFLEMAN
IN THE CONTINENTAL ARMY

Well, here comes the glory, the Major, so bashful, so famous, etc. He should come before the Captain, but never mind. I at first thought the Major cross and proud, but I was mistaken. He is about nineteen, nephew to the General, and acts as Major of Brigade to him; he cannot be extolled for the graces of person, but for those of the mind he may justly be celebrated; he is large in his person, manly, and an engaging countenance and address.

Finley is wretched ugly, but he went away last night, so shall not particularize him.

Nothing of any moment today; no acquaintance with the officers. Colonel Wood and Line and Gould dined with us. I was dressed in my chintz, and looked smarter than the night before.

Fourth Day, October 21st

I just now met the Major, very reserved; nothing but "Good morning," or "Your servant, madam"; but Furnival is most agreeable; he chats every opportunity, but luckily has a wife!

I have heard strange things of the Major. Worth a fortune of thirty thousand pounds, independent of anybody; the Major, moreover, is vastly bashful, so much so he can hardly look at the ladies. (Excuse me, good sir, I really thought you were not clever; if 'tis bashfulness only, we will drive that away.)

Third Day Eve, October 27th

When will Sally's admirers appear? Ah! that indeed. Why, Sally has not charms sufficient to pierce the heart of a soldier. But still I won't despair. Who knows what mischief I yet may do?

First Day Morn, October 31st

Colonel Wood was standing at a window with a young officer. He gave him a push forward, as much as to say, "Observe what fine girls we have here." For all I do not mention Wood as often as he deserves, it is not that we are not sociable; we are very much so, and he is often at our house, dines or drinks tea with us every day.

Liddy and I had a kind of an adventure with him this morn. We were in his chamber, chatting about our little affairs, and no idea of being interrupted; we were standing up, each an arm on a chest of drawers; the door banged open! Colonel Wood was in the room; we started, the color flew into our faces and crimsoned us over; the tears flew into my eyes. It was very silly, but his coming was so abrupt. He was between us and the door.

"Ladies, do not be scared, I only want something from my portmanteau; I beg you not to be disturbed."

We ran by him like two partridges, into Mama's room, threw ourselves into chairs, and reproached each other for being so foolish as to blush and look so silly. I was very much vexed at myself; so was Liddy. The Colonel laughed at us, and it blew over.

The army had orders to march today; the regulars accordingly did. General Smallwood had the command of the militia at that time, and they, being in the rear, were not to leave their encampment until Second Day.

Observe how militaryish I talk. No wonder, when I am surrounded by people of that order.

Second Day Morn, November 1st

Today the militia marches, and the General and officers leave us. Heigh ho! I am very sorry; for when you have been with agreeable people, 'tis impossible not to feel regret when they bid you adieu, perhaps forever. When they leave us we shall be immured in solitude.

The Major looks dull.

Second Day Noon

About two o'clock the General and Major came to bid us adieu. With Daddy and Mammy they shook hands very friendly; to us they bowed politely.

Our hearts were full. I thought Major was affected.

"Good-by, Miss Sally," spoken very low. He walked hastily and mounted his horse. They promised to visit us soon.

We stood at the door to take a last look, all of us very sober.

The Major turned his horse's head and rode back, dismounted. "I have forgot my pistols"; passed us, and ran upstairs.

He came swiftly back to us, as if wishing through inclination to stay, by duty compelled to go. He remounted his horse.

"Farewell, ladies, till I see you again," and cantered away.

We looked at him till the turn in the road hid him from our sight. "Amiable Major," "Clever fellow," "Good young man," was echoed from one to the other. I wonder whether we shall ever see him again. He has our wishes for his safety.

Third Day Morn, November 2d

It seems strange not to see our house as it used to be. We are very still. No rattling of wagons, glittering of muskets. The beating of the distant drum is all we hear.

Here I skip a week or two, nothing of consequence occurring. Some time since arrived two officers, Lieutenants Lee and Warring, Virginians. I had only the salutations of the morn from them.

Lee is not remarkable one way or the other, Warring an insignificant piece enough. Lee sings prettily, and talks a great deal: how good turkey hash and fried hominy is (a pretty discourse to entertain the ladies)—extols Virginia and execrates Maryland, which, by the by, I provoked them to; for though I admire both Virginia and Maryland, I laughed at the former and praised the latter. Ridiculed their manner of speaking. I took great delight in teasing them. I believe I did it sometimes ill-naturedly, but I don't care. They were not, I am certain almost, first-rate gentlemen. (How different from our other officers!) But they are gone to Virginia, where they may sing, dance, and eat turkey hash and fried hominy all day long, if they choose.

Nothing scarcely lowers a man in my opinion more than talking of eating, what they love and what they hate. Lee and Warring were proficients in this science. Enough of them.

December 5th, Sixth Day

Oh, gracious! Debby, I am all alive with fear. The English have come out to attack (as we imagine) our army. They are on Chestnut Hill, our army three miles this side. What will become of us, only six miles distant?

We are in hourly expectation of an engagement. I fear we shall be in the midst of it. Heaven defend us from so dreadful a sight. The Battle of Germantown, and the horrors of that day, are recent in my mind. It will be sufficiently dreadful if we are only in hearing of the firing, to think how many of our fellow-creatures are plunged into the boundless ocean of eternity, few of them prepared to meet their fate. But they are summoned before an all-merciful Judge, from whom they have a great deal to hope.

Seventh Day, December 6th

No firing this morn. I hope for one more quiet day.

First Day Afternoon, December 8th

Six months ago the bare idea of being within ten, aye twenty miles of a battle, would almost have distracted me. And now, though two such large armies are within six miles of us, we can be cheerful and converse calmly of it. It verifies the old proverb, that "Use is second nature."

Fifth Day Afternoon, December 11, 1777

Well, strange creature that I am, here have I been going on without giving thee an account of two officers—one who will be a principal character. Their names are Captain Lipscomb and a Mr. Tilly; the former a tall, genteel man, very delicate from indisposition, and has a softness in his countenance that is very pleasing, and has the finest head of hair that I ever saw; 'tis a light, shining auburn. The fashion of his hair was this—negligently tied and waving down his back. Well may it be said,

Loose flow'd the soft redundance of his hair.

He has not hitherto shown himself a lady's man, though he is perfectly polite.

Now let me attempt to characterize Tilly. He seems a wild, noisy mortal, though I am not much acquainted with him. He appears bashful when with girls. We dissipated the Major's bashfulness, but I doubt we have not so good a subject now. He is above the common size, rather genteel, an extreme pretty, ruddy face, hair brown, and a sufficiency of it, a very great laugher, and talks so excessively fast that he often begins sentences without finishing the last, which confuses him very much, and then he blushes and laughs, and in short, he keeps me in perpetual good humor; but the creature has not addressed one civil thing to me since he came.

But I have not done with his accomplishments yet, for he is a musician—that is, he plays on the German flute, and has it here.

Fifth Day Night

The family retired—take the adventures of the afternoon as they occurred.

Seaton and Captain Lipscomb drank tea with us. While we sat at tea the parlor door was opened, in came Tilly; his appearance was elegant; he had been riding; the wind had given the most beautiful glow to his cheeks and blown his hair carelessly round his face.

Oh, my heart, thought I, be secure!

The caution was needless; I found it without a wish to stray.

When the tea equipage was removed, the conversation turned on politics, a subject I avoid. I gave Betsy a hint. I rose, she followed, and we went to seek Liddy.

We chatted a few moments at the door. The moon shone with uncommon splendor. Our spirits were high. I proposed a walk; the girls agreed. When we reached the poplar tree, we stopped. Our ears were assailed by a number of voices.

"A party of light horse," said one.

"The English, perhaps; let's run home."

"No, no," said I, "be heroines."

At last two or three men on horseback came in sight. We walked on. The well-known voice of the Major saluted our hearing with "How do you do, ladies?"

We turned ourselves about with one accord. He, not relishing the idea of sleeping on the banks of the Schuylkill, had returned to the mill.

We chatted along the road till we reached our hospitable mansion. Stoddard dismounted, and went into Jesse's parlor. I sat there a half hour. He is very amiable.

Seaton, Lipscomb, Tilly, and my father, hearing of his return and impatient for the news, came in at one door, while I made my exit at the other.

I am vexed at Tilly, who has his flute and does nothing but play the fool. He begins a tune, plays a note or so, then stops. Well, after a while he begins again; stops again. "Will that do, Seaton? Hah! hah! hah!"

He has given us but two regular tunes since he arrived. I am passionately fond of music. How boyish he behaves.

Sixth Day, December 12th, 1777

I ran into Aunt's this morn to chat with the girls. Major Stoddard joined us in a few minutes.

I verily believe the man is fond of the ladies, and what is astonishing, he has not discovered the smallest degree of pride. Whether he is artful enough to conceal it under the veil of humility, or whether he has none, is a question; but I am inclined to think it the latter.

I really am of opinion that there are few of the young fellows of the modern age exempt from vanity, more especially those who are blessed with exterior graces. If they have a fine pair of eyes they are ever rolling them about; a fine set of teeth, mind they are great laughers, a genteel person, forever changing their attitudes to show them to advantage. Oh, vanity, vanity, how boundless is thy sway.

But to resume this interview with Major Stoddard. We were very witty and sprightly. I was darning an apron, upon which he was pleased to compliment me.

"Well, Miss Sally, what would you do if the British were to come here?"

"Do?" exclaimed I. "Be frightened just to death."

He laughed and said he would escape their rage by getting behind the representation of a British grenadier which we have upstairs. "Of all things, I should like to frighten Tilly with it. Pray, ladies, let's fix it in his chamber tonight."

"If thee will take all the blame, we will assist thee."

"That I will," he replied; and this was the plan.

We had bought some weeks ago a British grenadier from Uncle Miles's on purpose to divert us. It is remarkably well executed, six foot high, and makes a martial appearance. This we agreed to stand at the door that opens into the road (the house has four rooms on a floor, with a wide entry running through), with another figure that would add to the deceit. One of our servants was to stand behind them, others were to serve as the occasion offered.

After half an hour's converse, in which we raised our expectations to the highest pitch, we parted. If our scheme answers, I shall communicate in the eve. Till then, adieu. 'Tis dining hour.

Sixth Day Night

Never did I more sincerely wish to possess a descriptive genius than I do now. All that I can write will fall infinitely short of the truly diverting scene that I have been witness to tonight. But, as I mean to attempt an account, I had as well shorten the preface and begin the story.

In the beginning of the evening I went to Liddy and begged her to secure the swords and pistols which were in their parlor. The Marylander, hearing our voices, joined us. I told him of my proposal. Whether he thought it a good one or not I can't say, but he approved of it, and Liddy went in and brought her apron full of swords and pistols.

When this was done, Stoddard joined the officers. We girls went and stood at the first landing of the stairs. The gentlemen were very merry and chatting on public affairs, when Seaton's Negro (observe that Seaton, being indisposed, was apprised of the scheme) opened the door, candle in his hand, and said, "There's somebody at the door that wishes to see you."

"Who? All of us?" said Tilly.

"Yes, sir," answered the boy.

They all rose (the Major, as he afterwards said, almost dying with laughing) and walked into the entry, Tilly first, in full expectation of news.

The first object that struck his view was a British soldier. In a moment his ears were saluted with, "Is there any rebel officers here?" in a thundering voice.

Not waiting for a second word, he darted like lightning out at the front door, through the yard, bolted o'er the fence. Swamps, fences, thorn hedges, and plowed fields no way impeded his retreat. He was soon out of hearing.

The woods echoed with "Which way did he go? Stop him! Surround the house!" The amiable Lipscomb had his hand on the latch of the door, intending to attempt his escape; Stoddard, considering his indisposition, acquainted him with the deceit.

We females ran downstairs to join in the general laugh. I walked into Jesse's parlor. There sat poor Stoddard (whose sore lips must have received no advantage from this), almost convulsed with laughing, rolling in an armchair. He said nothing; I believe he could not have spoke.

"Major Stoddard," said I, "go call Tilly back. He will lose himself—indeed he will" (every word interrupted with a "Ha! Ha!").

At last he rose and went to the door, and what a loud voice could avail in bringing him back, he tried.

Figure to thyself this Tilly, of a snowy evening, no hat, shoes down at heel, hair untied, flying across meadows, creeks, and mudholes. Flying from what? Why, a bit of painted wood. But he was ignorant of what it was. The idea of being made a prisoner wholly engrossed his mind, and his last resource was to run.

After a while, we being in rather more composure, and our bursts of laughter less frequent yet by no means subsided, in full assembly of girls and officers Tilly entered.

The greatest part of my risibility turned to pity. Inexpressible confusion had taken entire possession of his countenance, his fine hair hanging disheveled down his shoulders, all splashed with mud; yet his fright, confusion, and race had not divested him of his beauty.

He smiled as he tripped up the steps, but 'twas vexation placed it on his features. Joy at that moment was banished from his heart. He briskly walked five or six steps, then stopped, and took a general survey of us all.

"Where have you been, Mr. Tilly?" asked one officer. (We girls were silent.)

"I really imagined," said Stoddard, "that you were gone for your pistols. I followed you to prevent danger" (an excessive laugh at each question, which it was impossible to restrain).

"Pray, where were your pistols, Tilly?"

He broke his silence by the following expression: "You may all go to the D—l." I never heard him utter an indecent expression before.

At last his good nature gained a complete ascendance over his anger, and he joined heartily in the laugh. I will do him the justice to say that he bore it charmingly. No cowardly threats, no vengeance denounced.

Stoddard caught hold of his coat. "Come, look what you ran from," and dragged him to the door.

He gave it a look, said it was very natural, and, by the singularity of his expressions, gave fresh cause for diversion. We all retired to our different parlors, for to rest our faces, if I may say so.

Well, certainly, these military folks will laugh all night. Such screaming I never did hear. Adieu tonight.

Seventh Day Morn, December 13th

I am fearful they will yet carry the joke too far. Tilly certainly possesses an uncommon share of good nature, or he could not tolerate these frequent teasings.

Ah, Deborah, the Major is going to leave us entirely—just going. I will see him first.

Seventh Day Noon

He has gone. I saw him pass the bridge. The woods, which you enter immediately after crossing it, hindered us from following him farther. I seem to fancy he will return in the evening.

Seventh Day Night

Stoddard has not come back. We shall not, I fancy, see him again for months, perhaps years, unless he should visit Philadelphia. We shall miss his agreeable company.

But what shall we make of Tilly? No civil things yet from him. Adieu tonight, my dear.

First Day Morn, December 14th

The officers yet here. No talk of their departure. They are very lively—Tilly's retreat the occasion (the principal one, at least).

First Day Night

Captain Lipscomb, Seaton, and Tilly, with Cousin Hannah Miles, dined with us today. Hannah's health seems established, to our great joy.

Such an everlasting laugher as Tilly I never knew. He caused us a good deal of diversion while we sat at table. He has not said a syllable to one of us young ladies since Sixth Day eve. He tells Lipscomb that the Major had the assistance of the ladies in the execution of the scheme. He tells a truth.

About four o'clock I was standing at the door, leaning my head upon my hand, when a genteel officer rode up to the gate and dismounted. "Your servant, ma'am," and gave me the compliment of his hat. Walked into Aunt's.

I went into our parlor. Soon Seaton was called. Many minutes had not elapsed before he entered with the same young fellow I had just seen. He introduced him by the name of Captain Smallwood. We seated ourselves. I then had an opportunity of seeing him.

He is a brother to General Smallwood. A very genteel, pretty little fellow, very modest, and seems agreeable, but no personal resemblance between him and the Major.

After tea, turning to Tilly, he said, "So, sir, I have heard you had like to have been made a prisoner last Friday night!"

"Pray, sir, who informed you?"

"Major Stoddard was my author."

"I fancy he made a fine tale of it. How far did he say I ran?"

"Two miles, and that you fell into the mill-dam!"

He raised his eyes and hands, and exclaimed, "What a confounded falsehood!"

The whole affair was again revived.

Our Tillian hero gave a mighty droll account of his retreat, as they call it. He told us that after he had got behind our kitchen he stopped for company, as he expected the others would immediately follow. "But I heard them scream, 'Which way did he go? Where is he?' 'Aye,' said I to myself, 'he is gone where you shan't catch him,' and off I set again."

"Pray," asked Mama, "did thee keep that lane between the meadows?"

"Oh, no, ma'am; that was a large road, and I might happen to meet some of them. When I reached yon thorn hedge I again stopped. As it was a cold night, I thought I would pull up my shoe heels, and tie my handkerchief around my head. I then began to have a suspicion of a trick, and hearing the Major hollo, I came back."

I think I did not laugh more at the very time than tonight at the rehearsal of it. He is so good-natured, and takes all their jokes with so good a grace, that I am quite charmed with him. He laughingly denounces vengeance against Stoddard. He will be even with him. He is in the Major's debt, but he will pay him.

Seventh Day Morn

O. Foulke arrived just now, and relateth as followeth: The army began their march at six this morn by their house. Our worthy General Smallwood breakfasted at Uncle Caleb's. He asked how Mr. and Mrs. Wister and the young ladies were, and sent his respects to us.

Our brave, our heroic General Washington was escorted by fifty of the Life Guard with drawn swords. Each day he acquires an addition to his goodness.

We have been very anxious to hear how the inhabitants have fared. I understand that General Arnold, who bears a good character, has the command of the city, and the soldiers conducted with great decorum. Smallwood says that they had the strictest orders to behave well; and I dare say they obeyed the order. I now think of nothing but returning to Philadelphia.

So shall now conclude this journal with humbly hoping that the Great Disposer of events, who has graciously vouchsafed to protect us to this day through many dangers, will still be pleased to continue his protection.

SALLY WISTER

North Wales, June 20, 1778

WAR IN THE WEST

Primarily the American Revolution was fought along the Atlantic seaboard. The British army drew its lifeblood from the Royal Navy, and never ventured too far from the coastal ports. Boston, New York, Savannah, Charleston, were the coveted prizes, and the springboards for the interior marches into Pennsylvania and New Jersey, South Carolina and Virginia. The defeat of Burgoyne in 1777 snapped off one British tentacle reaching into the American heartland from Canada, and the conquest of the Illinois posts by George Rogers Clark in 1779 snapped off another. Had the Western frontier buckled before an English invasion, the Continental Army would have been squeezed in a mortal pincers. War in the Western theater, therefore, deserves a greater emphasis than its few campaigns would seem to warrant.

Western fighting followed the patterns of border warfare rather than of pitched battle and strategic maneuver. Vast distances, tiny pockets of settlement, and the nomadic Indian tribes employed by the British determined the character of frontier conflict. The English possessed an immense asset in the Northwest posts acquired from France in 1763. From their forts at Niagara and Detroit they encouraged Iroquois raids and slaughter on the scattered villages in western New York and Pennsylvania, with or without the aid of Loyalists and regular troops. The patriots must defend themselves behind blockhouse and palisade until Washington could spare a regiment for a scouting party to lay waste the Iroquois villages. The Continental Army never succeeded in mounting an attack against Niagara or Detroit. To these posts the Indian raiders repaired, from as far south as Virginia and Kentucky, with prisoners and scalps to deliver to their allies. Daniel Boone was captured by Shawnees in the Blue Licks, after fighting off attacks on the frontier outposts at Boonsboro and Harrodsburg from 1775 to 1778, and taken north to Detroit. Operating out of Niagara, a Loyalist band under the hated Walter Butler descended with Seneca allies on Wyoming Valley in Pennsylvania and Cherry Valley in New York and butchered the frontier inhabitants, in the winter of 1778, in twin massacres that created as many infamous legends as the old Jersey. In consequence, the next year Washington sent General John Sullivan with five thousand men to invade the Seneca country and if possible assault Niagara, but he proceeded only as far as the Genesee River, laying waste the Indian cornfields and orchards but meeting few foes. So the Americans futilely diverted troops and supplies they badly needed to contain Howe in Philadelphia.

The threat from Detroit proved equally serious. Commanding the Great Lakes and the interior waterways from his strategic base, Lieutenant Governor Henry Hamilton relentlessly thrust at the open frontier with his redskin raiders, and earned the nickname of the "Hair-buyer." A brilliant exploit by a young frontiersman, George Rogers Clark, blunted the British effort to roll up the American flank anchored at Fort Pitt at the forks of the Ohio, and won for the new nation a vast inland territory. With a tiny band of men recruited by his own efforts, Clark set out from Kentucky in the spring of 1778 on a twelve-hundred-mile journey into the Illinois country, and secured the French settlements there with a clever display of diplomacy and force. Meanwhile Hamilton set out from Detroit in early October and recaptured the village of Vincennes. Clark was then faced with the alternative of withdrawing to Kentucky for reinforcements or attempting the hazardous overland and over-water march from Kaskaskia to Vincennes in the middle of winter to take Hamilton by surprise. (It is at this point that the present selection from his memoir commences.) His feat in crossing one hundred and eighty miles of seemingly impassable terrain, keeping up the morale of his men (half of them French), and capturing Hamilton's garrison in Vincennes on February 25, 1779, reads like a primitive saga.

Unfortunately, the follow-up campaign that Clark planned against Detroit never developed. Governor Jefferson of Virginia and General Washington, sympathetic as they were to the project, could spare him no forces, and the Western front relapsed into an indecisive state of raid and counterraid. Washington's commitments in the East and South left the Westerners virtually dependent upon their own resources, even after the surrender of Cornwallis, and so long as Detroit remained in British hands they suffered grievously. Weakness compelled them to abandon their forts in the Ohio country, and when even the friendly Delawares turned against the Americans, their situation grew ominous. Indian bands darted across the Ohio to plunder, burn, scalp, and carry off the settlers of western Pennsylvania and Virginia, who were reduced to farming alongside blockhouses and stockades. Sentinels stood on guard while the men worked in the fields, with their arms piled in a central spot ready for instant use. Under such conditions the whole border country from Fort Pitt south to the valleys of the Monongahela and the Youghiogheny and west to the Ohio River stood in danger. When General William Irvine assumed command of the Western Department under instructions from Washington, in March, 1782, he found Fort Pitt and the surrounding country in a calamitous condition.

Irvine acted quickly to save the fort and the people. He executed deserters, repaired the fort, and called a convention of the regular and militia officers and leading citizens. In consequence, defense plans were instituted calling for "flying" bodies of militia to patrol the frontiers, and an offensive was projected against the rallying center of the British Indian sorties, Sandusky. A volunteer militia force of several hundred men assembled in Mingo Bottom on May 20th under their elected commander, Colonel William Crawford, a prominent Westerner and old border fighter. The Irish and Scotch-Irish lads rode off in high spirits, in their belted hunting shirts, buckskin breeches, and moccasins, and carrying their tow cloth knapsacks, tomahawks, scalping knives, rifles, pouches, and powder horns. The little army clashed with the alerted and well-prepared Wyandots at Sandusky on June 4th. A fierce day's fighting left the issue undecided, but the appearance of Butler's Rangers, the hated Loyalist troop, decided Crawford to retreat. Heavy Indian crossfire galled the borderers next day as they turned back, and a number of stragglers were lost and captured. Crawford himself was taken and horribly tortured, while Dr. Knight, a surgeon, and John Slover, a guide, escaped to tell harrowing tales of their captivities.

The signing of the peace next year eased but did not terminate the difficulties of the border people, who lived under hazard until the British finally quitted Detroit and Niagara in 1796.

George Rogers Clark

George Rogers Clark (1752-1818) was born just outside Charlottesville, Virginia, of native Virginian stock, but from the age of twenty on he spent his time in the Kentucky and Ohio country, canoeing down the Ohio River, hunting, clearing land, surveying farms for settlers, and fighting as militia captain in Dunmore's War. His early years and his splendid physique prepared him perfectly for his major exploit. After the retaking of Vincennes, Clark vainly endeavored to raise a force to march on Detroit, even though backed by Washington and Jefferson, but he maintained his position in the West, and permanently blunted the British offensive. In the postwar years Clark lost his patriotic halo, largely as a result of an unsuccessful Indian expedition in 1786, and in the end, like Ethan Allen, he was accused of negotiating with a foreign government—in his case, of planning as a French general to take Louisiana from Spain.

At the request of James Madison, Clark labored over a memoir of his 1778-1779 campaigns ten years later, completing it by 1791. A journal he had previously written disappeared from his sight, but he referred to it in a letter to George Mason as follows:

> If I was sensible that You wou'd let no Person see this relation I wou'd give You a detail of our suffering for four days in crossing those waters, and the manner it was done; as I am sure You wou'd Credit; but it is too incredible for any Person to believe except those that are as well acquainted with me as You are or had experienced something similar to it.

The memoir lives up to this promise of incredible action, but the malformations of spelling and syntax prevented it from gaining an audience, although historians and novelists drew upon its vivid details (Winston Churchill, *The Crossing;* Maurice Thompson, *Alice of Old Vincennes*). It has been printed with partial editing by W. H. English in his *Conquest of the Country Northwest of the River Ohio 1778-1783* (Indianapolis and Kansas City, 1896), I, 457-555, and *literatim* by James A. James in the *Collections of the Illinois State Historical Library* (1912), VIII, 208-302. In his standard biography, *The Life of George Rogers Clark* (Chicago, c. 1928), James demonstrates the accuracy of the memoir (Appendix I, 474-494). Thanks to the inspiration of Milo M. Quaife, working from the manuscript in the Lyman C. Draper Collection in the Wisconsin Historical Society, the memoir was made available to the public in readable English, first in an edition of the Lakeside Classics in 1922, issued by R. R. Donnelley and Sons, Chicago, and then in conjunction with Governor Henry Hamilton's own account, under the title *The Capture of Old Vincennes. The Original Narratives of George Rogers Clark and of His Opponent Gov. Henry Hamilton*. Edited, with an Introduction and Notes, by Milo M. Quaife. (The Bobbs-Merrill Company, Indianapolis, c. 1927.) Recent scholarship has tended to regard Hamilton more favorably; see, e.g., John D. Barnhart, "A New Evaluation of Henry Hamilton and George Rogers Clark," *Mississippi Valley Historical Review*, XXXVII (March, 1951), 643-652.

In the selection that follows I have attempted a fairly literal rendering of the memoir, in the effort to recapture the flavor of Clark's highly individual style. This text is based on James, *op. cit.*, pp. 266-289, and I am indebted to Mr. Quaife's editorial notes.

THE MARCH FROM KASKASKIA TO VINCENNES

WE HAD THOUGHT, if we found there was no probability of keeping possession of our posts, to abandon them just on the approach of the enemy, whose numbers had considerably increased, return to Kentucky, and raise a force sufficient to intercept and prevent the English from returning again to Detroit. We knew the Indians were not fond of long campaigns and would leave them. But on the twenty-ninth of January, 1779, Mr. Vigo, then a Spanish merchant who had been at St. Vincennes, arrived and gave information that Governor Hamilton with thirty regulars, fifty French volunteers, Indian agents, interpreters, boatmen, etc., amounting to a considerable number, and about four hundred Indians, had in December last taken that post. As the season was so far advanced it was thought impossible to reach the Illinois, he had sent some of his Indians to Kentucky and to watch the Ohio, disbanded others, etc., with the understanding that the whole were to meet again in the spring, drive us out of the Illinois, and attack Kentucky in a body, joined by their Southern friends. All the goods had been taken from the merchants of St. Vincennes for the King's use. The English were repairing the fort and expected a reinforcement from Detroit in the spring, and appeared to have plenty of all kinds of stores. Although they were strict in their discipline he did not think they were under much apprehension of a visit, and believed that if we could get there undiscovered we might take the place. In short, we obtained all the information from this gentleman that we could wish for, as he had had good opportunity and had taken great pains to inform himself with a design to give intelligence.

We now viewed ourselves in a very critical situation, in a manner cut off from any intercourse between us and the rest of the continent. In the spring Hamilton, by a junction of his Northern and Southern Indians which he had prepared, would be at the head of such a force that nothing in this quarter could withstand his arms. Kentucky must immediately fall, and it would be well if the desolation would end there.

Even if we could make our way directly to Kentucky we were convinced that before we might raise a force sufficient to save that country it would be too late, as all the men there, joined by the troops we had, would not suffice, and to get timely succor from the interior frontiers was out of the question. We saw but one alternative: to attack the enemy in their quarters. If we were fortunate it would save the whole; if otherwise, we would be no worse off than if we should not make the attempt. We felt encouraged by the idea of the greatness of the consequences that would attend our success. The season of the year was also favorable, as the enemy could not suppose that we should be mad enough to attempt to march eighty leagues through a drowned country in the depth of winter, and would be off their guard and probably not think it worth while to keep out spies. Very likely if we could make our way successfully we might surprise them and pull through.

These and many other similar reasons induced us to resolve to attempt the enterprise, which view met with the approbation of every individual belonging to us. Orders were immediately issued for preparations. The whole country took fire at the alarm and every order was executed with cheerfulness by the inhabitants of every description, preparing provisions, encouraging volunteers, etc. etc., and as we had plenty of stores every man was completely rigged with all he could desire to withstand the coldest weather.

As we had for some time past been in a state of suspense we had partly prepared for some such event as this, and therefore were soon ready. The inhabitants of Kaskaskia being a little cowed since the affair of the supposedly intended siege, nothing was said to them on the subject of volunteers until the arrival of those from Cahokia. For these an expensive entertainment had been provided, to which they invited all their acquaintance of Kaskaskia. All little differences were thus made up, and by twelve o'clock the next day application was made to raise a company at Kaskaskia, which was granted and completed before night, the whole of the inhabitants exerting themselves in order to wipe off past coolness.

Everything being now ready, on the fifth of February, after receiving a lecture and absolution from the priest, we crossed the Kaskaskia River with one hundred and seventy men, marched about three miles, made camp where we lay until the eighth, and set out. The weather being wet (but fortunately not cold for the season) and a great part of the plains lying under water for several inches, marching proved difficult and very fatiguing.

My object now was to keep the men in spirits. I suffered them to shoot game on all occasions and feast on them in the manner of Indian war dances, each company in turn inviting the other to its feasts. This was the case every night, as the company that was to give it was always supplied with horses to lay up sufficient store of fresh meat in the course of the day, while I and my principal officers kept hailing on the woodsmen, shouting now and then, and running as much through the mud and water as any of them. Thus insensibly, without a murmur, were those men led on to the banks of the Little Wabash, which we reached on the thirteenth, through incredible difficulties far surpassing anything any of us had ever experienced (but nothing to what we had to go through). Frequently the pleasure of a day and the diversions of the night wore off the thought of the preceding day.

This place is called the "two Little Wabashes." They are three miles apart, and from the heights of the one to that of the other on the opposite shore is five miles; the whole stretch lies under water, generally about three feet in depth, never under two, and frequently four. We formed a camp on a height we found on the bank of the river and suffered our troops to amuse themselves. I viewed this sheet of water for some time with distrust, but accusing myself of doubting I immediately set to work without holding any consultation about it or suffering anybody else to do so in my presence. Accordingly I ordered a pirogue built at once, and acted as though crossing the water would be only a piece of diversion. As but few could work at a time, pains were taken to find amusement for the rest to keep them in high spirits, but the men were well prepared for this attempt, as they had frequently waded farther in water, although seldom above half leg deep. My anxiety to cross this place continually increased, for I saw that the crossing would at once fling us into a situation of a forlorn hope, as all ideas of a retreat would be in some measure done away. If after this was accomplished the men began to think seriously of what they had really suffered, they would prefer risking any seeming difficulty that might probably turn out favorably, than to attempt a retreat with the certainty of experiencing what they had already undergone (and if the weather should be freezing, an altogether impracticable venture, unless the ice would bear them).

In the evening of the fourteenth our vessel was finished, manned, and sent to explore the drowned lands, with private instructions what kind of report to make. If possible, they were to find some spot of dry land on the bank of the opposite small river. And this they did within about half an acre's distance, marking the trees back from thence to the camp, and so made a very favorable report.

Fortunately, the fifteenth happened to be a warm moist day for the season. The channel of the river where we lay extended about thirty yards in width. We built a scaffold on the opposite shore, which lay about three feet under water, ferried our baggage over, and put it there. Then our horses swam across and received their loads at the scaffold; by which time the troops were also brought across, and we began our march. Our vessel was loaded with the sick and we moved on cheerfully, every moment expecting to see dry land. This was not discovered until we came to the little dry spot just mentioned. This being a smaller branch than the other, the troops crossed immediately and marched on in the water as usual, in order to gain and take possession of the highest height they could discover. Our horses and baggage crossed as they had done at the former river and proceeded on, following the marked trail of the troops. (As tracks could not be seen in the water they had marked the trees.)

By evening we found ourselves encamped on a pretty height in high spirits. Each man was laughing at the other in consequence of something that had happened in the course of this ferrying business, as they called it, and the whole company at the great exploit they thought that they had accomplished. A little antic drummer afforded them great diversion by floating on his drum. All this we greatly encouraged, and they really began to think themselves superior to other men, and to feel that neither the rivers nor the seasons could stop their progress. Their whole conversation now turned on what they would do when they reached the enemy. They began to view the main Wabash as a creek, and made no doubt but such men as they could find a way to cross it. Soon they wound themselves up to such a pitch that they took St. Vincennes, divided the spoil, and before bedtime had far advanced on their route to Detroit.

This was doubtless pleasing to those of us that had more serious thoughts. We had as it were arrived in the enemy's country, with no possibility of a retreat if the enemy should discover and overpower us (except by the means of our galley if we should fall in with her). We were now convinced that the whole of the low country by the Wabash was drowned, so that the enemy could easily get to us if he discovered us and wished to risk an action. If he did not, we made no doubt of crossing the river by some means or other. Supposing that Captain Rogers had not got to his station agreeable to his appointment, we would if possible steal some vessels from houses opposite to the town, and so we flattered ourselves that all would be well, and marched on in high spirits.

On the seventeenth I dispatched Mr. Kennedy and three men to cross the river Embarrass (this river is six miles from St. Vincennes) and if possible to get some vessels in the vicinity of the town, but principally, if he could do so in safety, to procure some intelligence. He proceeded on his way, and getting to the Embarrass River found the country between that and the Wabash overflowed. We marched down below the mouth of the Embarrass, attempting in vain to get to the banks of the Wabash. Late in the night, finding a dry spot, we encamped, and were amused for the first time by the morning gun from the British garrison. We continued our march, and about two o'clock on the eighteenth gained the banks of the Wabash three leagues below

the town, where we encamped. I dispatched four men across the
river on a raft to find land and march to the town if possible,
and get some canoes privately. Captain McCarty with a few
men set out the next morning in a little canoe he had made for
the same purpose. Both parties returned without success. The
first could not get to land, and the Captain was driven back by
the appearance of a camp. The canoe was immediately dispatched
down the river to meet the galley, to give her orders to proceed
day and night. Determined to have every possible string to my
bow, I ordered more canoes to be built in a private place. While
not yet out of hopes of our boat arriving, I reasoned that if she
did not turn up, those canoes would augment our fleet, and if
she did not come before they were ready, they would answer our
purpose without her.

Many of our volunteers began for the first time to despair.
Some talked of returning, but in my present situation I felt past
all uneasiness. I laughed at them without persuading or ordering them to desist from any such attempt, but instead told them
I should be glad if they would go out and kill some deer. They
went, confused with such conduct. My own troops I knew had no
idea of abandoning an enterprise for the want of provisions while
there were plenty of good horses in their possession, and I knew
also that without any violence the volunteers could be detained
for a few days, in the course of which time our fate would be
known. I conducted myself in such a manner that caused everybody to believe I had no doubt of success, which kept up their
spirits. Hunters being out, they enjoyed every moment hopes of
getting a supply from them, and had the further hope of the
galley heaving in sight. I was sensible that if we should not be
discovered in two days we should effect the passage of the river.

On the twentieth the water guard decoyed on shore a boat with
five Frenchmen and some provisions on board, who were on their
way to join a party of hunters down the river. They informed
us that we were not discovered; that the inhabitants were well
disposed towards us; that the English had greatly strengthened
the fort, which was quite finished; that their numbers were nearly
the same as when Mr. Vigo left the place—in short, they gave us
every information we wished for. They told us of two vessels

adrift up the river, one of which Captain Worthington recovered, so that we now had two small vessels.

Early on the twenty-first the crossing of our troops commenced. We landed on a small rising called the Mamel, where we left our baggage. Captain J. Williams while searching for a passage gave chase to a canoe, but could not bring it to. The men that we had taken said it was impossible to make town that night or at all with our vessels, but recollecting what we had done we thought otherwise. We pushed into the water and marched a league to what is called the Upper Mamel, being frequently up to the arm-pits in water. Here we encamped. Our men remained in good spirits from the hopes of their fatigue soon being at an end and their wishes realized in getting in contact with the enemy.

This last march through the water so far outdid anything the Frenchmen could imagine that they were nearly rendered speech-less. They managed to say that the nearest land to us was a small league distant, called the Sugar Camp, on the bank of the river. A canoe was dispatched thence, and returned without finding a passage. I went in her myself, and sounding the water found it as deep as to my neck. I returned with the design of having the men transported on board the canoes to the Sugar Camp, al-though I knew this would take the whole day and ensuing night as the vessels would pass but slowly through the bushes, and the loss of so much time to men half starved was a matter of conse-quence. Now I would have given a good deal for a day's provision or for one of our horses.

I returned but slowly to the troops, giving myself time to think. On our arrival all ran to hear what was the report; every eye was fixed on me. Unfortunately, I spoke seriously to one of the officers —all became alarmed without knowing what I said. They ran from one to another bewailing their situation. I viewed their confusion for about one minute. Then whispering to those near me to do as I did, I suddenly took some water in my hand, poured powder over it, blacked my face, gave the war whoop, and marched into the water without saying a word. The party gasped and fell in one after another like a flock of sheep. I ordered those by me to begin a favorite song of theirs; it soon passed through the line, and the whole went on cheerfully.

I now intended to have them transported across the deepest part of the water, but when getting about waist-deep one of the men informed me that he thought he felt a path. We examined the spot and found it so, and concluded that it kept to the highest ground, which proved the case. By taking pains to follow this path we got to the Sugar Camp without the least difficulty, and what had alarmed us at the former place proved fortunate here, for we found about half an acre of dry ground, or at least ground not under water, where we took up our lodgings.

The Frenchmen that we had taken on the river appeared to be uneasy at our situation. They begged that they might be permitted to go in the two canoes to town in the night, saying that they would bring provisions from their own houses without a possibility of any person's knowing it, and offering that some of our men should go with them as a surety of their good conduct. They declared it impossible for us to march from that place until the water fell—which would be in a few days—for the plain before us for upwards of three miles was too deeply covered to cross. Some of them earnestly solicited that this might be done. I would by no means suffer it. I never could well account for this piece of obstinacy, and give satisfactory reasons to myself or anybody else why I denied a proposition apparently so easy to execute and of so much advantage to us, but something seemed to tell me that it should not be done, and it was not.

Most of the weather on this march was moist and warm for the season, but this night was the coldest we had had. In the morning the ice was from a half to three-quarters of an inch thick near the shores and in still water, but still it was the finest morning of our march. A little after sunrise I lectured the whole company. What I said to them I forget but it may be easily imagined, considering my affections for them at that time. I concluded by informing them that surmounting the plain then in full view and reaching the opposite woods would put an end to their fatigue, and that in a few hours they would have a sight of their long-wished-for object. Without waiting for any reply I stepped into the water. A huzza arose.

We generally marched through the water in a line, as being much the easiest way. Before a third of the men had entered I halted, and further to prove them, and having some suspicion of three or four, I hallooed to Major Bowman ordering him to fall in the rear with twenty-five men and put to death any man that refused to march, for we wanted no such person among us. The whole gave a cry of approbation that this was right, and on we went.

This was the most trying of all the difficulties we had experienced. I generally kept fifteen or twenty of the strongest men next to myself, and judged from my own feeling what must be that of the others. Getting toward the middle of the plain, the water about knee-deep, I found myself sensibly failing. As there were no trees or bushes here for the men to support themselves by, I doubted not that many of the weakest would be drowned. I ordered the canoes to make the land, discharge their loading, and ply backwards and forwards with all diligence to pick up the men. And further to encourage the party I sent some of the strongest men forward with orders, when they reached a certain distance, to pass the word back that the water was getting shallower, and when getting near the woods to cry out "Land!" This stratagem had its desired effect. The men thus encouraged exerted themselves almost beyond their abilities, the weak holding on to the stronger, and frequently one man was held up by two others. This was of infinite advantage to the weak, but the water never got shallower but continued deepening. On getting to the woods where they expected land I found the water up to my shoulders, but gaining those woods was of great consequence. All the little and weakly men hung to the trees and floated on the old logs until they were taken off by the canoes; the strong and tall got ashore and built fires. Many would reach the shore and fall exhausted with their bodies half in the water, not being able to support themselves. Fortunately, this proved a delightful dry spot of ground of about ten acres. We soon found that the fires answered no purpose, but that two strong men had to raise a weaker one by the arms in order to revive him, and the day being fine he would soon come to.

Then, as if designed by Providence, a canoe of Indian squaws and children coming up to the town crossed through part of this plain as a short cut, and was discovered by our canoes while they were out after our men. They gave chase, and took them. On board they found nearly half a quarter of buffalo, some corn, tallow, kettles, etc. This was a grand and invaluable prize. Broth was immediately made and served out to the weakest, but with great care. Most of the men got a little, but a great many would not taste it but gave their share to the weakly, jocosely saying something cheery to their comrades. This little refreshment, coupled with fine weather by the afternoon, gave new life to the party.

Crossing a narrow deep lake in the canoes and marching some distance, we came to a copse of timber called the Warrior's Island. We were now in full view of the fort and town at about two miles' distance, with not even a scrub tree between us.

THE ATTACK ON THE FORT

EVERY MAN feasted his eyes and forgot that he had ever suffered anything. All began to feel that what had passed was owing to good policy and nothing but what a man could bear and that a soldier had no right to complain, and so on, passing from one extreme to another, as is common in such cases. It was now we had to display our abilities. The plain between us and the town was not a perfect level, and the sunken ground was covered with water full of ducks. We observed several men on horseback out shooting them, within half a mile of us, and sent out an equal number of our active young Frenchmen to decoy and take one of them prisoner in such a manner as not to alarm the others; which they did. The information we obtained from this person was similar to what the Frenchmen we had taken on the river had told us, but he added that the British that evening had completed the wall of the fort, and that there were a good many Indians in town.

Our situation was now truly critical. No possibility existed of retreating in case of defeat. We lay in full view of a town that at this time had in it upwards of six hundred men, troops, inhabitants, and Indians. We were now in the situation that I had labored to get ourselves in. The idea of being made prisoner was foreign to almost every man, as they expected nothing but torture from the savages if they fell into their hands. Our fate was about to be determined, probably in a few hours. We knew that nothing but the most daring conduct could ensure success. I knew that a number of the inhabitants wished us well, and that

many were lukewarm to the interest of either side; also I learned
that the Grand Chief, son of the Tobacco, had but a few days
past openly declared in council with the British that he was
brother and friend to the Big Knives. All these were favorable
circumstances. As there was but little probability of our remaining undiscovered until dark, since great numbers of fowlers went
out in the evening and we could now see and hear them through
the plains around us, I determined to begin the enterprise immediately. Accordingly I wrote the following placard to the
inhabitants and sent it off by the prisoner just taken, who was
not permitted to see our numbers.

> To the Inhabitants:
>
> Gentlemen: Being now within two miles of your village with
> my army, determined to take your fort this night, and not
> being willing to surprise you, I take this step to request such
> of you as are true citizens and willing to enjoy the liberty I
> bring you to remain still in your houses; and that those (if
> any there be) that are friends to the King of England will in-
> stantly repair to the fort and join his troops and fight like
> men. If any such should hereafter be discovered that did not
> repair to the garrison they may depend on severe punishment.
> On the contrary those that are true friends to liberty may ex-
> pect to be well treated as such. I once more request that they
> may keep out of the streets, for every person found under
> arms on my arrival will be treated as an enemy.

I had various ideas on the supposed result of this letter. I
knew that it could do us no damage; that it would encourage our
friends, cause the lukewarm to decide, and astonish our enemies.
They would of course suppose our information good and our
forces so numerous that we were sure of success, and would never
dream that the idea of the army coming from Kentucky and not
from the Illinois was only a piece of parade. For they considered
it impossible for us to march from the Illinois, and thought that
my name was only being made use of. (This they firmly believed
until the next morning, when I was shown to them by a person
in the fort that knew me well.) Or possibly we were a flying party
that only made use of this stratagem to give ourselves time to retreat. This latter idea I knew would soon be done away with.

Several gentlemen sent their compliments to their friends
under borrowed names well known at St. Vincennes, as from per-

sons supposed to have been at Kentucky. The soldiers all had instructions that their common conversation when speaking of our own numbers should be such that a stranger overhearing must suppose there was near a thousand of us.

We anxiously viewed our messenger until he entered the town, and in a few minutes could discover by our glasses some stir in every street we could penetrate into, and great numbers running or riding out into the commons, we supposed in order to view us, which was the case. But what surprised us was that nothing had yet happened that had the appearance of the garrison's being alarmed, no drum nor gun sounding. We began to suppose that the information from our prisoner was false, and that the enemy already knew and was prepared for us. Every man had become impatient for action.

The moment was now arrived. A little before sunset we moved, and displayed ourselves in full view of the town. Crowds stood gazing at us. We were plunging ourselves into certain destruction or success. There was no middle way thought of. We had but little to say to our men, except to inculcate an idea of the necessity for obedience. We knew they did not want encouraging, and we felt that anything might be attempted with them that was possible for such a number, perfectly cool, under proper subordination, pleased with the prospect before them, and much attached to their officers. They all declared themselves convinced that an implicit obedience to orders was the only way to ensure success, and hoped that no mercy would be shown any person to violate them, but that he would immediately be put to death. Such language as this from the soldiers to persons in our situation must have been exceedingly agreeable.

We moved on slowly in full view of the town. As it was a point of some consequence to us to make ourselves appear as formidable as possible, in leaving our cover we marched and countermarched in such a manner that we appeared numerous. When we were raising volunteers in the Illinois, every person that set about the business had a set of colors given him, which he had brought along, giving us a total amount of ten or twelve pairs. These were displayed to the best advantage. The low plain we marched through was not a perfect level but had frequent risings in it seven or eight feet higher than the common level, which was covered with water, and as these risings generally ran in an oblique direction to the town, we took advantage of one of them to march through the water under it, and so completely prevented our men from being numbered. But our colors showed considerably above the height, as they were fixed to long poles procured for the purpose, and at a distance made no despicable appearance. Further, as our young Frenchmen had while we lay on the Warrior's Island decoyed and taken several fowlers with their horses, our officers were mounted on them and rode about, the more completely to deceive the enemy. In this manner we moved, and directed our march so that darkness fell before we had advanced more than halfway to the town. We then suddenly altered our direction and crossed intervening ponds where they could not have suspected us, and about eight o'clock gained the heights back of the town.

As there was yet no hostile appearance we grew impatient to have the cause unriddled. Lieutenant Bailey was ordered with fourteen men to march and fire on the fort, while the main body moved in a different direction and took possession of the strongest part of the town. Firing commenced on the fort, but the English did not believe it was an enemy, as drunken Indians frequently saluted the fort after night, until one of the men was shot down through a porthole as he was lighting his match. The drums now sounded and the business fairly commenced on both sides. Reinforcements were sent to attack the garrison, while other arrangements were being made in town.

We now found that the garrison had known nothing of us; that having finished the fort that evening, they had amused themselves at different games and had retired just before my letter arrived, as it was near roll call. After the placard was made public many of the inhabitants were afraid to go out of their houses for fear of giving offense, and not one dared give information.

The garrison was now completely surrounded. Our firing continued without intermission, except for about fifteen minutes a little before day, until nine o'clock the following morning, from the entire body of our troops joined by a few of the young men of the town that had got permission (except for fifty men kept as a reserve in case of casualties happening, which proved many and distracting in the course of the night). I had made myself fully acquainted with the situation of the fort, the town, and the parts relative to each. The cannon of the garrison was placed on the upper floors of strong blockhouses at each angle of the fort eleven feet above the surface, and the ports were so badly cut that many of our troops lay unharmed under their fire within twenty or thirty yards of the walls. They did no damage except to the buildings of the town, some of which they severely shattered. The gardens of St. Vincennes were very near the fort, and enclosed about two-thirds around with fencing, generally of good pickets well set and about six feet high. Where those were wanting breastworks were soon made by tearing down old houses, gardens, etc., so that those within had very little advantage over those without the fort, and not knowing the number of the enemy they thought themselves in a worse situation than they really were. Their musketry, employed in the dark against woodsmen covered by houses, palings, ditches, and the banks of the river, was of but little avail and did no damage to us, except for wounding a man or two. As we could not afford to lose men great care was taken to keep them sufficiently covered and to maintain a hot fire in order to intimidate as well as to destroy the enemy. The embrasures of their cannon were frequently shut, for our riflemen finding their range would pour in such volleys when they were opened that the English could not stand to the guns. Seven or eight of them in a short time were cut down. Our troops would continually abuse the enemy in order to aggravate them to open their ports and fire their cannon, that they might have the pleasure of cutting them down with their rifles, perhaps fifty of which might be leveled the moment the port flew open. And I believe if they had stood to their artillery that the greatest part of them would have been destroyed in the course of the night, as most of our men lay within thirty yards of the walls and in a few nearby houses and were as fully covered as those within the fort, and much more experienced in that mode of fighting. The flash of our guns directed them, but instantly our man moved his body; the moment there was the least appearance at one of their loopholes there would be perhaps a dozen guns fired at it. Sometimes we kept up an irregular fire as hot was possible from different directions for a few minutes, and then only a continual scattering fire at the ports as usual, whereupon a great noise and laughter immediately commenced in different parts of the town by the reserve parties, as if they had only fired on the fort a few minutes for amusement, until those continually firing at the fort were regularly relieved.

Conduct such as this kept the garrison eternally alarmed. They did not know what moment they might be stormed or sapped, as they could plainly discover that we had flung up some entrenchments across the streets and appeared to be very busily engaged under the bank of the river, which was within thirty feet of the walls. The situation of the magazine we well knew. Captain Bowman began some works in order to blow it up in case our artillery should arrive; but as we knew that we were daily liable to be overpowered by the numerous bands of Indians on the river in case they had again heartily joined the enemy (the certainty of which we were yet unacquainted with), we resolved to lose no time but to get the fort in our possession as soon as possible. We decided, if the vessel did not arrive in the meantime, to undermine the fort the ensuing night, and fixed on the spot and plan of executing this work, which we intended to commence the next day.

The Indians of different tribes who were inimical to us had left the town and neighborhood. Captain LaMothe continued to hover about in order if possible to make his way into the fort. Our parties continued in vain to attempt to surprise him, but a few of his men were taken, one of whom was Maisonville, a famous Indian partisan. Two lads that had captured him led him to a post in the street and fought from behind him as a breastwork, supposing that he would alarm the enemy and they would not fire at them for fear of killing him. An officer that discovered them at their amusement ordered them to untie Maisonville and take him to the guard, which they did, but did him no other damage. Almost all the persons that were most active in the department of Detroit were either in the fort or with Captain La-Mothe, and I became extremely uneasy for fear that he would not fall into our power, knowing that he would go off if he could effect his purpose. In the course of the night, finding that without some unforeseen accident the fort must inevitably be ours, and feeling that a reinforcement of twenty men, although considerable to them, would not be of great moment to us in the present situation of our affairs, and knowing that we had weakened them by killing or wounding many of their gunners, after some deliberation on the subject we concluded to risk the reinforcement in preference to LaMothe's going again among the Indians. As the garrison had at least a month's provisions, if it could hold out he might in the course of that time do us much damage.

A little before daylight the troops were withdrawn from the fort, except for a few parties of observation, and the firing totally ceased. Orders were given, in case LaMothe approached, not to alarm or fire on him without a certainty of killing or taking his whole party. In less than a quarter of an hour he passed within ten feet of an officer and small party that lay concealed. Ladders were flung over to them and as they mounted them our party shouted. Many of them fell from the top of the walls, some within and others outside, but as they were not fired on they all got over, much to the joy of their friends, as we easily discovered. But doubtless on considering the matter they must have been convinced that it was a scheme of ours to let them in and that we were so strong as to care but little about them, as the manner of their getting into the garrison clearly showed: our troops hollering and jeering at them while they mounted without firing at them, and our most blackguard soldiers frequently telling of the scheme and reason for suffering them to get into the fort, which on reflection they must have believed. But we knew that their knowledge of it could not now do us any damage but rather intimidate them. However, the garrison appeared much elated at the recovery of a valuable officer and party.

The firing immediately commenced on both sides with redoubled vigor, and I believe that more noise could not have been made by the same number of men. Their shouts could not be heard for the firearms but a continual blaze could be seen around the garrison, without much damage being done. A little before daylight our troops were drawn off to posts prepared for them about sixty to a hundred yards from the garrison, from which distance a loophole could scarcely be darkened but a rifle ball would pass through it. To have stood to their cannon would have meant destroying their men without a probability of doing much service. Our situations were nearly identical. It would have been imprudent in either party to have wasted their men unless some decisive stroke required it. Thus the attack continued until about nine o'clock in the morning of the twenty-fourth. Learning that the two prisoners the English had brought in the day before had a considerable number of letters with them, I supposed it an express that we expected about this time, which I knew to be of the greatest moment to us, as we had not received one since our arrival in the country. Not being fully acquainted with the character of our enemy, we were doubtful whether or not they might destroy those papers. To prevent this I sent a flag demanding the garrison, and desiring Governor Hamilton not to destroy them, with some threats in case he did should his garrison fall into my hands. His answer was that they were not disposed to be awed into anything unbecoming British subjects.

The firing commenced warmly for a considerable time, and we were obliged to be careful in preventing our men from exposing themselves too much. They were now much animated, having been refreshed during the flag talks, and frequently mentioned their wishes to storm the place and put an end to the business at once. This would at this time have been a piece of rashness. Our troops grew warm, and poured a heavy crossfire through every crack that could be discovered in any part of the fort. Several of the garrison were wounded and no possibility existed of standing near the embrasures. After some time, towards evening, a flag appeared with the following proposals.* I was greatly at a loss to conceive what reason Governor Hamilton could have for wishing a truce of three days on such terms as he proposed. A number said it was a scheme to get me into their possession. I had a different opinion and had no idea of his possessing such sentiments, as an act of that nature would infallibly ruin him. Rather I was convinced that he had some prospect of succor or of extricating himself in some other way. Although we had the greatest reason to expect a reinforcement in less than three days

* A three-day truce, and a private conference between the two commanding officers. "If Colonel Clark makes a difficulty of coming into the fort Lieutenant Governor Hamilton will speak to him before the gate." (Major Bowman's journal.)

that would at once put an end to the siege, I yet did not think it prudent to agree to the proposals and sent the following answer.*

We met at the church about eighty yards from the fort: Governor Hamilton, Major Hay, the Superintendent of Indian Affairs, and Captain Helm, who was their prisoner, Major Bowman, and myself. The conference then began. Various altercations took place for a considerable time.

The following articles were sent to the garrison, and an answer immediately returned.† The business being now nearly at an end, troops were posted in several strong houses around the garrison and patrolled during the night to prevent any deception that might be attempted. The remainder being off duty lay on their arms and for the first time for many days past got some rest.

During the conference a party of about twenty warriors had been sent to the Falls for scalps and prisoners, and was now discovered on their return as they entered the plains near the town. Not hearing any firing at this time, they had no suspicion of an enemy. Captain John Williams was ordered to meet and salute them. On meeting him the Indians supposed it a party of their friends coming to welcome them and gave the scalp and war whoop, and came on with all the parade of successful warriors. Williams did the same. Each approaching nearer, the Indians fired a volley in the air. The Captain did likewise. Coming within a few steps of each other, the chief stopped as if being suspicious. Captain Williams immediately seized him. The rest saw the mistake and ran. Fifteen of them were killed and made prisoners, and two partisans were put to death. The Indians tomahawked by the soldiers were flung into the river. We knew that nearly all of them were badly wounded, but as we yet had a more im-

* "Colonel Clark's compliments to Mr. Hamilton and begs leave to inform him that Colonel Clark will not agree to any other terms than that of Mr. Hamilton's surrendering himself and garrison prisoners at discretion. If Mr. Hamilton is desirous of a conference with Colonel Clark he will meet him at the church with Captain Helm." (Major Bowman's journal.)

† The fort and garrison to be surrendered by ten o'clock the next morning; the soldiers to receive three days' time to settle their affairs in Vincennes; the officers to retain their baggage. (Clark's contemporary journal.)

portant enemy to contend with there was no time for pursuit. After a few minutes in executing the business Captain Williams drew off his party and returned.

One reason why we did not wish to receive the garrison until the following morning was its being late in the evening before the capitulation was signed. The number of prisoners that we should have, when compared to our small force, made us feel the need of daylight to arrange matters to advantage. And as we knew we could now prevent any misfortune happening, since we could form such dispositions with our troops as to render the fort almost useless for defense, there could be of course no danger. Hence we supposed it prudent to let the British troops remain in the fort until the following morning. We should not ordinarily have had such suspicions and taken so much precaution, but I must confess that we could not help doubting the honor of men who could condescend to encourage the barbarity of the Indians —although almost every man had conceived a very favorable opinion of Governor Hamilton (and I believe what affected myself made some impression on the whole). I was happy to find that he never deviated while he stayed with us from that dignity of conduct that became an officer in his situation.

The morning of the twenty-fifth approaching, arrangements were made for receiving the garrison, and about ten o'clock it was delivered in form and everything immediately arranged to the best advantage. On viewing the inside of the fort and the stores I was astonished at its being given up in the manner it had been, but on weighing every circumstance I found that it was prudent and a lucky thing and probably saved the lives of many men on both sides; for the night past we inclined to attempt undermining the fort, and I found it would have required diligence to have prevented our success. If we had failed in this, I learned on further examination that our information was so good that in all probability the first hot shot after the arrival of our artillery would have blown up the magazine, and would at once have put an end to the business. Its situation and the quantity of powder it contained was such that it must have nearly destroyed the greater part of the garrison.

John Slover

John Slover as a boy of eight was seized in his home in New River, Virginia, by Miami Indians and carried off to southwestern Ohio with his mother, brother, and sisters. The savages killed his father, when he hallooed for them in his grief, and the two youngest children died on the march. His mother was afterwards exchanged, but Slover lived with the Miamis and Shawnees until he was twenty. Coming to Fort Pitt with his tribe to arrange a treaty in the fall of 1773, he met relatives who persuaded him, with difficulty, to resume the life of a white man. At the outbreak of the Revolution Slover enlisted in the Continental Army, and served fifteen months. On being discharged he married and settled in Westmoreland County, Pennsylvania. Knowing so well the country around the headwaters of the Sandusky River, and the character of the Indians, he was a natural choice to serve as guide for Crawford's invasion (see p. 239).

After escaping from the Wyandots and returning to Fort Pitt, the illiterate frontiersman narrated his experience to Hugh Henry Brackenridge, the novelist, who had just returned from study at Princeton. Brackenridge sent off the relations of Slover and Dr. Knight to his classmate, Philip Freneau, then editing the patriot weekly, *The Freeman's Journal*. The rancor of Brackenridge the frontier novelist met a match in the bitterness of Freneau the war poet, who had seen the inside of a British prison ship, and written about it in prose and verse. Freneau held the narratives from September, 1782, till the following spring hoping that General Guy Carleton would redeem his promise to Washington that Indian raids would cease. When they did not, Freneau published "The Narrative of the Perils and Sufferings of Dr. Knight and John Slover" in the issues of April 30, May 7, May 14, and May 28, 1783. They appeared in pamphlet form the same year, printed by Francis Bailey in Philadelphia. The present text is edited from pp. 36-60 of the Cincinnati, 1867, edition, published by U. P. James, reprinting the Nashville, 1843, edition: *Indian Atrocities, Narratives of the Perils and Sufferings of Dr. Knight and John Slover, among the Indians, during the Revolutionary War, with short memoirs of Col. Crawford & John Slover. And a letter from H. Brackinridge [sic] on the rights of the Indians, etc.*

INDIAN ATROCITIES

Having in the last war been a prisoner amongst the Indians many years, and so being well acquainted with the country west of the Ohio, I was employed as a guide in the expedition under

Colonel William Crawford against the Indian towns on or near the river Sandusky. It will be unnecessary for me to relate what is so well known, the circumstances and unfortunate events of that expedition; it will be sufficient to observe that, having on Tuesday the fourth of June [1782] fought the enemy near Sandusky, we lay that night in our camp, and the next day fired on each other at the distance of three hundred yards, doing little or no execution. In the evening of that day it was proposed by Colonel Crawford, as I have been since informed, to draw off with order; but at the moment of our retreat the Indians (who had probably perceived that we were about to retreat) firing alarm guns, our men broke and rode off in confusion, treading down those who were on foot, and leaving the wounded men, who supplicated to be taken with them.

I was with some others on the rear of our troops feeding our horses in the glade, when our men began to break. The main body of our people had passed by me a considerable distance before I was ready to set out. I overtook them before they crossed the glade, and was advanced almost in front. My company had endeavored to pass a morass, for coming up I found their horses had stuck fast in the morass, and endeavoring to pass, mine also in a short time stuck fast. (I ought to have said, the company of five or six men with which I had been immediately connected, and who were some distance to the right of the main body, had separated from me.) I tried a long time to disengage my horse, but in vain, until I could hear the enemy just behind me, and on each side. Here then I was obliged to leave him. The morass was so unstable that I sank up to the middle in it, and it was with the greatest difficulty that I got across. Having at length done so, I came up with the six men who had left their horses in the same manner I had done. Two of these, my companions, had lost their guns.

We traveled that night, making our course towards Detroit, with a view to shun the enemy, whom we conceived to have taken the paths by which the main body of our people had retreated. Just before day we got into a second deep morass, and were under the necessity of delaying until it was light to see our way through it. The whole of this day we traveled towards the Shawnee towns, with a view of throwing ourselves still farther out of the search of the enemy. About ten o'clock this day we sat down to eat a little, having tasted nothing from Tuesday, the day of our engagement, until this time, which was on Thursday, and now the only thing we had to eat was a scrap of pork to each. We had sat down by a warrior's path which we had not suspected, when eight or nine warriors appeared. Running off hastily, we left our baggage and provisions, but were not discovered by the party; skulking some time in the grass and bushes, we returned to the place and recovered our baggage. The warriors had hallooed as they passed, and were answered by others on our flanks.

In our journey through the glades (or wide extended dry meadows), about twelve o'clock this day we discovered a party of Indians in front, but by skulking in the grass and bushes we were not perceived by them. In these glades we were in great danger, as we could be seen at a great distance. In the afternoon of this day there fell a heavy rain. Traveling on we saw a party of the enemy about two hundred yards before us, but hiding ourselves in the bushes we had again the good fortune not to be discovered. This night we got out of the glades, having in the night crossed the paths by which we had advanced to Sandusky.

It was our design to leave all these paths to the right and to come in by the Tuscaroras. We would have made a much greater progress had it not been for two of our companions who were lame, the one having his foot burnt, the other with a swelling in his knee of a rheumatic nature.

On this day, which was the second after the retreat, one of our company, the person affected with the rheumatic swelling, was left behind some distance in a swamp. Waiting for him some time we saw him coming within one hundred yards, as I sat on the body of an old tree mending my moccasins, but taking my eye from him, I saw him no more. He had not observed our tracks, but had gone a different way. We whistled on our chargers, and afterwards hallooed for him, but in vain. Nevertheless, he was fortunate in missing us, for he afterwards came safe into Wheeling, which is a post of ours on the Ohio, about seventy miles below Fort Pitt. We traveled on until night, and were on the waters of the Muskingum from the middle of this day.

Having caught a fawn this day, we made fire in the evening

and had a repast, having in the meantime eaten nothing but the small bit of pork I mentioned before. We set off at break of day. About nine o'clock the third day we fell in with a party of the enemy about twelve miles from the Tuscaroras, which is about one hundred and thirty-five miles from Fort Pitt. They had come upon our tracks or had been on our flanks and discovered us, and then having got before, had waylaid us, and fired before we perceived them.

At the first fire one of my companions fell before me and another just behind me. These two had guns; there were six men in our company and four guns, two having been rendered useless by reason of the wet when coming through the swamp the first night; we had tried to discharge them but could not. When the Indians fired I ran to a tree, but an Indian, presenting himself fifteen yards before me, directed me to deliver myself up and I should not be hurt. My gun was in good order, but apprehending the enemy behind might discharge their pieces at me, I did not risk firing. This I had afterwards reason to regret when I found what was to be my fate, and also that the Indian before me presenting his gun was one of those who had just fired.

Two of my companions were taken with me in the same manner, the Indians assuring us we should not be hurt. But one in the company, James Paul, who had a gun in order, made his escape and has since come into Wheeling. One of these Indians knew me, and was of the party by whom I was taken in the last war. He came up and spoke to me, calling me by my Indian name, Mannuchothee, and upbraiding me for coming to war against them.

I will take a moment here to relate some particulars of my first captivity and my life since. I was taken from New River in Virginia by the Miamis, a nation called by us Picts, amongst whom I lived six years, afterwards being sold to a Delaware and by him put into the hands of a trader. I was carried amongst the Shawnees, with whom I continued six years, so that my whole time amongst these nations was twelve years, that is, from the eighth to the twentieth year of my age. At the treaty of Fort Pitt, in the fall preceding what is called Dunmore's War, which if I am right was in the year 1773 [1774], I came in with the Shawnee nation to the treaty, and met some of my relations at that place, who solicited me to relinquish the life of a savage. This I did with some reluctance, this manner of life having become natural to me, inasmuch as I had scarcely known any other. I enlisted as a soldier in the Continental Army at the commencement of the present war, and served fifteen months. Having been properly discharged I have since married, have a family, and am in communion with the church.

To return, the party by whom we were made prisoners had taken some horses and left them at the glades we had passed the day before. They had followed on our tracks from these glades. We returned there, found the horses, and rode to Wachatomakak, a town of the Mingoes and Shawnees. I think it was on the third day we reached the town. When we were approaching, the Indians in whose custody we were began to look sour, having been kind to us before and given us a little meat and flour to eat, which they had found or taken from some of our men on their retreat.

This town was a small one, we were told, about two miles distant from the main town, to which they intended to carry us. The inhabitants from this town came out with clubs and tomahawks, and struck, beat, and abused us greatly. They seized one of my two companions, stripped him naked, and blacked him with coal and water. This was the sign of being burnt; the man seemed to surmise it, and shed tears. He asked me the meaning of his being blacked, but I was forbid by the enemy, in their own language, to tell him what was intended. In English, which they spoke easily, having been often at Fort Pitt, they assured him he was not to be hurt. I know of no reason for making him the first object of their cruelty unless it was that he was the oldest.

A warrior had been sent to the great town to acquaint them with our coming and prepare them for the frolic, for on our coming to it the inhabitants came out with guns, clubs, and tomahawks. We were told that we had to run to the council house, about three hundred yards. The man that was blacked was about twenty yards before us in running the gantlet. They made him their principal object, men, women, and children beating him, and those who had guns firing loads of powder on him as he ran naked, putting the muzzles of the guns to his body, shouting, hallooing, and beating their drums in the meantime.

The unhappy man had reached the door of the council house, beat and wounded in a manner shocking to the sight—for having arrived before him we had it in our power to view the spectacle; it was indeed the most horrid that can be conceived. They had cut him with their tomahawks, shot his body black, burnt it into holes with loads of powder blown into him; a large wadding had made a wound in his shoulder whence the blood gushed.

Agreeable to the declaration of the enemy, when he first set out he had reason to think himself secure when he had reached the door of the council house. This seemed to be his hope, for coming up with great struggling and endeavors, he laid hold of the door, but was pulled back and drawn away by them; finding they intended no mercy but the putting him to death, he attempted several times to snatch or lay hold of some of their tomahawks, but being weak could not effect it. We saw him borne off, and they were a long time beating, wounding, and pursuing and killing him.

That same evening I saw the dead body of this man close by the council house. It was mangled cruelly, and the blood mingled with the powder was rendered black. A little later I saw him after he had been cut to pieces, and his limbs and head put on poles about two hundred yards outside the town. That evening also I saw the bodies of three others in the same black and mangled condition; these I was told had been put to death the same day, and just before we had reached the town. Their bodies as they lay were black, bloody, burnt with powder. Two of these were Harrison* and young Crawford.† I knew the visage of

* This was Colonel Harrison, son-in-law to Colonel Crawford, one of the first men in the Western country. He had been greatly active on many occasions in devising measures for the defense of the frontiers, and his character as a citizen in every way, then a young man, was distinguished and respectable. He had been a magistrate under the jurisdiction of Virginia, and I believe a delegate to the Assembly of that state. I know no man with whose grave, sedate manners, prudent conduct, good sense, and public spirit on all occasions I was more pleased. H.B.

† This was a son of Colonel Crawford. I do not remember to have seen him, nor was I acquainted with his character before the expedition, but have since been informed universally that he was a young man greatly and deservedly esteemed as a soldier and as a citizen. H.B.

Colonel Harrison, and I saw his clothing and that of young Crawford at the town. The third of these men I did not know, but believe to have been Colonel M. Cleland, the third in command
on the expedition. The next day the bodies of these men were
dragged to the outside of the town, and, their carcasses being
given to the dogs, their limbs and heads were stuck upon poles.

My surviving companion shortly after we had reached the
council house was sent to another town, and I presume he was
burnt or executed in the same manner.

In the evening the men assembled in the council house. This
is a large building about fifty yards in length, twenty-five yards
wide, and sixteen feet in height, built of split poles covered with
bark. Their first object was to examine me, which they could do
in their own language, inasmuch as I could speak the Miami,
Shawnee, and Delaware languages, which I had learned during
my early captivity in the last war. I found I had not forgotten
these languages, especially the two former, as well as my native
tongue.

They began with interrogating me concerning the situation of
our country. What were our provisions? Our numbers? The state
of the war between us and Britain? I informed them Cornwallis
had been taken, which next day, when Matthew Elliot came with
James Girty,* he affirmed to be a lie, and the Indians seemed to
give full credit to his declarations.

Hitherto I had been treated with some appearance of kindness, but now the enemy began to alter their behavior towards
me. Girty had informed them that when he asked me how I liked
to live there, I had said that I intended to take the first opportunity to take a scalp and run off. It was, to be sure, very probable that if I had such intention, I would communicate it to
him. Another man had come to me with a story of having lived
on the south branch of the Potomac in Virginia and having three
brothers there, and pretended he wanted to get away, but I suspected his design; nevertheless he reported that I had consented

* These men, Elliot and Girty, were inhabitants of the Western country, and since the commencement of the war for some time professed an
attachment to America, then went off to the Indians. They are of that
horrid brood called refugees, and whom the Devil has long since marked
for his own property. H.B.

to go. In the meantime I was not tied and could have escaped, but having nothing to put on my feet, I waited some time longer to provide for this.

I was invited every night to the war dance, which they usually continued until almost day. I could not comply with their desire, believing these things to be the service of the Devil.

The council lasted fifteen days, fifty to one hundred warriors being usually in council and sometimes more. Every warrior is admitted to these councils, but only the chiefs or head warriors have the privilege of speaking. The head warriors are accounted such from the number of scalps and prisoners they have taken. The third day McKee* was in council, and afterwards was generally present. He spoke little, and did not ask any questions or speak to me at all. He lives about two miles out of town, has a house built of square logs with a shingle roof; he was dressed in gold-laced clothes. I had seen him at the former town through which I passed.

I think it was on the last day of the council save one that a speech came from Detroit, brought by a warrior who had been counseling with the commanding officer at that place. The speech had been long expected, and was in answer to one some time before sent from the town to Detroit. It was in a belt of wampum, and began by addressing them, "My children," and then inquiring why they continued to take prisoners. "Provisions are scarce; when prisoners are brought in we are obliged to maintain them, and still some of them are running away and carrying tidings of our affairs. When any of your people fall into the hands of the rebels, they show no mercy; why then should you take prisoners? Take no more prisoners, my children, of any sort; man, woman, or child."

Two days after, a party from every nearby nation being collected, it was determined to take no more prisoners of any sort. They had held a large council, and the determination was that even if it were possible they could find a child of a span of three inches long, they would show no mercy on it. At the conclusion of the council it was agreed upon by all the tribes present, viz.:

* This man before the war was an Indian agent for the British. He was put on parole, broke it, went to the Indians, and has since continued violently to incite them to make war against us. H.B.

the Tawas, the Chippewas, the Wyandots, the Mingoes, the Delawares, the Shawnees, the Munsees, and a part of the Cherokees, that should any of the nations who were not present take any prisoners, these would rise against them, take away the prisoners, and put them to death.

In the course of these deliberations I understood what was said perfectly. They laid plans against our settlements of Kentucky, the Falls, and towards Wheeling. These it will be unnecessary for me to mention in this narrative, more especially as the Indians finding me to have escaped, and knowing that I would not fail to communicate these designs, will be led to alter their resolutions.

There was one council held at which I was not present. The warriors had sent for me as usual, but the squaw with whom I lived would not suffer me to go, but hid me under a large quantity of skins. It may have been from an unwillingness that I should hear in council the determination in respect to me, that I should be burnt.

About this time twelve men were brought in from Kentucky, three of whom were burnt on this day. The remainder were distributed to other towns, and all, as the Indians informed me, were burnt. This was after the speech came from Detroit.

On the day after, I saw an Indian who had just come into town, and who said that one of the prisoners he was bringing to be burnt, and who he said was a doctor, had made his escape from him. I knew this must have been Dr. Knight, who went as surgeon of the expedition. The Indian had a wound four inches long in his head, which he acknowledged the doctor had given him; he was cut to the skull. His story was that he had untied the doctor, being asked by him to do so, the doctor promising that he would not go away; that while he was employed in kindling the fire the doctor snatched up the gun, had come behind and struck him; that he then made a stroke at the doctor with his knife, who laid hold of it, and his fingers were cut almost off, the knife being drawn through his hand; that he gave the doctor two stabs, one in the back, the other in the belly. He said the doctor was a great, big, tall, strong man. Being now adopted in an Indian family, and having some confidence for my safety, I took the liberty to contradict this, and said that I knew the doctor, who was a weak, little man. The other warriors laughed immoderately, and did not seem to credit him.

The day after the council I have mentioned, about forty warriors, accompanied by George Girty, came early in the morning round the house where I was. The squaws gave me up. I was sitting before the door of the house; they put a rope round my neck, tied my arms behind my back, stripped me naked, and blacked me in the usual manner. George Girty, as soon as I was tied, d—d me, and said that I now should get what I had deserved many years. I was led away to a town distant about five miles, to which a messenger had been dispatched to desire them to prepare to receive me. Arriving at this town, I was beaten with clubs and the pipe ends of their tomahawks, and was kept for some time tied to a tree before a house door. In the meanwhile the inhabitants set out to another town about two miles distant, where I was to be burnt, and where I arrived about three o'clock in the afternoon.

Here also was a council house, part of it covered and part of it without a roof. In the part without the cover, but with sides built up, there stood a post about sixteen feet in height, and in the middle of the house around the post there were three piles of wood built about three feet high and four feet from the post. Being brought to the post, my arms were tied behind me, and the thong or cord with which they were bound was fastened to the post. A rope also was put about my neck, and tied to the post about four feet above my head. During the time they were tying me, piles of wood were kindled and began to flame.

Death by burning, which appeared to be now my fate, I had resolved to sustain with patience. The divine grace of God had made it less alarming to me, for on my way this day I had been greatly exercised in regard to my latter end. I knew myself to have been a regular member of the church, and to have sought repentance for my sins, but though I had often heard of the faith of assurance, I had known nothing of it personally. But early this day, instantaneously, by a change wrought upon me sudden and perceivable as lightning, an assurance of my peace made with God sprung up in mind. The following words were the subject of my meditation: "In peace thou shalt see God. Fear not those who can kill the body. In peace shalt thou depart." I was on this occasion, by a confidence in mind not to be resisted, fully assured of my salvation. This being the case I was willing, satisfied, and glad to die.

I was tied to the post, as I have already said, and the flame was now kindled. The day was clear, not a cloud to be seen. If there were clouds low in the horizon, the sides of the house prevented me from seeing them, but I heard no thunder, nor observed any sign of approaching rain. Just as the fire of one pile began to blaze, the wind rose; from the time they began to kindle the fire and to tie me to the post until the wind began to blow was about fifteen minutes. The wind blew a hurricane, and the rain followed in less than three minutes. The rain fell violently, and the fire, though it began to blaze considerably, was instantly extinguished. The rain lasted about a quarter of an hour.

When it was over the savages stood amazed, and were a long time silent. At last one said, "We will let him alone till morning, and take a whole day's frolic in burning him." The sun at this time was about three hours high. It was agreed upon, and untying the rope about my neck they made me sit down, and began to dance round me. They continued dancing in this manner until eleven o'clock at night, in the meantime beating, kicking, and wounding me with their tomahawks and clubs.*

At last one of the warriors, the Half Moon, asked if I was sleepy. I answered yes. The head warrior then chose out three warriors to take care of me. I was taken to a blockhouse, where my arms were tied until the cord was hid in the flesh; they were tied in two places, around the wrist and above the elbows. A rope was fastened about my neck and tied to a beam of the house, but slack enough to permit me to lie down on a board. The three warriors were constantly harassing and troubling me, saying, "How will you like to eat fire tomorrow? You will kill no more Indians now." I was in expectation of their going to sleep, when at length, about an hour before daybreak, two lay down, while the third smoked a pipe, talked to me, and asked the same painful questions. About half an hour after, he also lay down; I

---

* I observed marks on Slover when I saw him, which was eight or ten days after he came in, particularly a wound above his right eyebrow, which he had received with the pipe end of a tomahawk; but his back and body generally had been injured. H.B.

heard him begin to snore. Instantly I went to work, and as my arms were perfectly dead with the cord, I laid myself down upon my right arm, which was behind my back, and keeping it fast with my fingers, which had still some life and strength, I slipped the cord from my left arm over my elbow and my wrist. One of the warriors now got up and stirred the fire. I was apprehensive that I should be examined, and thought it was over with me, but my hopes revived when he lay down again. I then attempted to unloose the rope about my neck; tried to gnaw it, but it was in vain, as it was as thick as my thumb and as hard as iron, being made of a buffalo hide. I wrought with it a long time, gave it out, and could see no relief. At this time I saw daybreak and heard the cock crow. I made a second attempt, almost without hope, pulling the rope by putting my fingers between it and my neck (it was a noose with two or three knots tied over it), when to my great surprise it came easily untied.

I slipped over the warriors as they lay, and having got out of the house, looked back to see if there was any disturbance. I then ran through the town into a cornfield; in my way I saw a squaw with four or five children lying asleep under a tree: Going in a different way into the field, I untied my arm, which was greatly swollen and had turned black. Having observed a number of horses in the glade as I ran through it, I went back to catch one, and on my way found a piece of an old rug or quilt hanging on a fence, which I took with me. Having caught the horse, and using the rope with which I had been tied for a halter, I rode off. The horse was strong and swift, and the woods being open and the country level, about ten o'clock that day I crossed the Scioto River at a place, by computation, fifty full miles from the town. I had rode about twenty-five miles on this side of the Scioto by three o'clock in the afternoon, when the horse began to fail, and could no longer go on a trot. I instantly left him, and on foot ran about twenty miles farther that day, making in the whole the distance of near one hundred miles. In the evening I heard hallooing behind me, and for this reason did not halt until about ten o'clock at night, when I sat down, was extremely sick, and vomited; but when the moon rose, which might have been about two hours after, I went on and traveled until day.

During the night I had a path, but in the morning I judged it prudent to forsake the path and take a ridge for the distance of fifteen miles, in a line at right angles to my course, putting back as I went along, with a stick, the weeds which I had bent, lest I should be tracked by the enemy. I lay the next night on the waters of Muskingum. The nettles had been troublesome to me after my crossing the Scioto, having nothing to defend myself with but the piece of a rug which I had found and which while I rode I used under me by way of a saddle. The briars and thorns were now painful too, and prevented me from traveling in the night until the moon appeared. In the meantime I was prevented from sleeping by the mosquitoes, for even in the day I was under the necessity of traveling with a handful of bushes to brush them from my body.

The next night I reached Cushakim and next day came to Newcomer's Town. There I got about seven raspberries, which were the first thing I ate from the morning the Indians had taken me to burn me until this time, which was now about three o'clock the fourth day. I felt hunger very little, but was extremely weak. I swam Muskingum River at Oldcomer's Town, the river being two hundred yards wide; having reached the bank I sat down, looked back, and thought I had a start of the Indians if any should pursue. That evening I traveled about five miles; next day came to Stillwater, a small river, in a branch of which I caught two small crawfish to eat. Next night I lay within five miles of Wheeling, but had not slept a wink during this whole time, sleep being rendered impossible by the mosquitoes, which it was my constant employment to brush away. Next day came to Wheeling, and saw a man on the island in the Ohio opposite to that post, and calling to him and asking for particular persons who had been on the expedition, and telling him I was Slover, at length, with great difficulty, I persuaded him to come over and bring me across in his canoe.

THE CLOSING SHOTS

*Following the failure of the British attempt in the winter of 1777-
1778 to crush the American armies in New York and Pennsylvania, the scenes of battle shift southward. The Southern states
had virtually escaped the impact of war in its first four years.
Now Clinton, permanently established in New York, began to
probe the one untested region of rebelling states with expedition-
ary forces. If England should not conquer her colonies, she might
at any rate detach four rich prizes in Georgia, the Carolinas, and
Virginia. Great wealth, in tobacco, slaves, and well-watered land,
lay in the South. Many prosperous planters tended toward Loyal-
ism, through fear or natural Anglophilism. A small white popula-
tion (Georgia had only seventeen thousand whites), especially
laggard in raising Continentals, indicated weakness.*

*The flourishing seaports of Savannah and Charleston promptly
attracted the British strategists. Savannah fell easily in the closing days of 1778, and General Lincoln handed over Charleston
to Clinton after a four months' siege, on May 12, 1780, in a crushing and costly defeat. Two months later another major disaster
overcame the patriots, when Gates, given command of Continental troops who had been marching to relieve Charleston, fled
at the head of his broken army from Cornwallis at Camden. And
in October, 1780, and January, 1781, British forces under Leslie
and the traitor Arnold pillaged an inert Virginia, whom all the
energies of Governors Patrick Henry and Thomas Jefferson could
not bestir. The British blueprints for Southern conquest seemed
on the verge of realization.*

*Unpredictably, the fortunes of Cornwallis began to dip after
Camden, and little more than a year later he yielded up his army
to Washington and Lafayette in a mortal defeat. Various factors
account for the renewal of American energies. As had happened
in every theater of war, farmer-patriots sprang up from the countryside to grapple with the invader. Tarleton's butchery of Virginia militia at Waxhaws, an action praised by Cornwallis; the*

severe military rule imposed on South Carolina; and the groveling collaboration of rich planters with the British conquerors—all stung the back-country and "overmountain" men into sharp reprisal. Converging swiftly through the woods and swamps on some Tory or redcoat post, they struck audaciously and melted away, unhindered by baggage trains and supply problems. The nucleus of a new Continental Army led by clever Nathanael Greene began marching south to harry Cornwallis, with militia gathering around him on the way. Cornwallis and his men fell prey to what had become a general British ailment, the desire for loot and plunder, rather than military objectives, and the Southern campaign dwindled into a series of petty raids, all further inflaming the patriots. Contrary to Clinton's planning, Cornwallis turned north for the rich pickings in Virginia, a state where the British possessed no strategic port. And slowly French power came into play, as supplies of louis d'or arrived in Philadelphia, and the French army at Newport and navy in the West Indies for once began to mesh with the Americans.

The elements for a gigantic coup had taken form, and the fortunes of war gave them substance. Clinton expected an attack on New York, and false dispatches that fell into his hands confirmed his suspicion. Instead of sending aid to Cornwallis, he requested aid. Washington himself favored the New York enterprise, and in that respect Clinton guessed right, but French pressure had changed Washington's mind. De Grasse was willing to take off a couple of weeks from his West Indies prizetaking during the hurricane season, but he saw no future in attacking a British fleet in New York harbor, when he could sail into empty Virginia waters. It happened that Admiral Hood looked in at Chesapeake Bay on his way from the West Indies to New York, where he arrived on August 28, 1781, and saw nothing of his French foe. But De Grasse dropped anchor in the Bay on August 30th, and by that narrow margin the French enjoyed undisputed mastery of the Chesapeake. Both the British army and the British navy had been fooled, and when Washington and Lafayette marched south from Philadelphia to join Greene, the jaws of the trap closed neatly. Bottled in the cul-de-sac of the Yorktown peninsula by an enemy twice his number, Cornwallis speedily *capitulated, and the ships Clinton sent tardily to his relief turned back to New York on hearing the news. By luck, by clever co-ordination, and by a boldness in seizing on the Earl's mistakes, the Americans with their French allies captured a second British army. The King had lost his colonies.*

James Thacher

A spectacular description of the siege of Yorktown occurs in the *Diary of the American Revolution* by James Thacher (1754-1844), which far exceeds in literary finish any other Revolutionary journal. The obvious fact is that Thacher, a physician who wrote nine books on varied subjects, polished his actual diary of 1775-1783 for the volume he published in 1823, and turned it rather into a memoir, filled with rolling periods and elegant patriotic sentiments. Nevertheless the authentic note of the eyewitness does sound through the pages, as Thacher describes the battle of the kegs, the Wyoming Valley Massacre, the execution of Major André, the British atrocities at New London, and the glory of Cornwallis's defeat and surrender at Yorktown, Virginia, in October, 1781, the passage which is reproduced here.

Thacher was born in Barnstable, Massachusetts, a descendant of seventeenth-century Puritan settlers. His father, a farmer, had little means, but the son apprenticed at sixteen to Dr. Abner Hersey, and served all through the war in a medical capacity; at Yorktown he was surgeon to a corps of light infantry led by Colonel Alexander Scammell. In 1784 he began regular practice at Plymouth, where he gained a wide reputation through his medical dictionary and medical handbooks (*American Medical Biography*, 1828; *The American New Dispensatory*, 1810; *American Modern Practice*, 1817). He also wrote on beekeeping, orchard cultivation, hydrophobia, the town history of Plymouth, and the Salem witchcraft hysteria, which he analyzed from a pathological point of view. His portrait shows a small, sharp, Yankee face, with thin lips, straight hair, and a fancy white ruff; he is described as a slight, agile person.

The selection given here comes from the first edition, *A Military Journal during the American Revolutionary War, from 1775-1783* (Boston, Richardson & Lord, 1823), 339-348.

October 8th, and 9th, 1781. The duty of our troops has been for several days extremely severe. Our regiment labors in the trenches every other day and night, where I find it difficult to avoid suffering by the cold, having no other covering than a single blanket in the open field. We erected a battery last night in front of our first parallel, without any annoyance from the enemy. Two or three of our batteries being now prepared to open on the town [Yorktown], His Excellency General Washington put the match

17. JAMES THACHER

to the first gun, and a furious discharge of cannon and mortars immediately followed, and Earl Cornwallis has received his first salutation.

From the 10th to the 15th, a tremendous and incessant firing from the American and French batteries is kept up, and the enemy return the fire, but with little effect. A red-hot shell from the French battery set fire to the *Charon,* a British forty-four-gun ship, and two or three smaller vessels at anchor in the river, which were consumed in the night. From the bank of the river I had a fine view of this splendid conflagration. The ships were enwrapped in a torrent of fire, which, spreading with vivid brightness among the combustible rigging, and running with amazing rapidity to the tops of the several masts, while all around was thunder and lightning from our numerous cannon and mortars, and in the darkness of night, presented one of the most sublime and magnificent spectacles which can be imagined. Some of our shells, overreaching the town, are seen to fall into the river and, bursting, throw up columns of water like the spouting of the monsters of the deep.

We have now made further approaches to the town, by throwing up a second parallel line, and batteries within about three hundred yards. This was effected in the night, and at daylight the enemy were roused to the greatest exertions. The engines of war have raged with redoubled fury and destruction on both sides; no cessation day or night. The French had two officers wounded and fifteen men killed or wounded, and among the Americans two or three were wounded. I assisted in amputating a man's thigh. The siege is daily becoming more and more formidable and alarming, and His Lordship must view his situation as extremely critical, if not desperate.

Being in the trenches every other night and day, I have a fine opportunity of witnessing the sublime and stupendous scene which is continually exhibiting. The bomb shells from the besiegers and the besieged are incessantly crossing each other's paths in the air. They are clearly visible in the form of a black ball in the day, but in the night they appear like a fiery meteor with a blazing tail, most beautifully brilliant, ascending majestically from the mortar to a certain altitude, and gradually descending to the spot where they are destined to execute their work of destruction. It is astonishing with what accuracy an experienced gunner will make his calculations, that a shell shall fall within a few feet of a given point and burst at the precise time, though at a great distance. When a shell falls, it whirls round, burrows, and excavates the earth to a considerable extent, and, bursting, makes dreadful havoc around. I have more than once witnessed fragments of the mangled bodies and limbs of the British soldiers thrown into the air by the bursting of our shells; and by one from the enemy, Captain White of the Seventh Massachusetts Regiment and one soldier were killed and another wounded near where I was standing. About twelve or fourteen men have been killed or wounded within twenty-four hours. I attended at the hospital, amputated a man's arm, and assisted in dressing a number of wounds.

The enemy having two redoubts, about three hundred yards in front of their principal works, which enfiladed our entrenchment and impeded our approaches, it was resolved to take possession of them both by assault. The one on the left of the British garrison, bordering on the banks of the river, was assigned to our brigade of light infantry, under the command of the Marquis de la Fayette. The advanced corps was led on by the intrepid Colonel Hamilton, who had commanded a regiment of light infantry during the campaign, and assisted by Colonel Gimat. The assault commenced at eight o'clock in the evening, and the assailants bravely entered the fort with the point of the bayonet without firing a single gun. We suffered the loss of eight men killed and about thirty wounded, among whom Colonel Gimat received a slight wound in his foot, and Major Gibbs, of His Excellency's guard, and two other officers were slightly wounded. Major Campbell, who commanded in the fort, was wounded and taken prisoner, with about thirty soldiers; the remainder made their escape. I was desired to visit the wounded in the fort, even before the balls had ceased whistling about my ears, and saw a sergeant and eight men dead in the ditch. A captain of our infantry, belonging to New Hampshire, threatened to take the life of Major Campbell, to avenge the death of his favorite, Colonel Scammell, but Colonel Hamilton interposed, and not a man was killed after he ceased to resist. During the assault the

British kept up an incessant firing of cannon and musketry from their whole line.

His Excellency General Washington and Generals Lincoln and Knox, with their aides (having dismounted), were standing in an exposed situation waiting the result. Colonel Cobb, one of General Washington's aides, solicitous for his safety, said to His Excellency, "Sir, you are too much exposed here, had you not better step a little back?"

"Colonel Cobb," replied His Excellency, "if you are afraid, you have liberty to step back."

The other redoubt on the right of the British lines was assaulted at the same time by a detachment of the French, commanded by the gallant Baron de Viominel. Such was the ardor displayed by the assailants that all resistance was soon overcome, though at the expense of nearly one hundred men killed and wounded. Of the defenders of the redoubt, eighteen were killed, and one captain and two subaltern officers and forty-two rank and file captured. Our second parallel line was immediately connected with the two redoubts now taken from the enemy, and some new batteries were thrown up in front of our second parallel line, with a covert way and angling work approaching to less than three hundred yards of their principal forts. These will soon be mantled with cannon and mortars, and when their horrid thundering commences, it must convince His Lordship that his post is not invincible, and that submission must soon be his only alternative. Our artillery men, by the exactness of their aim, make every discharge take effect, so that many of the enemy's guns are entirely silenced and their works are almost in ruins.

16th. A party of the enemy consisting of about four hundred men, commanded by Colonel Abercrombie, about four in the morning made a vigorous sortie against two unfinished redoubts occupied by the French. They spiked up seven or eight pieces of cannon, and killed several soldiers, but the French advanced and drove them from the redoubts, leaving several killed and wounded.

Our New England troops have now become very sickly. The prevalent diseases are intermittent and remittent fevers, which are very prevalent in this climate during the autumnal months.

17th. The whole of our works are now mounted with cannon and mortars. Not less than one hundred pieces of heavy ordnance have been in continual operation during the last twenty-four hours. The whole peninsula trembles under the incessant thunderings of our infernal machines. We have leveled some of their works in ruins and silenced their guns; they have almost ceased firing. We are so near as to have a distinct view of the dreadful havoc and destruction of their works, and even see the men in their lines torn to pieces by the bursting of our shells.

But the scene is drawing to a close. Lord Cornwallis, at length realizing the extreme hazard of his deplorable situation, and finding it in vain any longer to resist, has this forenoon come to the humiliating expedient of sending out a flag, requesting a cessation of hostilities for twenty-four hours, that commissioners may be appointed to prepare and adjust the terms of capitulation. Two or three flags passed in the course of the day, and General Washington consented to a cessation of hostilities for two hours only, that His Lordship may suggest his proposals, as a basis for a treaty. They being in part accepted, a suspension of hostilities will be continued till tomorrow.

18th. It is now ascertained that Lord Cornwallis, to avoid the necessity of a surrender, had determined on the bold attempt to make his escape in the night of the 16th with a part of his army into the country. His plan was to leave sick and baggage behind, and to cross with his effective force over to Gloucester Point, there to destroy the French legion and other troops, and to mount his infantry on their horses and such others as might be procured, and thus push their way to New York by land. A more preposterous and desperate attempt can scarcely be imagined. Boats were secretly prepared, arrangements made, and a large proportion of his troops actually embarked and landed on Gloucester Point when, from a moderate and calm evening, a most violent storm of wind and rain ensued. The boats with the remaining troops were all driven down the river, and it was not till the next day that his troops could be returned to the garrison at York.

At an early hour this forenoon General Washington communicated to Lord Cornwallis the general basis of the terms of capitulation which he deemed admissible, and allowed two hours for his reply. Commissioners were soon after appointed to prepare the particular terms of agreement. The gentlemen appointed by General Washington are Colonel Laurens, one of his aides-de-camp, and Viscount Noailles of the French army. They have this day held an interview with the two British officers on the part of Lord Cornwallis, the terms of capitulation are settled, and being confirmed by the commanders of both armies, the royal troops are to march out tomorrow and surrender their arms. It is a circumstance deserving of remark that the Colonel Laurens who is stipulating for the surrender of a British nobleman at the head of a royal army is the son of Mr. Henry Laurens, our Ambassador to Holland, who, being captured on his voyage, is now in close confinement in the Tower of London.

19th. This is to us a most glorious day, but to the English one of bitter chagrin and disappointment. Preparations are now making to receive as captives that vindictive, haughty commander, and that victorious army, who by their robberies and murders have so long been a scourge to our brethren of the Southern states. Being on horseback, I anticipate a full share of satisfaction in viewing the various movements in the interesting scene. The stipulated terms of capitulation are similar to those granted to General Lincoln at Charleston the last year. The captive troops are to march out with shouldered arms, colors cased, and drums beating a British or German march, and to ground their arms at a place assigned for the purpose. The officers are allowed their side arms and private property, and the generals and such officers as desire it are to go on parole to England or New York. The marines and seamen of the King's ships are prisoners of war to the navy of France, and the land forces to the United States. All military and artillery stores to be delivered up unimpaired. The royal prisoners to be sent into the interior of Virginia, Maryland, and Pennsylvania in regiments, to have rations allowed them equal to the American soldiers, and to have their officers near them. Lord Cornwallis to man and dispatch the *Bonetta* sloop of war with dispatches to Sir Henry Clinton at New York without being searched, the vessel to be returned and the hands accounted for.

At about twelve o'clock, the combined army was arranged and drawn up in two lines, extending more than a mile in length. The Americans were drawn up in a line on the right side of the road, and the French occupied the left. At the head of the former the great American commander, mounted on his noble courser, took his station, attended by his aides. At the head of the latter was posted the excellent Count Rochambeau and his suite. The French troops, in complete uniform, displayed a martial and noble appearance; their band of music, of which the timbrel formed a part, is a delightful novelty, and produced while marching to the ground a most enchanting effect. The Americans, though not all in uniform, nor their dress so neat, yet exhibited an erect soldierly air, and every countenance beamed with satisfaction and joy. The concourse of spectators from the country was prodigious, in point of numbers probably equal to the military, but universal silence and order prevailed.

It was about two o'clock when the captive army advanced through the line formed for their reception. Every eye was prepared to gaze on Lord Cornwallis, the object of peculiar interest and solicitude, but he disappointed our anxious expectations; pretending indisposition, he made General O'Hara his substitute as the leader of his army. This officer was followed by the conquered troops in a slow and solemn step, with shouldered arms, colors cased, and drums beating a British march. Having arrived at the head of the line, General O'Hara, elegantly mounted, advanced to His Excellency the Commander-in-Chief, taking off his hat, and apologized for the nonappearance of Earl Cornwallis. With his usual dignity and politeness His Excellency pointed to Major General Lincoln for directions, by whom the British army was conducted into a spacious field where it was intended they should ground their arms. The royal troops, while marching through the line formed by the allied army, exhibited a decent and neat appearance as respects arms and clothing, for their commander opened his store and directed every soldier to be furnished with a new suit complete, prior to the capitulation. But in their line of march we remarked a disorderly and unsoldierly conduct, their step was irregular, and their ranks frequently broken. But it was in the field when they came to the last act of the drama that the spirit and pride of the British soldier was put to the severest test; here their mortification could not be concealed. Some of the platoon officers appeared to be exceedingly chagrined when giving the word "Ground arms," and I am a witness that they performed this duty in a very unofficerlike manner, and that many of the soldiers manifested a sullen temper, throwing their arms on the pile with violence, as if determined to render them useless. This irregularity, however, was checked by the authority of General Lincoln.

After having grounded their arms and divested themselves of their accouterments, the captive troops were conducted back to Yorktown and guarded by our troops till they could be removed to the place of their destination. The British troops that were stationed at Gloucester surrendered at the same time and in the same manner to the command of the Duke de Luzerne. This must be a very interesting and gratifying transaction to General Lincoln, who, having himself been obliged to surrender an army to a haughty foe the last year, has now assigned him the pleasing duty of giving laws to a conquered army in return, and of reflecting that the terms which were imposed on him are adopted as a basis of the surrender in the present instance.

It is a very gratifying circumstance that every degree of harmony, confidence, and friendly intercourse subsisted between the American and French troops during the campaign, no contest existing except an emulous spirit to excel in exploits and enterprise against the common enemy, and a desire to be celebrated in the annals of history for an ardent love of great and heroic actions. We are not to be surprised that the pride of the British officers is humbled on this occasion, as they have always entertained an exalted opinion of their own military prowess, and affected to view the Americans as a contemptible, undisciplined rabble. But there is no display of magnanimity when a great commander shrinks from the inevitable misfortunes of war, and when it is considered that Lord Cornwallis has frequently appeared in splendid triumph at the head of his army by which he is almost adored, we conceive it incumbent on him cheerfully to participate in their misfortunes and degradations, however humiliating. But it is said he gives himself up entirely to vexation and despair.

18. DEFEATED BRITISH ARMIES

A. Encampment of Burgoyne's Convention Army at Charlottesville, Va.,
Following the Surrender

B. Surrender of Cornwallis at Yorktown, October 19, 1781

POSTWAR

The American Revolution did not completely end with the sign-ing of the peace treaty at Paris on December 3, 1783. Even in the military sense, border warfare continued until Wayne's victory at Fallen Timbers in 1794. In the realm of social and constitu-tional change, the forces stimulated by the Revolution main-tained their momentum throughout the '80's. New state constitu-tions emasculated the power of governors and exalted that of the lower assembly. Royalty and nobility were swept off American soil. The Established Church of England became an independent church in the United States, and the Congregational Church established in Northern states gradually lost its preferential treat-ment. In the physical adjustment required to tie up loose ends of the war, certain affairs dragged on. Homeless Loyalists, seeking compensation under terms of the peace, found American courts cynical toward their claims. In reprisal, or by way of excuse, the British garrisons lingered on in the strategic Northwest forts they had bound themselves to vacate, and continued their in-citing of Indian tribes against frontier settlements. Not until 1796 did English soldiers quit American territory.

Emotional and sentimental traditions hallowed by the Revolu-tionary struggle lived on in the minds of postwar Americans. Anglophobia and Francophilism affected the diplomacy of the first years of the new Constitutional government, and endured into the nineteenth and twentieth centuries in such policies as "twisting the lion's tail" and such symbols as "Lafayette, we are here!" A process of mythology would eventually enshrine patriot leaders and their battlegrounds, Lexington and Concord, Bunker Hill and Valley Forge, Saratoga and Yorktown, but obedient students would remember little of the march to Quebec, the Bat-tle of Long Island, the siege of Charleston, the rout at Camden. Ethan Allen, George Rogers Clark, and Tom Paine would be-come demigods in the national pantheon—after their lifetimes. For American veterans did not immediately profit from the glories of Revolution. They returned to their farms and work-benches to fight inflationary prices in a damaged economy, or to hunt jobs. England no longer opened her ports freely to American goods; states levied tariffs against each other; the prof-iteers extorted and speculated, and angry ex-soldiers in Massa-chusetts picked up their guns again to march on the courts and save their farms from the mortgagor. Patriot stock fell low in the immediate postwar years. Sam Adams never gained an elective office; the name of Tom Paine became anathema to Federalist gentlemen; Ethan Allen and George Rogers Clark were branded traitors for dallying with the governments of England and France. Pensions were not granted until an act of 1818, and then privates received only eight dollars a month. The neglect that veterans complained of in their memoirs and autobiographies began with the very cessation of war. Elijah Fisher, on being discharged from the Jersey *in April, 1783, begged help from "gentlefolks" in New York, who told him times were poor. "I said then, What do you think of us poor prisoners that have neither money nor friends and have been long absent from our homes? Then some of them would pity us and would give us something, some half a dollar, some a quarter, some less, some nothing but frowns." Fisher sailed for Boston, but could find no work there, and sat down in the marketplace self-pityingly. But on reflection he decided he was more fortunate than many others, and would do his best and trust in Providence.* And such indeed was the cold comfort for many a poor veteran.*

Elijah Fisher reasoned with good Yankee common sense, for other patriots, maimed and broken, would gladly have filled his shoes. Israel Potter spent forty years trying to reach his homeland, and found little reason for joy when he returned. No old soldier had as strange and sad a tale to tell as he.

* Quoted in Charles K. Bolton, *The Private Soldier Under Washington* (London, 1902), 247-248.

Israel Potter

All we know about Israel Ralph Potter (1744-1826?) is what he has told us in his personal history. He was born in Cranston, Rhode Island, ran away from home at eighteen because of a family dispute over his girl, knocked about in the wilds of Connecticut helping to clear and survey land, shipped to sea in merchantmen and whalers, worked as a farm laborer, and enlisted in a company of minute men in 1774. When it was called to arms he fought at Bunker Hill and assisted in the siege of Boston. To prevent supplies from reaching the Tories by sea, Washington armed several vessels and called for soldier volunteers to man them. Accordingly Potter went aboard the brigantine *Washington*, and sailed from Plymouth (the point at which his narrative as here given commences). The *Washington* was promptly captured by a British patrol, and Potter never saw his homeland again until 1823.

The text that follows is edited from the original edition, *Life and Remarkable Adventures of Israel R. Potter, (A Native of Cranston, Rhode-Island). Who was a soldier in the American Revolution.* Providence, printed for Henry Trumbull, 1824. Another imprint reads, "Printed by J. Howard, for I. R. Potter." The latter was reprinted in the *Magazine of History*, Extra Number 16 (1911), with an editorial foreword. Melville's story "Israel Potter" was published in book form in 1855 in New York, and appeared in an unauthorized edition in 1865 under the title *The Refugee*.

WE SET SAIL about the eighth of December, but had been out but three days when we were captured by the enemy's ship *Foy*, of twenty guns, who took us all out and put a prize crew on board the *Washington*. The *Foy* proceeded with us immediately to Boston Bay, where we were put on board the British frigate *Tartar* and orders given to convey us to England.

When two or three days out I projected a scheme (with the assistance of my fellow-prisoners, seventy-two in number) to take the ship, in which we should undoubtedly have succeeded, as we had a number of resolute fellows on board, had it not been for the treachery of a renegade Englishman, who betrayed us. As I was pointed out by this fellow as the principal in the plot, I was ordered in irons by the officers of the *Tartar*, and in this situation I remained until the arrival of the ship at Portsmouth (England), when I was brought on deck and closely examined, but protesting my innocence. What was very fortunate for me in the course of the examination, the person by whom I had been betrayed, having been proved a British deserter, his story was discredited and I was relieved of my irons.

The prisoners were now all thoroughly cleansed and conveyed to the marine hospital on shore, where many of us took the small-pox the natural way from some whom we found in the hospital affected with that disease, and which proved fatal to nearly one-half our number. From the hospital those of us who survived were conveyed to Spithead and put on board a guard ship. There I had been confined with my fellow-prisoners about one month, when I was ordered into the boat to assist the bargemen (in consequence of the absence of one of their gang) in rowing the Lieutenant on shore. As soon as we reached the shore and the officer landed, it was proposed by some of the boat's crew to resort for a few moments to an alehouse in the vicinity, to treat themselves to a few pots of beer; which being agreed to by all, I thought this a favorable opportunity, and the only one that might present, to escape from my floating prison, and felt determined not to let it pass unimproved. Accordingly, as the boat's crew were about to enter the house, I expressed a necessity of my separating from them a few moments, to which they (not suspecting any design) readily assented. As soon as I saw them all snugly in and the door closed, I gave speed to my legs, and ran, as I then concluded, about four miles without once halting. I steered my course toward London, as by mingling with the crowd there I thought it probable that I should be least suspected.

When I had reached the distance of about ten miles from where I quit the bargemen (and beginning to think myself in little danger of apprehension, should any of them be sent by the Lieutenant in pursuit of me), as I was leisurely passing a public house I was noticed and hailed by a naval officer at the door with "Ahoy, what ship?"

"No ship," was my reply.

On this he ordered me to stop, but I took no other notice than to observe to him that if he would attend to his own business I would proceed quietly about mine. This rather increasing than diminishing his suspicions that I was a deserter, garbed as I was, he gave chase. Finding myself closely pursued and unwilling again to be. made a prisoner, if it were possible to escape, I had once more to trust to my legs, and should have again succeeded had not the officer, on finding himself likely to be distanced, set up a cry of "Stop thief!" This brought numbers out of their houses and workshops, who, joining in the pursuit, succeeded after a chase of nearly a mile in overhauling me.

Finding myself once more in their power, and a perfect stranger to the country, I deemed it vain to attempt to deceive them with a lie, and therefore made a voluntary confession to the officer that I was a prisoner of war, and related to him in what manner I had that morning made my escape. By the officer I was conveyed back to the inn and left in custody of two soldiers. The former, previous to retiring, observed to the landlord that he believed me to be a true-blooded Yankee, and requested him to supply me at his expense with as much liquor as I should call for.

The house was thronged early in the evening by many of the "good and faithful subjects of King George," who had assembled to take a peep at the "Yankee rebel" (as they termed me) who had so recently taken an active part in the rebellious war then raging in His Majesty's American provinces—while others came apparently to gratify a curiosity in viewing, for the first time, an "American Yankee," whom they had been taught to believe a kind of nondescript being of much less refinement than the ancient Britons, and possessing little more humanity than the buccaneers.

As for myself I thought it best not to be reserved, but to reply readily to all their inquiries, for my mind was wholly employed in devising a plan to escape from the custody of my keepers. So far from manifesting a disposition to resent any of the insults offered me or my country, to prevent any suspicions of my designs I feigned myself not a little pleased with their observations, and in no way dissatisfied with my situation. As the officer had left orders with the landlord to supply me with as much liquor as I should be pleased to call for, I felt determined to make my keepers merry at his expense, if possible, as the best means that I could adopt to effect my escape.

The loyal group having attempted in vain to irritate me by their mean and ungenerous reflections, one observed that he had frequently heard it mentioned that the Yankees were extraordinary dancers, and proposed that I should entertain the company with a jig, to which I expressed a willingness to assent (with much feigned satisfaction) if a fiddler could be procured. Fortunately for them there was one residing in the neighborhood, who was soon introduced, when I was obliged (although much against my own inclination) to take the floor—with the full determination, however, that if John Bull was to be thus diverted at the expense of an unfortunate prisoner of war, Uncle Jonathan should come in for his part of the sport before morning, by showing them a few Yankee steps which they had little dreamed of.

By my performances they were soon satisfied that in this kind of exercise I should suffer but little in competition with the most nimble-footed Briton among them, nor would they release me until I had danced myself into a state of perfect perspiration. This, however, so far from being any disadvantage to me, I considered all in favor of my projected plan to escape—for while I was pleased to see the flowing bowl passing merrily about, and not unfrequently brought in contact with the lips of my two keepers, the state of perspiration that I was in prevented its producing on me any intoxicating effects.

The evening being now far spent and the company mostly retiring, my keepers (who, to use a sailor's phrase, I was happy to discover "half seas over") much to my dissatisfaction furnished me with a pair of handcuffs and spread a blanket by the side of their bed, on which I was to repose for the night. I feigned myself very grateful to them for having humanely furnished me with a comfortable bed, stretched myself on it with much apparent unconcern, and remained quiet about one hour, when I was sure that the family had all retired to bed. The important moment had now arrived in which I was resolved to carry my premeditated plan into execution, or die in the attempt. For certain I was that if I let this opportunity pass unimproved, I might have cause to regret it when it was too late: I should most assuredly be conveyed early in the morning back to the floating prison from which I had so recently escaped, and where I might possibly remain confined until America should obtain her independence, or the differences between Great Britain and her American provinces were adjusted. Yet should I in my attempt to escape meet with more opposition from my keepers than what I had calculated from their apparent state of inebriety, the contest I well knew would be very unequal; they were two full-grown stout men, with whom (if they were assisted by no others) I should have to contend handcuffed! But after mature deliberation I resolved that, however hazardous the attempt, it should be made, and that immediately.

After remaining quiet, as I before observed, until I thought it probable that all had retired to bed in the house, I intimated to my keepers that I was under the necessity of requesting permission to retire for a few moments to the back yard. Both instantly arose and reeling toward me seized each an arm, and proceeded to conduct me through a long and narrow entry to the back door, which was no sooner unbolted and opened by one of them than I tripped up the heels of both and laid them sprawling, and in a moment was at the garden wall seeking a passage whereby I might gain the public road. A new and unexpected obstacle now presented, for I found the whole garden enclosed with a smooth bricken wall, of the height of twelve feet at least, and was prevented by the darkness of the night from discovering an avenue leading therefrom. In this predicament, my only alternative was either to scale this wall handcuffed as I was, and without a moment's hesitation, or to suffer myself to be made a captive of again by my keepers, who had already recovered their feet and were bellowing like bullocks for assistance. Had it not been a very dark night, I must certainly have been discovered and retaken by them. Fortunately, before they had succeeded in rallying the family, in groping about I met with a fruit tree situated within ten or twelve feet of the wall, which I ascended as expeditiously as possible, and by an extraordinary leap from the branches reached the top of the wall, and was in an instant on the opposite side.

The coast being now clear, I ran to the distance of two or three miles with as much speed as my situation would admit of. My next object now was to rid myself of my handcuffs, which, fortunately proving none of the stoutest, I succeeded in doing after much painful labor. It was now as I judged about twelve o'clock, and I had succeeded in reaching a considerable distance from the inn from which I had made my escape, without hearing or seeing anything of my keepers, whom I had left staggering about in the garden in search of their "Yankee captive." It was indeed to their intoxicated state, and the extreme darkness of the night, that I imputed my success in evading their pursuit.

I saw no one until about the break of day, when I met an old man, tottering beneath the weight of his pickax, hoe, and shovel, clad in tattered garments, and otherwise the picture of poverty and distress. He had just left his humble dwelling, and was proceeding thus early to his daily labor; and as I was now satisfied that it would be very difficult for me to travel in the daytime garbed as I was, in a sailor's habit, without exciting the suspicions of His Royal Majesty's pimps, who (I had been informed) were constantly on the lookout for deserters, I applied to the old man, miserable as he appeared, for a change of clothing, offering those which I then wore for a suit of inferior quality and less value. This I was induced to do at that moment as I thought that, whatever might have been his suspicions as to my motives in wishing to exchange my dress, self-interest would prevent his communicating them. The old man, however, appeared a little surprised at my offer, and after a short examination of my pea jacket, trousers, etc., expressed a doubt whether I would be willing to exchange them for his "church suit," which he represented as something worse for wear, and not worth half so much as those I then wore. Taking courage, however, from my assurances that a change of dress was my only object, he deposited his tools by the side of a hedge and invited me to accompany him to his house, which we soon reached and entered.

Here a scene of poverty and wretchedness presented which exceeded everything of the kind that I had ever before witnessed. The internal appearance of the miserable hovel I am confident would suffer in a comparison with any of the meanest stables of our American farmers. There was but one room, in one corner of which was a bed of straw covered with a coarse sheet, and on which reposed his wife and five small children. I had heard much of the impoverished and distressed situation of the poor in England, but the present presented an instance of which I had formed no conception. Little indeed did I then think that it would be my lot, before I should meet with an opportunity to return to my native country, to be placed in an infinitely worse situation! But alas, such was my hard fortune.

The first garment presented by the poor old man, of his best, or "church suit," as he termed it, was a coat of very coarse cloth, and containing a number of patches of almost every color but that of the cloth of which it was originally made. The next was a waistcoat and a pair of smallclothes, which appeared each to have received a bountiful supply of patches to correspond with the coat. The coat I put on without much difficulty, but the two other garments proved much too small for me, and when I had succeeded with considerable difficulty in putting them on, they set so taut as to cause me some apprehension that they might even stop the circulation of blood! My next exchange was my buff cap for an old rusty large-brimmed hat.

The old man appeared very much pleased with his bargain, and represented to his wife that he could now accompany her to church much more decently clad. He immediately tried on the pea jacket and trousers, and seemed to give himself very little concern about their size, although I am confident that one leg of the trousers was sufficiently large to admit his whole body. But however ludicrous his appearance in his new suit, I am confident that it could not have been more so than mine, garbed as I was like an old man of seventy! From my old friend I learned the course that I must steer to reach London, the towns and villages that I should have to pass through, and the distance thereto, which was between seventy and eighty miles. He likewise represented to me that the country was filled with soldiers who were on the constant lookout for deserters, for whom they received a stipulated reward.

After enjoining it on the old man not to give any information of me, should he meet on the road anyone who should inquire for such a person, I took my leave of him and again set out with a determination to reach London, thus disguised, if possible. I traveled about thirty miles that day, and at night entered a barn in hopes to find some straw or hay on which to repose for the night, for I had not money sufficient to pay for a night's lodging at a public house, had I thought it prudent to apply for one. In my expectation to find either hay or straw in the barn I was sadly disappointed, for I soon found that it contained not a lock of either, and after groping about in the dark in search of something that might serve for a substitute, I found nothing better than an undressed sheepskin. With no other bed on which to repose my wearied limbs I spent a sleepless night, cold, hungry, and weary, and impatient for the arrival of the morning's dawn, that I might be enabled to pursue my journey.

At break of day I again set out and soon found myself within the suburbs of a considerable village, in passing which I was fearful there would be some risk of detection. To guard myself as much as possible against suspicion I furnished myself with a crutch and, feigning myself a cripple, hobbled through the town without meeting with any interruption. In two hours after, I arrived in the vicinity of another still more considerable village, but fortunately for me, at the moment I was overtaken by an empty baggage wagon bound to London. Again feigning myself very lame, I begged of the driver to grant a poor cripple the indulgence to ride a few miles, to which he assented. I concealed myself by lying prostrate on the bottom of the wagon, until we had passed quite through the village. Then, finding the wagoner disposed to drive much slower than what I wished to travel, after thanking him for the kind disposition which he had manifested to oblige me, I quit the wagon, threw away my crutch, and traveled with a speed calculated to surprise the driver with so sudden a recovery of the use of my legs. The reader will perceive that I had now become almost an adept at deception, which I would not, however, have so frequently practiced had not self-preservation demanded it.

As I thought there would be in my journey to London infinitely more danger of detection in passing through large towns or villages than in confining myself to the country, I avoided them as much as possible. When I found myself once more on the borders of one, apparently of much larger size than any that I had yet passed, I though it most expedient to take a circuitous route to avoid it; in attempting which, I met with an almost insurmountable obstacle, that I little dreamed of. When nearly abreast of the town I found my route obstructed by a ditch, of upwards of twelve feet in breadth, and of what depth I could not determine. As there was now no other alternative left me but to leap this ditch or to retrace my steps and pass through the town, after a moment's reflection I determined to attempt the former, although it would be attempting a feat of activity that I supposed myself incapable of performing; yet, however incredible it may appear, I assure my readers that I did effect it, and reached the opposite side with dry feet!

I had now arrived within about sixteen miles of London when, night approaching, I again sought lodging in a barn. It contained a small quantity of hay, and afforded me a tolerable comfortable night's rest. By the dawn of day I arose somewhat refreshed, and resumed my journey with the pleasing prospect of reaching London before night. But while encouraged and cheered by these pleasing anticipations, an unexpected occurrence blasted my fair prospects. I had succeeded in reaching in safety a distance so great from the place where I had been last held a prisoner, and within so short a distance of London, the place of my destination, that I began to think myself out of danger. Then, as I was passing through the town of Staines (within a few miles of London) about eleven o'clock in the forenoon, I was met by three or four British soldiers, whose notice I attracted, and who, unfortunately for me, discovered by the collar (which I had not taken the precaution to conceal) that I wore a shirt which exactly corresponded with those uniformly worn by His Majesty's seamen. Not being able to give a satisfactory account of myself, I was made a prisoner of, on suspicion of being a deserter from His Majesty's service, and was immediately committed to the Round House, a prison, so called, appropriated to the confinement of runaways and those convicted of small offenses. I was committed in the evening, and to secure me the more effectually I was handcuffed, and left supperless by my unfeeling jailor, to pass the night in wretchedness.

I had now been three days without food (with the exception of a single two-penny loaf) and felt myself unable much longer to resist the cravings of nature. My spirits, which until now had armed me with fortitude, began to forsake me—indeed I was at this moment on the eve of despair when, calling to mind that grief would only aggravate my calamity, I endeavored to arm my soul with patience, and habituate myself as well as I could to woe. Accordingly I roused my spirits, and banishing for a few moments these gloomy ideas, I began to reflect seriously on the methods how to extricate myself from this labyrinth of horror. My first object was to rid myself of my handcuffs, which I succeeded in doing after two hours' hard labor, by sawing them across the grating of the window. Having my hands now at liberty, the next thing to be done was to force the door of my apartment, which was secured on the outside by a hasp and padlock. I devised many schemes but for the want of tools to work with was unable to carry them into execution. However, I at length succeeded with the assistance of no other instrument than the bolt of my handcuffs, with which, thrusting my arm through a small window or aperture in the door, I forced the padlock, and as there was now no other barrier to prevent my escape, after an imprisonment of about five hours I was once more at large.

It was now as I judged about midnight, and although enfeebled and tormented with excessive hunger and fatigue, I set out with the determination of reaching London, if possible, early the ensuing morning. At break of day I reached and passed through Brentford, a town of considerable note and within six miles of the capital, but so great was my hunger at this moment that I was under serious apprehension of falling a victim to absolute starvation. In my youth I had read accounts of the dreadful effects of hunger, which had led men to the commission of the most horrible excesses, but I never thought that fate would thereafter doom me to an almost similar situation.

When I made my escape from the prison ship six English pennies was all the money that I possessed. With two I had purchased a two-penny loaf the day after I had escaped from my keepers at the inn, and the other four still remained in my possession, as I had not met with a favorable opportunity since to purchase food of any kind. Having now arrived at the distance of one and a half miles from Brentford, I met with a laborer employed in building a rail fence, to whom my deplorable situation induced me to apply for work, or for information of anyone in the neighborhood that might be in want of a hand to work at farming or gardening. He informed me that he did not wish himself to hire, but that Sir John Millet, whose seat he represented as but a short distance, was in the habit of employing many hands at that season of the year (which was in the spring of 1776), and he doubted not but that I might there meet with employment.

My spirits revived a little, at even a distant prospect of obtaining something to alleviate my sufferings, and I started in quest of the seat of Sir John, agreeable to the directions which I had received. In attempting to follow them I mistook my way and proceeded up a graveled and beautifully ornamented walk, which unconsciously led me directly to the garden of the Princess Amelia. I had approached within view of the royal mansion when a glimpse of a number of "redcoats" who thronged the yard satisfied me of my mistake, and caused me to make an instantaneous and precipitate retreat, being determined not to afford any more of their mess an opportunity of boasting of the capture of a "Yankee rebel." Indeed, a wolf or bear of the American wilderness could not be more terrified or panic-stricken at the sight of a firebrand than I then was at that of a British redcoat!

Having succeeded in making good my retreat from the garden of Her Highness without being discovered, I took another path which led me to where a number of laborers were employed in shoveling gravel, and to whom I repeated my inquiry if they could inform me of anyone in want of help.

"Why in troth, friend" (answered one in a dialect peculiar to the laboring class of people of that part of the country), "me master, Sir John, hires a goodly many, and as we've a deal of work now, maybe he'll hire you; 'spose he stop a little with us until work is done, he may then gang along, and we'll question Sir John, whither him be wanting another like us or no!"

Although I was sensible that an application of this kind might lead to a discovery of my situation, whereby I might be again deprived of my liberty and immured in a loathsome prison, yet there was now no other alternative left me but to seek in this way something to satisfy the cravings of hunger. I concluded, as the honest laborer had proposed, to await until they had completed their work, and then to accompany them home to ascertain the will of Sir John.

As I had heard much of the tyrannical and domineering disposition of the rich and purse-proud of England, who were generally the lords of the manor and the particular favorites of the Crown, it was not without feeling a very considerable degree of diffidence that I introduced myself into the presence of one whom I strongly suspected to be of that class. But, what was peculiarly fortunate for me, a short acquaintance was sufficient to satisfy me that, as regarded this gentleman, my apprehensions were without cause. I found him walking in his front yard in company with several other gentlemen; on being made acquainted with my business, his first inquiry was whether I had a hoe, or money to purchase one, and on being answered in the negative, he requested me to call early the ensuing morning, and he would endeavor to furnish me with one.

It is impossible for me to express the satisfaction that I felt at this prospect of a deliverance from my wretched situation. I was now by so long fasting reduced to such a state of weakness that my legs were hardly able to support me, and it was with extreme difficulty that I succeeded in reaching a baker's shop in the neighborhood, where with my four remaining pennies, which I had reserved for a last resource, I purchased two two-penny loaves.

After four days of intolerable hunger, the reader may judge how great must have been my joy to find myself in possession of even a morsel to appease it. Although five times the quantity of the "staff of life" would scarcely have satisfied my appetite, yet as I thought it improbable that I should be indulged with a mouthful of anything to eat in the morning I concluded to eat then but one loaf, and to reserve the other for another meal. But having eaten one, so far from satisfying, it seemed rather to increase my appetite for the other; the temptation was irresistible, the cravings of hunger predominated and would not be satisfied until I had devoured the remaining one.

The day was now far spent and I was compelled to resort with reluctance to a carriage house, to spend another night in misery. I found nothing therein on which to repose my wearied limbs but the bare floor, which was sufficient to deprive me of sleep, however much exhausted nature required it; my spirits were, however, buoyed up by the pleasing consolation that the succeeding day would bring relief. As soon as daylight appeared, I hastened to await the commands of one who, since my first introduction, I could not but flatter myself would prove my benefactor, and afford me that relief which my pitiful situation so much required. It was an hour much earlier than the domestics were in the habit of arising, and I had been a considerable time walking back and forth in the barnyard before any made their appearance. It was now about four o'clock, and the stable-man

informed me that eight o'clock was the usual hour in which
the laborers commenced their day's work. He granted me permission to repose myself on some straw beneath the manger, until
they should be in readiness to depart to commence their day's
work. In these four hours I had a more comfortable nap than any
that I had enjoyed the four preceding nights.

At eight o'clock precisely all hands were called, and preparations made for a commencement of the labors of the day. I was
furnished with a large iron fork and a hoe and ordered by my
employer to accompany them, and although my strength at this
moment was hardly sufficient to enable me to bear even so light
a burden, yet I was unwilling to expose my weakness, so long as
it could be avoided. But the time had now arrived in which it
was impossible for me any longer to conceal it, and I had to confess to my fellow-laborers that such had been my state of poverty
that (with the exception of the four small loaves of bread) I had
not tasted food for four days! I was not, I must confess, displeased
to witness the evident pity and commiseration which this woeful
declaration appeared to excite in their minds, as I had supposed
them too much accustomed to witness scenes of misery and distress to have their feelings much affected by a brief recital of my
sufferings and deprivations. But in justice to them I must say
that, although a very illiterate, I found them (with a few exceptions) a humane and benevolent people.

About eleven o'clock we were visited by our employer, Sir
John. He, noticing me particularly, and perceiving the little progress I made in my labor, observed that although I had the appearance of being a stout hearty man, yet I either feigned myself
or really was a very weak one! One of my friendly fellow-laborers
immediately remarked that it was not surprising I lacked
strength, as I had eaten nothing of consequence for four days.
Mr. Millet appeared at first little disposed to credit the fact, but
on being assured by me that it was really so, he put a shilling into
my hand and bid me go immediately and purchase to that
amount in bread and meat—a request which the reader may suppose I did not hesitate to comply with.

Having made a tolerable meal, and feeling somewhat refreshed
thereby, I was on my return when I was met by my fellow-laborers on their return home, four o'clock being the hour in which

they usually quit work. As soon as we arrived, some victuals were ordered for me by Sir John. When the maid presented a much smaller quantity that what her benevolent master supposed sufficient to satisfy one who had been four days fasting, she was ordered to return and bring out the platter and the whole of its contents, and I was requested to eat my fill. But I ate sparingly to prevent the dangerous consequences which might have resulted from voracity in my debilitated state.

My light repast being over, one of the men was ordered by my hospitable friend to provide for me a comfortable bed in the barn, where I spent the night on a couch of clean straw, more sweetly than ever I had done in the days of my better fortune. I arose early much refreshed, and was preparing after breakfast to accompany the laborers to their work when Sir John, smiling, bid me return to my couch and there remain until I was in a better state; indeed, the generous compassion and benevolence of this gentleman was unbounded. After having on that day partaken of an excellent dinner, which had been provided expressly for me, and the domestics having been ordered to retire, I was not a little surprised to hear myself thus addressed by him.

"My honest friend, I perceive that you are a seafaring man, and your history probably is a secret which you may not wish to divulge; but whatever circumstances may have attended you, you may make them known to me with the greatest safety, for I pledge my honor I will never betray you."

Having experienced so many proofs of the friendly disposition of Mr. Millet, I could not hesitate a moment to comply with his request, and without attempting to conceal a single fact, made him acquainted with every circumstance that had attended me since my first enlistment as a soldier. After expressing his regret that there should be any of his countrymen found so void of the principles of humanity as to treat thus an unfortunate prisoner of war, he assured me that so long as I remained in his employ he would guarantee my safety—adding that notwithstanding (in consequence of the unhappy differences which then prevailed between Great Britain and her American colonies) the inhabitants of the latter were denominated rebels, yet they were not without their friends in England, who wished well to their cause, and would cheerfully aid them whenever an opportunity should present. He represented the soldiers (whom it had been reported to me were constantly on the lookout for deserters) as a set of mean and contemptible wretches, little better than lawless banditti, who, to obtain the fee awarded by government for the apprehension of a deserter, would betray their best friends.

Having been generously supplied with a new suit of clothes and other necessaries by Mr. M., I contracted with him for six months to superintend his strawberry garden, in the course of which, so far from being molested, I was not suspected by even his own domestics of being an American. At the expiration of the six months, by the recommendation of my hospitable friend, I got a berth in the garden of the Princess Amelia, where, although among my fellow-laborers the American rebellion was not unfrequently the topic of their conversation, and the "d—d Yankee rebels" (as they termed them) frequently the subjects of their vilest abuse, I was little suspected of being one of that class. I must confess that it was difficult to suppress the indignant feelings occasioned by hearing my countrymen spoken of so disrespectfully, but as a single word in their favor might have betrayed me, I could only secretly indulge the hope that I might before the conclusion of the war have an opportunity to repay them in their own coin, with interest.

I remained in the employ of the Princess about three months, and then in consequence of a misunderstanding with the overseer, I hired myself to a farmer in a small village adjoining Brentford, where I had not been three weeks employed before rumor was afloat that I was a Yankee prisoner of war! From whence the report arose, or by what it was occasioned, I never could learn. It no sooner reached the ears of the soldiers than they were on the alert, seeking an opportunity to seize my person. Fortunately, I was apprised of their intentions before they had time to carry them into effect; I was, however, hard pushed, and sought for by them with a diligence and perseverance that certainly deserved a better cause. I had many hairbreadth escapes, and most assuredly should have been taken had it not been for the friendship of those who, I suspect, felt not less friendly to the cause of my country but dare not publicly avow it.

I was at one time traced by the soldiers in pursuit of me to the house of one of this description, in whose garret I was concealed, and was at that moment in bed. They entered and inquired for me. On being told that I was not in the house they insisted on searching, and were in the act of ascending the chamber stairs for that purpose when, seizing my clothes, I passed up through the scuttle and reached the roof of the house, and from thence half naked passed to those of the adjoining ones to the number of ten or twelve, and succeeded in making my escape without being discovered.

Being continually harassed by night and day by the soldiers, and driven from place to place without an opportunity to perform a day's work, I was advised by one whose sincerity I could not doubt to apply for a berth as a laborer in the garden of His Royal Majesty, situated in the village of Kew, a few miles from Brentford. There, under the protection of His Majesty, it was represented to me that I should be perfectly safe, as the soldiers dare not approach the royal premises to molest anyone therein employed. This person was so friendly as to introduce me himself to the overseer, as an acquaintance who possessed a perfect knowledge of gardening. But he carefully concealed the fact of my being American born, and the suspicion entertained by some of my being a prisoner of war who had escaped the vigilance of my keepers.

The overseer concluded to receive me on trial. It was here that I had not only frequent opportunities to see His Royal Majesty in person, in his frequent resorts to this, one of his country retreats, but once had the honor of being addressed by him. The fact was that I had not been one week employed in the garden before the suspicion of my being either a prisoner of war or a spy in the employ of the American rebels was communicated, not only to the overseer and other persons employed in the garden, but even to the King himself! As I was one day busily engaged with three others in graveling a walk, I was unexpectedly accosted by His Majesty, who with much apparent good nature inquired of me my country.

"An American born, may it please Your Majesty," was my reply (taking off my hat, which he requested me instantly to replace on my head).

"Ah!," continued he with a smile, "an American, a stubborn,

a very stubborn people indeed! And what brought you to this country, and how long have you been here?"

"The fate of war, Your Majesty—I was brought to this country a prisoner about eleven months since." And thinking this a favorable opportunity to acquaint him with a few of my grievances, I briefly stated to him how much I had been harassed by the soldiers.

"While you are here employed they will not trouble you," was the only reply he made, and passed on.

The familiar manner in which I had been interrogated by His Majesty had, I must confess, a tendency in some degree to prepossess me in his favor. I at least suspected him to possess a disposition less tyrannical and capable of better views than what had been imputed to him, and so I had frequently heard it represented in America: that, uninfluenced by such of his ministers as unwisely disregarded the reiterated complaints of the American people, he would have been foremost to have redressed their grievances, of which they so justly complained.

I continued in the service of His Majesty's gardener at Kew about four months. When the season arrived in which the work of the garden required less laborers, I with three others was discharged, and the day after engaged myself for a few months to a farmer in the town and neighborhood where I had been last employed. But not one week had expired before the old story of my being an American prisoner of war was revived and industriously circulated, and the soldiers (eager to obtain the proffered bounty) like a pack of bloodhounds were again on the track seeking an opportunity to surprise me. The house wherein I had taken up my abode was several times thoroughly searched by them, but I was always so fortunate as to discover their approach in season to make good my escape by the assistance of a friend. To so much inconvenience, however, did this continual apprehension and fear subject me, that I was finally half resolved to surrender myself a prisoner to some of His Majesty's officers and submit to my fate, whatever it might be, when by an unexpected occurrence, and the seasonable interposition of Providence in my favor, I was induced to change my resolution.

When driven almost to a state of despondency by continual

alarms and fears of falling into the hands of a set of desper-
adoes, who for a very small reward would willingly have un-
dertaken the commission of almost any crime, I received a
message from a gentleman of responsibility of Brentford (J.
Woodcock, Esq.), requesting me to repair immediately to his
house. The invitation I was disposed to pay but little attention
to, as I viewed it nothing more than a plan of my pursuers to
decoy and entrap me. But on learning from my confidential
friend that the gentleman who had sent the message was one
whose loyalty had been doubted, I was induced to comply with
the request.

I reached the house of Squire Woodcock about eight o'clock in
the evening. After receiving from him at the door assurances
that I might enter without fear or apprehension of any design
on his part against me, I suffered myself to be introduced into a
private chamber, where were seated two other gentlemen who
appeared to be persons of no mean rank, and proved to be no
other than Horne Tooke and James Bridges, Esquires. As all
three of these gentlemen have long since paid the debt of nature,
and are placed beyond the reach of such as might be disposed
to persecute or reproach them for their disloyalty, I can now with
perfect safety disclose their names—names which ought to be dear
to every true American.

After having (by their particular request) furnished these gentlemen with a brief account of the most important incidents of
my life, I underwent a very strict examination, as they seemed
determined to satisfy themselves, before they made any important
advances or disclosures, that I was a person in whom they could
repose implicit confidence. Finding me firmly attached to the interest of my country, so much so as to be willing to sacrifice even
my life if necessary in her behalf, they began to address me with
less reserve. They bestowed the highest encomiums on my countrymen for the bravery which they had displayed in their recent
engagements with the British troops, as well as for their patriotism in publicly manifesting their abhorrence and detestation of
the ministerial party in England, who to alienate their affections
and to enslave them had endeavored to subvert the British Constitution. Finally they inquired of me if (to promote the interests
of my country) I should have any objection to take a trip to Paris

on an important mission, if my passage and other expenses were
paid and a generous compensation allowed me for my trouble,
and which in all probability would lead to the means whereby
I might return to my country.

I replied that I should have none.

After having enjoined upon me to keep everything which they
had communicated a profound secret, they presented me with a
guinea and a letter for a gentleman in White Waltham (a country
town about thirty miles from Brentford), which they requested
me to reach as soon as possible, and there remain until they
should send for me, and by no means to fail to arrive at the
precise hour that they should appoint.

After partaking of a little refreshment I set out at twelve
o'clock at night, and reached White Waltham at half-past eleven
the succeeding day, and immediately waited on and presented
the letter to the gentleman to whom it was directed. He gave me
a very cordial reception, and I soon found he was as real a friend
to America's cause as the three gentlemen I had just quitted. It
was from him that I received the first information of the evacuation of Boston by the British troops, and of the Declaration of
Independence by the American Congress. Indeed, he appeared
to possess a knowledge of almost every important transaction in
America since the memorable Battle of Bunker Hill. It was
to him that I was indebted for many particulars which I might
otherwise have remained ignorant of, as I have always found it a
principle of the Britons to conceal everything calculated to
diminish or tarnish their fame as a "great and powerful nation."

I remained in the family of this gentleman about a fortnight,
when I received a letter from Squire Woodcock, requesting me
to be at his house without fail precisely at two o'clock the morning ensuing. Accordingly, I packed up and started immediately
for Brentford, and reached the house of Squire Woodcock at the
appointed hour. I found there, in company with the latter, the
two gentlemen whose names I have before mentioned, and who
now made known the object of my mission to Paris—which was
to convey in the most secret manner possible a letter to Dr.
Franklin. Everything was in readiness, and a chaise ready harnessed which was to convey me to Charing Cross waited at the
door. I was presented with a pair of boots made expressly for me,

and for the safe conveyance of the letter of which I was to be the bearer; one of them contained a false heel, in which the letter was deposited, and was to be thus conveyed to the Doctor. After again repeating my former declarations, that whatever might be my fate they should never be exposed, I departed and was conveyed in quick time to Charing Cross. There I took the post coach for Dover and from thence was immediately conveyed in a packet to Calais, and in fifteen minutes after landing started for Paris, which I reached in safety, and delivered to Dr. Franklin the letter of which I was the bearer.

What were the contents of this letter I was never informed and never knew, but had little doubt that it contained important information relative to the views of the British Cabinet as regarded the affairs of America. Although I well knew that a discovery while within the British dominions would have proved equally fatal to me as to the gentlemen by whom I was employed, yet I most solemnly declare that to be serviceable to my country at that important period was much more of an object with me than the reward which I had been promised, however considerable it might be.

My interview with Dr. Franklin was a pleasing one. For nearly an hour he conversed with me in the most agreeable and instructive manner, listened to the tale of my sufferings with much apparent interest, and seemed disposed to encourage me with the assurance that if the Americans should succeed in their grand object, and firmly establish their independence, they would not fail to remunerate their soldiers for their services. But, alas! as regards myself, these assurances have not as yet been verified! I am confident, however, that had it been a possible thing for the great and good man (whose humanity and generosity have been the theme of infinitely abler pens than mine) to have lived to this day, I should not have petitioned my country in vain for a momentary enjoyment of that provision which has been extended to so great a portion of my fellow-soldiers, whose hardships and deprivations in the cause of their country could not, I am sure, have been half so great as mine!

After remaining two days in Paris, letters were delivered to me by the Doctor to convey to the gentlemen by whom I had been employed, and which for their better security as well as my own I deposited, like the other, in the heel of my boot. To the great satisfaction of my friends I reached Brentford in safety, and without exciting the suspicion of anyone as to the important (although somewhat dangerous) mission that I had been engaged in. I remained secreted in the house of Squire Woodcock a few days, and then by his and the two other gentlemen's request made a second trip to Paris, and in delivering my letters was equally as fortunate as in my first. If I succeeded in returning in safety to Brentford this trip, I was (agreeable to the generous proposal of Dr. Franklin) to return immediately to France, from whence he was to procure me a passage to America. But although in my return I met with no difficulty, yet, as if fate had selected me as a victim to endure the miseries and privations which afterward attended me, but three hours before I reached Dover to engage a passage for the third and last time to Calais, all intercourse between the two countries was prohibited!

My flattering expectations of being enabled soon to return to my native country were thus by an unforeseen circumstance completely destroyed. I returned immediately to the gentlemen by whom I had been last employed, to advise with them what it would be best for me to do in my then unpleasant situation. For indeed, as all prospects were now at an end of meeting with an opportunity very soon to return to America, I could not bear the idea of remaining any longer in a neighborhood where I was so strongly suspected of being a fugitive from justice, and under continual apprehension of being retaken and immured like a felon in a dungeon.

These gentlemen advised me to repair immediately to London, where, employed as a laborer, if I did not imprudently betray myself they thought there was little probability of my being suspected of being an American. This advice I readily accepted as the plan exactly accorded with my opinion. These gentlemen supplied me with money sufficient to defray my expenses, and entrusted me with five guineas to convey and distribute among a number of Americans then confined as prisoners of war in one of the city prisons.

I reached London late in the evening and the next day engaged board at five shillings per week at a public house in Lombard Street, where under a fictitious name I passed for a farmer from Lincolnshire. My next object was to find my way to the prison where were confined as prisoners of war a number of my countrymen, in order to distribute the five guineas from their friends at Brentford. I found the prison without much trouble, but it was with very considerable difficulty that I gained admittance, and not until I had presented the turnkey with a considerable fee would he consent to indulge me. The reader will suppose that I must have been very much surprised when, as soon as the door of the prisoners' apartment was opened and I had passed the threshold, one of them exclaimed with much apparent astonishment, "Potter! Is that you? How in the name of Heaven came you here?" An exclamation like this by one of a number to whom I supposed myself a perfect stranger caused me much uneasiness for a few moments, as I expected nothing less than to recognize in this man some one of my old shipmates, who had undoubtedly a knowledge of my being a prisoner of war, and of having been confined as such on board the ship at Spithead. But in this I soon found to my satisfaction that I was mistaken. After viewing for a moment the person by whom I had been thus addressed, I discovered him to be no other than my old friend Sergeant Singles, with whom I had been intimately acquainted in America. As the exclamation was in the presence of the turnkey, lest I should have the key turned upon me and be considered as lawful a prisoner as any of the rest, I hinted to my friend that he certainly mistook me (a Lincolnshire farmer) for another person, and by a wink gave him to understand that a renewal of our acquaintance or an exchange of civilities would be more agreeable to me at some other time. I now as I had been requested divided the money as equally as possible among them, and to prevent the suspicions of the keeper I represented to them in a feigned dialect peculiar to the laboring people of the shire towns that "me master was owing a little trifle or so to a rebel trader of one of His Majesty's American provinces, and was 'quested by him to pay the balance and so to his brother Yankee rebels here imprisoned."

I found the poor fellows (fifteen in number) confined in a dark filthy apartment of about eighteen feet square, and which I could not perceive contained anything but a rough plank bench of about ten feet in length, and a heap of straw with one or two tattered, filthy-looking blankets spread thereon, which was probably the only bedding allowed them. Although their situation was such as could not fail to excite my pity, yet I could do no more than lament that it was not in my power to relieve them. How long they remained thus confined or when exchanged I could never learn, as I never to my knowledge saw one of them afterwards.

For four or five days after I reached London I did very little more than walk about the city, viewing such curiosities as met my eye. Then, reflecting that remaining thus idle I should not only be very soon out of funds but should run the risk of being suspected and apprehended as belonging to one of the numerous gangs of pickpockets which infest the streets of the city, I applied to an Intelligence Office for a coachman's berth. This I was so fortunate as to procure at fifteen shillings per week. My employer (J. Hyslop, Esq.), although rigid in his exactions, was punctual in his payments, and by my strict prudence and abstinence from the numerous diversions of the city I was enabled in the six months which I served him to lay up more cash than what I had earned the twelve months preceding. The next business in which I engaged was that of brickmaking, and which, together with that of gardening, I pursued in the summer seasons almost exclusively for five years, in all which time I was not once suspected of being an American. Yet I must confess that my feelings were not unfrequently most powerfully wrought upon, by hearing my countrymen dubbed with cowardice, and by those too who had been thrice flogged or frightened by them when attempting to ascend the heights of Bunker Hill.

I should now pass over the five years that I was employed as above mentioned, as checkered by few incidents worth relating, were it not for one or two circumstances of some little importance that either attended me or came within my own personal knowledge. The reader has undoubtedly heard that the city of London and its suburbs is always more or less infested with gangs of nefarious wretches, who come under the denomination of robbers, pickpockets, shoplifters, swindlers, beggars, etc., who are constantly prowling the streets in disguise, seeking opportunities to surprise and depredate on the weak and unguarded. Of these the first class form no inconsiderable portion, and contrive to elude and set at defiance the utmost vigilance of government. In the daytime they disperse each to his avocation, as, the better to blind the scrutinizing eye of justice, they make it a principle to follow some laborious profession; at night they assemble to proceed on their nocturnal rounds, in quest of those whose well-stored pockets promise them a reward equal to the risk they run in obtaining it. As I was one evening passing through Hyde Park, with five guineas and a few pennies in my pocket, I was stopped by six of these lawless footpads who, presenting pistols to my breast, demanded my money. Fortunately for me, I had previously disposed the guineas in a private pocket of my pantaloons, for their better security; thrusting their hands into my other pockets and finding me in possession of but a few English pennies, they took them and decamped. I hastened to Bow Street and lodged information of the robbery with the officers, who to my no little surprise informed me that mine was the fifth instance of information of similar robberies by the same gang, which had been lodged with them that evening! Runners had been sent in every direction in pursuit of them, but with what success I could never learn.

Despairing of meeting with a favorable opportunity to return to America until the conclusion of peace, and the prospects of a continuation of the war being as great then (by what I could learn) as at any period from its commencement, I became more reconciled to my situation, and contracted an intimacy with a young woman whose parents were poor but respectable, and whom I soon after married. I took a small ready-furnished chamber in Red Cross Street, where with the fruits of my first hard earnings I was enabled to live tolerably comfortably for three or four years —when, by sickness and other unavoidable circumstances, I was doomed to endure miseries uncommon to human nature.

In the winter of 1781, news was received in London of the surrender of the army of Lord Cornwallis to the French and American forces! The receipt of news of an event so unexpected operated on the British ministers and members of Parliament like a tremendous clap of thunder. Deep sorrow was evidently depicted in the countenances of those who had been the most strenuous advocates for the war. Never was there a time in which I longed more to exult, and to declare myself a true-blooded

Yankee. And what was still more pleasing to me was to find my-self even surpassed in expressions of joy and satisfaction by my wife at news which, while it went to establish the military fame of my countrymen, was so calculated to humble the pride of her own! Greater proofs of her regard for me and my country I could not require.

The ministerial party in Parliament who had been the insti-gators of the war, and who believed that even a view of the bright glistening muskets and bayonets of John Bull would frighten the leather-aproned Yankees to a speedy submission, began now to harbor a more favorable opinion of the courage of the latter. His Majesty repaired immediately to the House of Peers and opened the sessions of Parliament; warm debates took place, on account of the ruinous manner in which the American war was continued, but Lord North and his party appeared yet unwill-ing to give us the contest. The capitulation of Cornwallis had, however, one good effect, as it produced the immediate release of Mr. Laurens from the Tower, and although it did not put an immediate end to the war, yet all hopes of conquering America from that moment appeared to be given up by all except North and his adherents.

There was no one engaged in the cause of America that did more to establish her fame in England, and to satisfy the high-boasting Britons of the bravery and unconquerable resolution of the Yankees, than the bold adventurer Captain Paul Jones, who for ten or eleven months kept all the western coast of the island in alarm. He boldly landed at Whitehaven, where he burnt a ship in the harbor, and even attempted to burn the town. Nor was this to my knowledge the only instance in which the Britons were threatened with a very serious conflagration by the instiga-tion of their enemies abroad. A daring attempt was made by one James Aitkin, commonly known in London by the name of John the Painter, to set fire to the royal dock and shipping at Ports-mouth, and would probably have succeeded had he not impru-dently communicated his intentions to one who, for the sake of a few guineas, shamefully betrayed him. Poor Aitkin was imme-diately seized, tried, condemned, executed, and hanged in his chains. Every means was used to extort from him a confession by whom he had been employed, but without any success; it was, however, strongly suspected that he had been employed by the French, as it was about the time that they openly declared them-selves in favor of the Americans.

With regard to Mr. Laurens, I ought to have mentioned that as soon as I heard of his capture on his passage to Holland, and of his confinement in the Tower, I applied for and obtained per-mission to visit him in his apartment, and (with some distant hopes that he might point out some way in which I might be enabled to return to America) I stated to him every particular as regarded my situation. He seemed not only to lament very much my hard fortune but also, to use his own words, "that America should be deprived of the services of such men, at the important period too when she most required them." He in-formed me that he was himself held a prisoner, and knew not when or on what conditions he would be liberated, but should he thereafter be in a situation to assist me in obtaining a passage to America, he should consider it a duty which he owed to his country to do it.

Although I succeeded in obtaining by my industry a tolerable living for myself and family, yet so far from becoming reconciled to my situation, I was impatient for the return of peace, when (as I then flattered myself) I should once more have an oppor-tunity to return to my native country. I became every day less attached to a country where I could not meet with anything (with the exception of my little family) that could compensate me for the loss of the pleasing society of my kindred and friends in America. Born among a moral and humane people, and having in my early days contracted their habits and a considerable num-ber of their prejudices, it would be unnatural to suppose that I should not prefer their society to either that of rogues, thieves, pimps, and vagabonds, or of a more honest but an exceedingly oppressed and forlorn people.

I found London as it had been represented to me, a large and magnificent city, filled with inhabitants of almost every descrip-tion and occupation—and such a one indeed as might be pleasing to an Englishman delighting in tumult and confusion, and ac-customed to witness scenes of riot and dissipation, as well as those of human affliction; or to one who, for the sake of variety, would be willing to imprison himself within the walls of a bed-

lam, where continual noise would deafen him, where the un-
wholesomeness of the air would affect his lungs, and where the
closeness of the surrounding buildings would not permit him to
enjoy the enlivening influence of the sun! There is not, perhaps,
another city of its size in the whole world, the streets of which
display a greater contrast in the wealth and misery, the honesty
and knavery of its inhabitants, than the city of London. The
eye of the passing stranger unaccustomed to witness such scenes
is at one moment dazzled by the appearance of pompous wealth,
with it splendid equipage; at the next he is solicited by apparently the most wretched of human beings, to impart a single
penny for the relief of his starving family. Among the latter class
there are many, however, who so far from being the real objects
of charity that they represent themselves to be, actually possess
more wealth than those who sometimes benevolently bestow it.
These vile impostors, by every species of deception that was ever
devised or practiced by man, aim to excite pity and compassion,
and to extort charity from those unacquainted with their easy
circumstances. They possess the faculty of assuming any character
that may best suit their purpose, sometimes hobbling with a
crutch and exhibiting a wooden leg, or "an honorable scar of a
wound, received in Egypt, at Waterloo, or at Trafalgar, fighting
for their most gracious sovereign and master King George."

Independent of these there is another species of beggars, the
gypsies, who form a distinct clan, and will associate with none
but those of their own tribe. They are notorious thieves as well
as beggars, and constantly infest the streets of London to the
annoyance of strangers and those who have the appearance of
being wealthy. They have no particular home or abiding place,
but encamp about in open fields or under hedges, as occasion
requires; they are generally of a yellow complexion, and converse
in a dialect peculiar only to themselves. Their thieving propen-
sities not infrequently leads them to kidnap little children whenever an opportunity presents. Then, by a dye changing their complexion to one that corresponds with their own, they represent
them as their own offspring, and carry them about half naked on
their backs to arouse the pity of those from whom they beg
charity.

The city is infested with a still higher order of rogues, denominated pickpockets or cutpurses, who carry on their nefarious practices while garbed like gentlemen, and introduce themselves into the most fashionable circles. Many of them are persons who once sustained respectable characters but who, by extravagance and excesses, have reduced themselves to want and find themselves obliged at last to have recourse to pilfering and thieving.

Thus have I endeavored to furnish the reader with the particulars of a few of the vices peculiar to a large portion of the inhabitants of the city of London. To these might be added a thousand other misdemeanors of a less criminal nature, daily practiced by striplings from the age of six to the hoary-headed of ninety. This I assure my readers is a picture correctly delineated and not too highly wrought of a city famous for its magnificence and where I was doomed to spend more than forty years of my life.

In September, 1783, the glorious news of a definitive Treaty of Peace having been signed between the United States and Great Britain was publicly announced in London. On the minds of those who had been made rich by the war the unwelcome news operated apparently like a paralytic stroke, while those whose views had been inimical to the cause of America, and had sought refuge in England, attempted to disguise their disappointment and dejection under a veil of assumed cheerfulness. As regarded myself, I can only say that had an event so long and ardently wished by me taken place but a few months before, I should have hailed it as the epoch of my deliverance from a state of oppression and privation that I had already too long endured.

An opportunity indeed now presented for me to return once more to my native country after so long an absence, had I possessed the means. But such was the high price demanded for a passage, and such had been my low wages and the expenses attending the support of even a small family in London, that I found myself at this time in possession of funds hardly sufficient to defray the expense of my own passage, and much less that of my wife and child. Hence the only choice left me was either to desert them, and thereby subject them (far separated from me) to the frowns of an uncharitable people, or to content myself to remain with them and partake of a portion of that wretchedness which even my presence could not avert. When the affairs of the

American government had become so far regulated as to support a Consul at the British Court, I might indeed have availed myself individually of the opportunity which presented of procuring a passage home at the government's expense; but as this was a privilege that could not be extended to my wife and child, my regard for them prevented my embracing the only means provided by my country for the return of her captured soldiers and seamen.

To make the best of my hard fortune, I became as resigned and reconciled to my situation as circumstances would admit of, flattering myself that fortune might at some unexpected moment decide in my favor. I had become an expert workman at brickmaking, at which business and at gardening I continued to work for very small wages, for three or four years after the peace, but still found my prospects of a speedy return to my country by no ways flattering. The peace had thrown thousands who had taken an active part in the war out of employ; London was thronged with them. In preference to starving, they required no other consideration for their labor than a humble living, which had a lamentable effect in reducing the wages of the laboring class. Among this class I must rank myself, and from this period ought I to date the commencement of my greatest miseries, which never failed to attend me in a greater or less degree until that happy moment when, favored by Providence, I was permitted once more to visit the peaceful shores of the land of my nativity.

When I first entered the city of London I was almost stunned, while my curiosity was not a little excited, by what is termed the "cries of London." The streets were thronged by persons of both sexes and of every age, crying each the various articles which they were exposing for sale, or for jobs of work at their various occupations. I little then thought that this was a mode I should be obliged myself to adopt to obtain a scanty pittance for my needy family, but such indeed proved to be the case. The great increase of laborers produced by the cessation of hostilities had so great an effect in the reduction of wages that the trifling consideration now allowed me by my employers for my services, in the line of business in which I had been several years engaged, became insufficient to enable me to procure a humble sustenance. Having in vain sought for more profitable business, I was induced to apply to an acquaintance for instruction in the art of chair making, which I partially obtained from him for a trifling consideration.

It was now (in the year 1789) that I assumed a line of business very different from that in which I had ever before been engaged. Fortunately for me, I possessed strong lungs, which I found very necessary in an employment the success of which depended, in a great measure, in being enabled to drown the voices of others engaged in the same occupation by my own. "Old chairs to mend" became now my constant cry through the streets of London, from morning to night; and although I found my business not so profitable as I could have wished, yet it yielded a tolerable support for my family some time, and probably would have continued so to have done were it not for the almost constant illness of my children. Thus afflicted by additional cares and expenses, I was obliged, to alleviate the sufferings of my family, to contract some trifling debts which it was not in my power to discharge.

I now became the victim of additional miseries. I was visited by a bailiff employed by a creditor, who, seizing me with the claws of a tiger, dragged me from my poor family and inhumanly thrust me into prison! Indeed, no misery that I ever before endured equaled this: separated from those dependent on me for the necessaries of life, and placed in a situation in which it was impossible for me to afford them any relief! Fortunately for me at this melancholy moment my wife enjoyed good health, as it was to her praiseworthy exertions that her poor helpless children, as well as myself, owed our preservation from a state of starvation. This good woman had become acquainted with many who had been my customers, to whom she made known my situation, and the sufferings of my family, and these had the humanity to furnish me with work during my confinement. The chairs were conveyed to and from the prison by my wife, and this way I was enabled to support myself and to contribute something to the relief of my afflicted family. I had in vain represented to my unfeeling creditor my inability to satisfy his demands, and the suffering conditions of those wholly dependent on me. Unfortunately for me, he proved to be one of those human beasts who, having no soul, take pleasure in tormenting that of others; who never feel but in their own misfortunes, and never rejoice but in the afflictions of others. Of such beings, so disgraceful to human nature, I assure the reader London contains not an inconsiderable number.

After having for four months languished in a horrid prison, I was liberated therefrom a mere skeleton; the mind afflicted had tortured the body, so much is the one in subjection to the other. I returned sorrowful and dejected to my distressed family, whom I found in very little better condition. We now from necessity took up our abode in an obscure situation near Moorfields, where, by my constant application to business, I succeeded in earning daily a humble pittance for my family—barely sufficient, however, to satisfy the cravings of nature; and to add to my burdens, some one of my family was almost always indisposed.

However wretched my situation, there were many others at this period, with whom I was particularly acquainted, whose sufferings were greater if possible than my own, and whom want and misery drove to the commission of crimes that in any other situation they would probably not have been guilty of. Such was the case of the unfortunate Bellamy, who was capitally convicted and executed for a crime which distresses in his family, almost unexampled, had in a moment of despair compelled him to commit. He was one who had seen better days, was once a commissioned officer in the army, but being unfortunate was obliged to quit the service to avoid the horrors of a prison, and was thrown on the world, without a single penny or a single friend. The distresses of his family were such that they were obliged to live for a considerable time deprived of all sustenance except what they could derive from scanty and precarious meals of potatoes and milk. In this situation his unfortunate wife was confined in childbed. Lodging in an obscure garret, she was destitute of every species of those conveniences almost indispensable with females in her condition, being herself without clothes, and to procure a covering for her newborn infant all their resources were exhausted. In this situation his wife and child must inevitably have starved were it not for the loan of five shillings which he walked from London to Blackheath to borrow. At his trial he made a solemn appeal to Heaven, as to the truth of every particular as above stated. So far from wishing to exaggerate a single fact, he had suppressed many more instances of calamity scarcely to be paralleled. After the disgrace brought upon himself by this single transaction, life could not be a boon he would be anxious to solicit, but nature pleaded in his breast for a deserving wife and helpless child. All, however, was ineffectual; he was condemned and executed pursuant to his sentence.

I have yet one or two more melancholy instances of the effects of famine to record, the first of which happened within a mile of my then miserable habitation. A poor widow woman, who had been left destitute with five small children, and who had been driven to the most awful extremities of hunger, overpowered at length by the pitiful cries of her wretched offspring for a morsel of bread, in a fit of despair rushed into the shop of a baker in the neighborhood, and seizing a loaf of bread bore it off to the relief of her starving family. She was in the act of dividing it among them when the baker, who had pursued her, entered and charged her with the theft. The charge she did not deny, but pleaded the starving condition of her miserable family in palliation of the crime. The baker, noticing a platter on the table containing a quantity of roasted meat, pointed to it as a proof that she could not have been driven to such an extremity by hunger—but his surprise may be better imagined than described when, being requested by the half-distracted mother to approach and inspect more closely the contents of the platter, he found it to consist of the remains of a roasted dog, which she informed him had been her only food and that of her poor children for the three preceding days! The baker, struck with so shocking a proof of the poverty and distress of the desolate family, humanely contributed to their relief until they were admitted into the hospital.

I was not personally acquainted with the next family, but I well knew one who was, and who communicated to me the following melancholy particulars of its wretched situation, which I now present to my readers as another proof of the deplorable situation of the poor in England after the close of the American war. The minister of a parish was sent for to attend the funeral of a deceased person in his neighborhood. Being conducted to the apartment which contained the corpse (and which was the only one possessed by the unhappy family), he found that it was so low he was unable to stand upright in it. In a dark corner of the room stood a three-legged stool supporting a coffin of rough

boards, which contained the body of the dead mother, who
had the day previous expired in labor for the want of assistance.
The father was sitting on a little stool over a few coals of fire
and endeavoring to keep the infant warm in his bosom; five of his
seven children, half naked, were asking their father for a piece
of bread, while another about three years old was standing over
the corpse of his mother, and crying, as he was wont to do, "Take
me, take me, Mama!" "Mama is asleep," said one of his sisters
with tears in her eyes, "Mama is asleep, Johnny, don't cry, the
good nurse has gone to beg you some bread and will soon return." In a few minutes an old woman, crooked with age and
clothed in tatters, came hobbling into the room with a two-penny
loaf in her hand and, after heaving a sigh, calmly set down and
divided the loaf as far as it would go among the poor famished
children. This she observed was the only food they had tasted for
the last twenty-four hours. By the kind interposition of the
worthy divine, a contribution was immediately raised for the
relief of this wretched family.

I might add many more melancholy instances of the extreme
poverty and distress of the poor of London with which I was personally acquainted, but to return to the tale of my own sufferings.

While hundreds were daily becoming the victims of hunger
and starvation, I was enabled by my industry to obtain a morsel each day for my family, although this morsel, which was
to be divided among four, would many times have proved insufficient to have satisfied the hunger of one. I seldom ever failed
from morning to night to cry "Old chairs to mend" through the
principal streets of the city, but many times with very little success. If I obtained four chairs to rebottom in the course of one
day I considered myself fortunate indeed, but instances of such
good luck were very rare; it was more frequent that I did not
obtain a single one and, after crying the whole day until I made
myself hoarse, was obliged to return to my poor family at night
empty-handed.

So many at one time engaged in the same business that had I
not resorted to other means my family must inevitably have
starved. While crying "Old chairs to mend," I collected all the
old rags, bits of paper, nails, and broken glass which I could
find in the streets, and deposited them in a big bag which I

carried with me for that purpose. These produced me a trifle,
and that trifle when other resources failed procured me a morsel
of bread or a few pounds of potatoes for my poor wife and children. Yet I murmured not at the dispensation of the Supreme
Arbiter of allotments, who had assigned to me so humble a line
of duty—although I could not have believed, once, that I should
ever have been brought to such a state of humiliating distress.

In February, 1793, war was declared by Great Britain against
the republic of France, and although war is a calamity that ought
always to be regretted by friends of humanity, yet no event could
have happened at that time productive of so much benefit to me
as this. It was the means of draining the country of those soldiers
who had been thrown out of employ by the peace. This evil was
now removed; the old soldiers preferred an employment more in
character with themselves to doing the drudgery of the city.
Great inducements were held out to them to enlist, and the army
was not long retarded in its operations for want of recruits. My
prospects in being enabled to earn something to satisfy the calls
of nature became now more flattering. The great number that
had been employed during the peace in a business similar to my
own were now reduced to half, which enabled me to obtain such
an extra number of jobs at chair mending that I no longer found
it necessary to collect the scrapings of the streets. I was now
enabled to purchase for my family two or three pounds of fresh
meat each week, an article to which (with one or two exceptions)
we had been strangers for more than a year, having subsisted
principally on potatoes, oatmeal bread, salt fish, and rarely a
little skim milk.

Had not other afflictions attended me, I should not have had
much cause to complain of very extraordinary hardships or privations from this period until the conclusion of the war in 1817.
My family had increased, and to add to my cares there was
scarcely a week passed but that some one of them was not seriously indisposed. Of ten children I had the misfortune to bury
seven under five years of age and two more after they had arrived
to the age of twenty. My last and only child now living it pleased
the Almighty to spare to me, to administer help and comfort to
his poor afflicted parent, and without whose assistance I should
(so far from having been enabled once more to visit the land of

my nativity) ere this have paid the debt of nature in a foreign land, and that too by a death no less horrible than that of starvation.

As my life was unattended with any very extraordinary circumstances from the commencement of the war until the re-establishment of monarchy in France, and the cessation of hostilities on the part of Great Britain in 1817, I shall commence on the narration of my unparalleled sufferings from the latter period.

The peace produced similar effects to that of 1783. Thousands were thrown out of employ and the streets of London thronged with soldiers seeking means to earn a humble subsistence. The cry of "Old chairs to mend" (and that too at a very reduced price) was reiterated through the streets of London by numbers who but the month before were at Waterloo fighting the battles of their country. This so seriously affected my business that to obtain food for my family I was obliged once more to collect scraps of rags, paper, glass, and such other articles of however trifling value that I could find in the streets.

At this distressing period instances of thefts and daring robberies increased throughout Great Britain threefold. Bands of highwaymen and robbers hovered about the vicinity of London in numbers which almost defied suppression. Many were taken and executed or transported, but this seemed to render the rest only the more desperately bold and cruel, while housebreaking and assassination were daily perpetrated with new arts and outrages in the very capital. Nor was the starving condition of the honest poor, who were to be met with at all times of day and in every street, seeking something to appease their hunger, less remarkable. Unable to procure by any means within their power sustenance sufficient to support nature, some actually became the victims of absolute starvation, as the following instance will show. A poor man exhausted by want dropped down in the street. Those who were passing, unacquainted with the frequency of such melancholy events, at first thought him intoxicated; but after languishing half an hour he expired. On the following day an inquest was held on the body, and the verdict of the jury not giving satisfaction to the coroner, they adjourned to the next day. In the interim two respectable surgeons were engaged to open the body, in which not a particle of nutriment was to be found except a little yellow substance, supposed to be grass or some crude vegetable which the poor man had swallowed to appease the cravings of nature. This lamentable proof confirmed the opinion of the jury that he died for want of the necessaries of life, and gave their verdict accordingly.

Miserable as was the fate of this man and many others, mine was but little better, and would ultimately have been the same had it not been for the assistance afforded me by my only remaining child, a lad but seven years of age. I had now arrived at an advanced age of life, and although possessing an extraordinary constitution for one of my years, yet by my incessant labors to obtain subsistence for my family I brought on myself a severe fit of sickness, which confined me three weeks to my chamber. In this time my only sustenance was the produce of a few half-pennies which my poor wife and little son had been able to earn each day by disposing of matches of their own make, and in collecting and disposing of the articles of small value to be found thinly scattered in the streets. In three weeks it was the will of Providence so far to restore to me my strength as to enable me once more to move abroad in search of something to support nature.

The tenement which I at this time rented and which was occupied by my family was a small and wretched apartment of a garret, for which I had obligated myself to pay sixpence per day. This was to be paid at the close of every week, and in case of failure (agreeable to the laws or customs of the land) my furniture was liable to be seized. In consequence of my illness and other misfortunes, I fell six weeks in arrears for rent. Returning one evening with my wife and son from the performance of our daily task, my kind readers may judge what my feelings must have been to find our room stripped of every article of however trifling value that it contained! Alas, oh heavens, to what a state of wretchedness were we now reduced! If there were anything wanting to complete our misery, this additional drop to the cup of our afflictions more than sufficed. Although the real value of all that they had taken from me, or rather robbed me of, would not if publicly disposed of have produced a sum probably exceeding five dollars, yet it was our all, except a few tattered garments that we had on our backs. Not an article of bedding of any kind was left us on which to repose at night, or a chair or stool on which we could rest our wearied limbs. But, as destitute as we were, and naked as they had left our dreary apartment, we had no other abiding place.

With a few halfpennies which were jointly our hard earnings of that day I purchased a peck of coal and a few pounds of potatoes; while the former furnished us with a little fire, the latter served for the moment to appease our hunger. From a poor family in the adjoining room I was obliged with the loan of a wooden bench, which served as a seat and a table, on which we partook of our homely fare. In this woeful situation, hovering over a few half-consumed coals, we spent a sleepless night. The day's dawn brought additional afflictions. My poor wife had until this period borne her troubles without a sigh or a murmur, and passed through hardships and sorrows which nothing but the Supreme Giver of patience and fortitude, and her perfect confidence in him, could have enabled her to sustain; yet so severe and unexpected a stroke as the last she could not withstand. I found her in the morning gloomy and dejected, and so extremely feeble as to be hardly able to descend the stairs.

We left our miserable habitation in the morning, with hopes that the wretched spectacle that we presented, weak and emaciated as we were, would move some to pity and induce them to impart that relief which our situations so much required. It would, however, be almost endless to recount the many rebuffs we met with in our attempts to crave assistance. Some few indeed were more merciful, and whatever their opinion might be of the cause of our misery, the distress they saw us in excited their charity, and for their own sakes were induced to contribute a trifle to our wants. We alternately happened among savages and Christians, but even the latter, too much influenced by appearances, were very sparing of their bounty.

With the small trifle that had been charitably bestowed on us we returned at night to our wretched dwelling, which, stripped as it had been, could promise us but little more than a shelter, and where we spent the night very much as the preceding one. Such was the debilitated state of my poor wife the ensuing morning, produced by excessive hunger and fatigue, as to render it certain that the hand of death, in mercy to her, was about to release her from her long and unparalleled sufferings. The attendance that the helpless situation of my poor wife now demanded it was not within my power to afford her, as early the next day I was reluctantly driven by hunger abroad in search of something that might contribute to our relief. I left my unfortunate companion, attended by no other person but our little son, destitute of fuel and food, and stretched on an armful of straw, which I had been so fortunate as to provide myself with the day preceding. The whole produce of my labors this day (which I may safely say was the most melancholy one of my life) amounted to no more than one shilling! This I laid out to the best advantage possible, in the purchase of a few of the necessaries which the situation of my sick companion most required.

I ought to have mentioned that, previous to this sad period, when most severely afflicted I had been two or three times driven to the necessity of making application to the Overseers of the Poor of the parish in which I resided, for admittance into the almshouse, or for some assistance, but never with any success, being always put off by them with some evasive answer or frivolous pretense. Sometimes they charged me with being an impostor, and said that laziness more than debility and real want had induced me to make the application. At other times I was told that being an American born, I had no lawful claim on the government of that country for support; that I ought to have made application to the American Consul, whose business it was to assist such of his countrymen whose situations required it.

But such now was my distress that I was induced to renew my application to the Overseer for assistance, representing to him the deplorable situation of my family, who were actually starving for the want of that sustenance which it was not in my power to procure for them. And—what I thought would most probably affect his feelings—I described to him the peculiar and distressing situation of my wife, the hour of whose dissolution was apparently fast approaching. But I soon found that I was addressing one who possessed a heart callous to the feelings of humanity. The same cruel observations were made as before, that I was a vile impostor who was seeking to obtain that support in England which my own country had withheld from me; that the American

Yankees had fought for and obtained their independence, and yet were not independent enough to support their own poor; that Great Britain would find enough to do, was she to afford relief to every d—d Yankee vagabond that should apply for it! Fortunately for this abusive British scoundrel, I possess not now that bodily strength and activity which I could once boast of, or the villain (whether within His Majesty's dominions or not) should have received on the spot a proof of "Yankee independence" for his insolence!

Failing in my attempts to obtain the assistance which the lamentable situation of my wife required, I had recourse to other means. I waited on two or three gentlemen in my neighborhood, who had been represented to me as persons of humanity, and entreated them to visit my miserable dwelling to satisfy themselves of the state of my wretchedness, especially that of my dying companion. They complied with my request, and were introduced to a scene which for misery and distress they declared surpassed everything that they had ever before witnessed. They accompanied me immediately to the principal supervisor of the poor of the parish, and described to him the misery which they had just seen. Thereupon an order was issued to have my wife conveyed to the hospital, which was directly done, and where she was comfortably provided for. But alas, the relief which her situation had so much required had been too long deferred. Her deprivation and sufferings had been too great to admit of her now being restored to her former state of health, or relieved by anything that could be administered. After her removal to the hospital she lingered a few days in a state of perfect insensibility, and then closed her eyes forever on a world where for many years she had been the unhappy subject of almost constant affliction.

My situation was now truly a lonely one, bereaved of my wife and all my children except one. He, although little more than seven years of age, was a child of great sprightliness and activity, and possessed a perfect knowledge of the chair-bottoming business, by which he earned not only enough (when work could be obtained) to furnish himself with food but contributed much to the relief of his surviving parent when confined by illness and infirmity.

We continued to live in the apartment from which my wife had been removed until I was so fortunate as to be able to rent a ready-furnished apartment, as it was termed, at four shillings and sixpence per week. Apartments of this kind were uncommon in London and were intended to accommodate poor families, situated as we were, who had been so unfortunate as to be stripped of everything but the clothes on their backs by their unfeeling landlords. These "ready-furnished rooms" were nothing but miserable apartments in garrets, and contained but few more conveniences than what many of our common prisons in America afford: a bunk of straw, with two or three old blankets, a couple of chairs, and a rough table about three feet square, with an article or two of ironware in which to cook our victuals (if we should be so fortunate as to obtain any). But even with these few conveniences, the room was comparatively a palace to the one we had for several weeks past inhabited.

When my health would permit I seldom failed to visit daily the most public streets of the city, and from morning to night cry for old chairs to mend, accompanied by my son Thomas with a bundle of flags. If we were so fortunate as to obtain a job of work more than we could complete in the day, with the permission of the owner I would convey the chairs on my back to my humble dwelling, and with the assistance of my little son improve the evening to complete the work, which would produce us a few halfpennies to purchase something for our breakfast the next morning. But it was very seldom that instances of this kind occurred. It was more frequently the case that after crying for old chairs to mend the whole day, we were obliged to return home hungry and weary, and without a single halfpenny in our pockets, there to fast until the succeeding day. And indeed there were some instances in which we were compelled to fast two or three days successively, without being able to procure a single job of work. The rent I had obligated myself to pay every night, and frequently when our hunger was such as hardly to be endured, I must needs reserve the few pennies that I possessed for this purpose.

In our most starving condition, when every other plan failed, my little son would adopt the expedient of sweeping the public causeways leading from one walk to the other. Thus he would

19. ISRAEL POTTER AND HIS SON
Crying "Old Chairs to Mend" in the Streets of London

labor the whole day, with the expectation of receiving no other reward than what the gentlemen who had occasion to cross would bestow in charity, which seldom amounted to more than a few pennies. Sometimes the poor boy would toil in this way the whole day, without being so fortunate as to receive a single halfpenny. It was then he would return home sorrowful and dejected and, while he attempted to conceal his own hunger, with tears in his eyes would lament his hard fortune in not being able to obtain something to appease mine. While he was thus employed I remained at home, but not idle, being busily engaged in making matches, with which (when he returned home empty-handed) we were obliged, fatigued as we were, to visit the markets to offer for sale, and where we had sometimes to tarry until eleven o'clock at night before we could meet with a single purchaser.

One stormy night of a Saturday I visited the market with my son for this purpose, and after exposing ourselves to the chilling rain until past ten o'clock without being able either of us to sell a single match, I advised the youth, being thinly clad, to return home, feeling disposed to tarry myself a little while longer in hopes that better success might attend me. Having already fasted one day and night, it was indispensably necessary that I should obtain something to appease our hunger the succeeding day (Sunday) or, what seemed almost impossible, endure longer its torments. I remained until the clock struck eleven, the hour at which the market closed, and yet had met with no better success. It is impossible to describe the sensation of despondency which overwhelmed me at this moment. I now considered it as certain that I must return home with nothing wherewith to satisfy our craving appetites, and with my mind filled with the most heart-rending reflections I was about to set out, when Heaven seemed pleased to interpose in my behalf, and to send relief when I little expected it. Passing a beef stall, I attracted the notice of the butcher, who, viewing me emaciated by long fastings, and clad in tattered garments from which the water was fast dripping, judged no doubt by my appearance that on no one could charity be more properly bestowed, and threw into my basket a beef's heart with the request that I would depart with it immediately for my home, if any I had! I will not attempt to describe the joy that I felt on this occasion. I hastened home with a much lighter heart than what I had anticipated, and when I arrived, the sensations of joy exhibited by my little son on viewing the prize that I bore produced effects as various as extraordinary; he wept, then laughed and danced with transport.

The reader must suppose that while I found it so extremely difficult to earn enough to preserve us from starvation, I had little to spare for clothing and other necessaries. That this was really my situation I think no one will doubt when I positively declare that to such extremities was I driven, being unable to pay a barber for shaving me, I was obliged to adopt the expedient for more than two years of clipping my beard as close as possible with a pair of scissors. As strange and laughable as the circumstance may appear to some, I assure the reader that I state facts, and exaggerate nothing. As regarded our clothes, I can say no more than that they were the best that we could procure, and were such as persons of our situation were obliged to wear; they served to conceal our nakedness, but would have proved insufficient to have protected our bodies from the weather of a colder climate. Such indeed was sometimes our miserable appearance, clad in tattered garments, that while engaged in our employment of crying for old chairs to mend, a few halfpennies unsolicited were bestowed on us in charity. An instance of this kind happened one day as I was passing through Threadneedle Street. A gentleman, perceiving by the appearance of the shoes that I wore that they were about to quit me, put a half crown in my hand and bid me go and cry "Old shoes to mend!"

In long and gloomy winter evenings, when unable to furnish myself with any other light than that emitted by a little fire of sea coal, I would attempt to drive away melancholy by amusing my son with an account of my native country, and of the many blessings there enjoyed by even the poorest class of people: of their fair fields, producing a regular supply of bread; their convenient houses, to which they could repair after the toils of the day, to partake of the fruits of their labor, safe from the storms and the cold, and where they could lay down their heads to rest without any to molest them or to make them afraid. Nothing could have been better calculated to excite animation in the mind of the poor child than the account so flattering of a country which had given birth to his father, and to which he had re-

ceived my repeated assurances he should accompany me as soon
as an opportunity should present. After expressing his fears that
the happy day was yet far distant, with a deep sigh he would exclaim, "Would to God it was tomorrow!"

About a year after the decease of my wife I was taken extremely
ill, insomuch that at one time my life was despaired of, and had
it not been for the friendless and lonely situation in which such
an event would have placed my son, I should have welcomed the
hour of my dissolution and viewed it as a consummation rather
to be wished than dreaded. For so great had been my sufferings
of mind and body, and the miseries to which I was still exposed,
that life had really become a burden to me; indeed, I think it
would have been difficult to have found on the face of the earth
a being more wretched than I had been for the three years past.

During my illness my only friend on earth was my son Thomas,
who did everything within the power of his age to do. Sometimes
by crying for old chairs to mend (for he had become as expert
a workman at this business as his father) and sometimes by sweeping the causeways, and making and selling matches, he succeeded in earning each day a trifle sufficient to procure for me
and himself a humble sustenance. When I had so far recovered
as to be able to creep abroad, and the youth had been so fortunate
as to obtain a good job, I would accompany him, although very
feeble, and assist him in conveying the chairs home. It was on
such occasions that my dear child would manifest his tenderness
and affection for me, by insisting, if there were four chairs, that
I should carry but one, and he would carry the remaining three,
or in that proportion if a greater or lesser number.

From the moment that I had informed him of the many blessings enjoyed by my countrymen of every class, I was almost constantly urged by my son to apply to the American Consul for a
passage. It was in vain I told him that if such an application were
attended with success, it must cause our separation, perhaps forever, as he would not be permitted to accompany me at the expense of the government. "Never mind me," he would reply. "Do
not, Father, suffer any more on my account; if you can succeed
in obtaining a passage to a country where you can enjoy the
blessings that you have described to me, I may hereafter be so

fortunate as to meet with an opportunity to join you, and if not, it will be a consolation to me, whatever my afflictions may be, to think that yours have ceased." My ardent wish to return to American was not less than that of my son, but I could not bear the thoughts of a separation, or of leaving him behind exposed to all the miseries peculiar to the friendless poor of that country; he was a child of my old age, from whom I had received too many proofs of his love and regard.

I was indeed unacquainted with the place of residence of the American Consul. I had made frequent inquiries, but found no one that could inform me correctly where he might be found. But so anxious was my son that I should spend the remnant of my days in that country where I should receive, if nothing more, a Christian burial at my decease, and bid adieu forever to a land where I had spent so great a portion of my life in sorrow, and many years had endured the lingering tortures of protracted famine, that he ceased not to inquire of everyone with whom he was acquainted, until he obtained the wished-for information. Having learned the place of residence of the American Consul, and fearful of the consequence of delay, he would give me no peace until I promised that I would accompany him there the succeeding day, if my strength would admit of it; for although I had partially recovered from a severe fit of sickness, yet I was still so weak and feeble as to be scarcely able to walk.

My son did not forget to remind me early the next morning of my promise, and rather to gratify him than with an expectation of meeting with much success, I set out with him, feeble as I was, for the Consul's. The distance was about two miles, and before I had succeeded in reaching half the way I had wished myself a dozen times safe home again, and had it not been for the strong persuasions of my son to the contrary, I certainly should have returned. I was never before so sensible of the effects of my long sufferings, which had left me scarcely strength sufficient to move without the assistance of my son, who, when he found me reeling or halting through weakness, would support me until I had recovered enough to proceed.

Such was the state of my weakness that, although we started early in the morning, it was half-past three when we reached the

Consul's office, when I was so much exhausted as to be obliged to ascend the steps on my hands and knees. Fortunately, we found the Consul in.

On my addressing him and acquainting him with the object of my visit, he seemed at first unwilling to credit the fact that I was an American born. But after interrogating me some time as to the place of my nativity, the cause which first brought me to England, etc., he seemed to be more satisfied. He observed, however, on learning that the lad who accompanied me was my son, that he could procure a passage for me but not for him, as being born in England, the American government would consider him a British subject, and under no obligation to defray the expense of his passage. And as regarded myself, he observed that he had his doubts, so aged and infirm did I appear to be, whether I should live to reach America, if I should attempt it.

I cannot say that I was much surprised at the observations of the Consul, as they exactly agreed with what I had anticipated. Anxious as I then felt to visit once more my native country, I determined not to attempt it unless I could be accompanied by my son, and expressed myself to this effect to the Consul. The poor lad appeared nearly overcome with grief when he saw me preparing to return without being able to effect my object. Indeed, so greatly was he affected, and such the sorrow that he exhibited, that he attracted the notice (and I believe I may add the pity) of the Consul, who, after making some few inquiries as regarded his disposition, age, etc., observed that he could furnish the lad with a passage at his own expense, if I would consent to his living with a connection of his (the Consul's) on his arrival in America. "But," continued he, "in such a case you must be awhile separated, for it would be imprudent for you to attempt the passage until you have gained more strength. I will pay your board, where by better living than you have been latterly accustomed to, you may have a chance to recruit. But your son must take passage on board the *London* packet, which sails for Boston the day after tomorrow."

Although but a few moments previous my son would have thought no sacrifice too great in obtaining passages to America, yet when he found that instead of himself, I was to be left for a while behind, he appeared at some loss how to determine. But on being assured by the Consul that if my life was spared I should soon join him, he consented. The Consul furnished him with a few necessary articles of clothing, and the next day I accompanied him on board the packet which was to convey him to America. After giving him the best advice that I was capable of as regarded his behavior and deportment while on his passage, and on his arrival in America, I took my leave of him and saw him not again until I met him on the wharf on my arrival at Boston.

When I parted with the Consul he presented me with half a crown, and directions where to apply for board. It was at a public inn where I found many American seamen who like myself were boarded there at the Consul's expense, until passages could be obtained for them to America. I was treated by them with much civility, and by hearing them daily recount their various and remarkable adventures, as well as by relating my own, I passed my time more agreeably than what I probably should have done in other society.

In eight weeks I was so far recruited by good living as in the Consul's opinion to be able to endure the fatigues of a passage to my native country, and one was procured for me on board the ship *Carterian,* bound to New York. We set sail on the fifth of April, 1823, and after a passage of forty-two days arrived safe at our port of destination.

After having experienced in a foreign land so much ill-treatment, and for no other fault than that of being an American, I could not but flatter myself that when I bid adieu to that country I should no longer be the subject of unjust persecution. But the sad reverse which I experienced while on board the *Carterian* convinced me of the incorrectness of my conclusions. For my country's sake, I am happy that I have it in my power to say that the crew of this ship was not composed altogether of Americans; there was a mixture of all nations, and among them some so vile and destitute of every humane principle as to delight in sporting with the infirmities of one whose gray locks ought at least to have protected him. By these unfeeling wretches (who deserve not the name of sailors) I was not only shamefully ill-used on the passage but was robbed of some necessary articles of clothing, which had been charitably bestowed on me by the American Consul.

We arrived in the harbor of New York about midnight, and such were the pleasing sensations produced by the reflection that on the morrow I should be privileged to walk once more on American ground after an absence of almost fifty years, and that but a short distance now separated me from my dear son, that it was in vain I attempted to close my eyes to sleep. Never was the morning's dawn so cheerfully welcomed by me. I solicited and obtained the permission of the Captain to be early set on shore. On reaching it I did not forget to offer up my unfeigned thanks to that Almighty Being who had not only sustained me during my heavy afflictions abroad but had finally restored me to my native country. The pleasure that I enjoyed in viewing the streets thronged by those who, although I could not claim as acquaintances, I could greet as my countrymen, was unbounded. I felt a great regard for almost every object that met my eye, because it was American.

Great as was my joy on finding myself once more among my countrymen, I felt not a little impatient for the arrival of the happy moment when I should be able to meet my son. Agreeable to the orders which I received from the American Consul, I applied to the Customs House in New York for a passage from thence to Boston, and with which I was provided on board a regular packet which sailed the morning ensuing. In justice to the Captain, I must say that I was treated by him as well as by all on board with much civility. We arrived at the long wharf in Boston after a short and pleasant passage. I had been informed by the Consul, previous to leaving London, of the name of the gentleman with whom my son probably lived, and a fellow-passenger on board the packet was so good as to call on him and inform him of my arrival. In less than fifteen minutes after receiving the information my son met me on the wharf. Readers, you will not believe it possible for me to describe my feelings correctly at this joyful moment! If you are a parent, you may have some conception of them, but a faint one, however, unless you and an only and beloved child have been placed in a similar situation.

After acquainting myself with the state of my boy's health, my next inquiry was whether he found the country as I had described it, and how he esteemed it. "Well, extremely well," was his reply. "Since my arrival I have fared like a prince. I have meat every day, and have feasted on American puddings and pies (such as you used to tell me about) until I have become almost sick of them!" He immediately conducted me to the house of the gentleman with whom he lived, by whom I was treated with much hospitality. In the afternoon of the day succeeding (by the earnest request of my son) I visited Bunker Hill, which he had a curiosity to view, having heard me speak so frequently of it while in London as the place where the memorable battle was fought and in which I received my wounds.

I continued in Boston about a fortnight, and then set out on foot to visit my native state. My son accompanied me as far as Roxbury, when I was obliged reluctantly to part with him, and proceeded myself no farther on my journey that day than Jamaica Plains, where at a public house I tarried all night. From thence I started early the next morning and reached Providence about five o'clock in the afternoon, and obtained lodging at a public inn in High Street.

It may not be improper here to acquaint my readers that I had left my father possessed of very considerable property, to which at his decease I thought myself entitled to a portion equal to that of the other children. As my father was very economical in the management of his affairs, I knew this could amount to a very considerable sum. It was to obtain my share, if possible, that I became extremely anxious to visit immediately the place of my nativity. Accordingly, the day after I arrived in Providence I hastened to Cranston, to seek my connections if any were to be found, and if not, to seek among the most aged of the inhabitants someone who had not forgotten me, and who might be able to furnish me the sought-for information. But, alas, too soon were blasted my hopeful expectations of finding something in reserve for me, that might have afforded me a humble support the few remaining days of my life. A distant relative informed me that my brothers had many years since removed to a distant part of the country; that having credited a rumor in circulation of my death, at the decease of my father they had disposed of his real estate and divided the proceeds equally among themselves! This was another instance of adverse fortune that I had not anticipated. It was indeed a circumstance so foreign to my mind that I felt myself for the first time unhappy since my return to my native land, and even believed myself now doomed to endure, among my own countrymen (for whose liberties I had fought and bled), miseries similar to those that had attended me for many years in Europe. With these gloomy forebodings I returned to Providence, and contracted for board with the gentleman at whose house I had lodged the first night of my arrival in town, and to whom I shall feel till death under the deepest obligations that gratitude can dictate. For I can truly say of him that "I was a stranger and he took me in, I was hungry and naked, and he fed and clothed me."

As I had never received any remuneration for services rendered and hardships endured in the cause of my country, I was now obliged, as my last resort, to petition Congress to be included with the few surviving soldiers of the Revolution they had been pleased to grant pensions. And I would to God that I could add, for the honor of my country, that the application met with its deserving success. But, although accompanied by the deposition of a respectable gentleman (which deposition I have thought proper to annex to my narrative) satisfactorily confirming every fact as therein stated, yet on no other principle than that I was absent from the country when the pension law was passed, my petition was *rejected!* Reader, I have been for forty years (as you will perceive by what I have stated in the foregoing pages) subject, in a foreign country, to almost all the miseries with which poor human nature is capable of being afflicted; yet in no one instance did I ever feel such a depression of spirits as when the fate of my petition was announced to me. I love too well the country which gave me birth, and entertain too high a respect for those employed in its government, to reproach them with ingratitude; yet it is my sincere prayer that this strange and unprecedented circumstance, of withholding from me that reward which they have so generally bestowed on others, may never be told in Europe, or published in the streets of London, lest it reach the ears of some who had the effrontery to declare to me personally that for the active part I had taken in the "rebellious war" misery and starvation would ultimately be my reward!

To conclude. Although I may be again unfortunate in a renewal of my application to government for that reward to which my services so justly entitle me, yet I feel thankful that I am

privileged (after enduring so much) to spend the remainder of
my days among those who I am confident are possessed of too
much humanity to see me suffer. And this I am sensible I owe to
the Divine Goodness, which graciously condescended to support
me under my numerous afflictions, and finally enabled me to return to my native country in the seventy-ninth year of my age.
For this I return unfeigned thanks to the Almighty, and hope to
give during the remainder of my life convincing testimonies of
the strong impression which those afflictions made on my mind,
by devoting myself sincerely to the duties of religion.

FOUR histories of the American Revolution have appeared in recent years. John C. Miller, *Triumph of Freedom, 1775-1783* (Boston: Little, Brown & Co., 1948), presents a full panorama of civilian as well as military life. Willard M. Wallace, *Appeal to Arms, A Military History of the American Revolution* (New York: Harper & Brothers, 1951), is a technical treatment. Lynn Montross, *Rag, Tag and Bobtail, The Story of the Continental Army 1775-1783* (New York: Harper & Brothers, 1952), another study by a specialist in military history, disputes Wallace on certain points, especially in taking credit from Benedict Arnold and awarding it to Horatio Gates. Christopher Ward, *The War of the Revolution,* ed. John R. Alden (2 vols., New York: The Macmillan Co., 1952), traces the land campaigns in still greater detail.

The following special studies afford background for the selections in this volume. Chapter 1: Harold Murdock, *The Nineteenth of April 1775* (Boston, 1923), and Allen French, *The Day of Concord and Lexington* (Boston, 1925). Chapter 2: Danske Dandridge, *American Prisoners of the Revolution* (Charlottesville, Va., 1911), and Francis Abell, *Prisoners of War in Britain 1756 to 1815* (Oxford University Press, 1914). Chapter 3: Claude H. Van Tyne, *The Loyalists in the American Revolution* (New York, 1902). Chapter 4: Charles O. Paullin, *The Navy of the American Revolution* (Chicago, 1906), and Gardner W. Allen, *A Naval History of the American Revolution* (2 vols., Boston & New York, 1913). Chapter 5: Hoffman Nickerson, *The Turning Point of the Revolution* (Boston, 1928), and Alfred Hoyt Bill, *Valley Forge: The Making of an Army* (New York, 1952). Chapter 6: John D. Barnhart, *Henry Hamilton and George Rogers Clark in the American Revolution* (Crawfordsville, Indiana, 1951), and Consul W. Butterfield, *History of George Rogers Clark's Conquest of the Illinois and the Wabash Towns 1778 and 1779* (Columbus, Ohio, 1904), and idem, *An Historical Account of the Expedition against Sandusky under Col. William Crawford in 1782* (Cincinnati, 1883). Chapter 7: H. P. Johnston, *The Yorktown Campaign and the Surrender of Cornwallis, 1781* (New York, 1881). Chapter 8: Richard Chase, *Herman Melville, A Critical*

Study (New York, 1949), 176-184, "Israel in the Wilderness," and Leon Howard, *Herman Melville, A Biography* (Berkeley and Los Angeles, 1951), 150, 213, 214, 278.

REVOLUTIONARY NARRATIVES

The following selected list is intended to document the discussion of patriot memoirs in the Introduction. Many diaries, journals, and logbooks from Revolutionary times, never intended for publication, have been printed by state historical societies and similar outlets; these are listed in detail in William Mathews, *American Diaries*, Berkeley & Los Angeles, 1945, 108-161.

ALLEN, ETHAN. *A narrative of Colonel Ethan Allen's captivity, from the time of his being taken by the British, near Montreal, on the 25th day of September, in the year 1775 to the time of his exchange, on the 6th day of May, 1778: containing, his voyages and travels, with the most remarkable occurrences respecting himself, and many other continental prisoners, particularly the destruction of the prisoners at New York, by General Sir William Howe, in the years 1776 and 1777. Interspersed with some political observations. Written by himself and now published for the information of the curious of all nations.* Philadelphia, printed and sold by Robert Bell, in Third Street, 1779.

ANDROS, THOMAS. *The old Jersey captive: or, A narrative of the captivity of Thomas Andros, (now pastor of the church in Berkley,) on board the old Jersey prison ship at New York, 1781. In a series of letters to a friend, suited to inspire faith and confidence in a particular divine providence.* Boston, W. Pierce, 1833.

BECKER, JOHN P. (?). *The sexagenary, or Reminiscences of the American Revolution.* Albany, W. C. Little and O. Steele, 1833.

BLATCHFORD, JOHN. *Narrative of remarkable occurrences, in the life of John Blatchford, of Cape-Ann, commonwealth of Massachusetts. Containing, his treatment in Nova-Scotia, the West-Indies, Great Britain, France, and the East-Indies, as a prisoner in the late war. Taken from his own mouth.* New-London: printed by T. Green, 1788.

BROOKE, FRANCIS TAGLIAFERRO. *A family narrative, being the reminiscences of a revolutionary officer, afterwards judge of the court of appeals; written for the information of his children.* Richmond, Va., Macfarlane & Fergusson, 1849.

BURNHAM, JONATHAN. *The life of Col. Jonathan Burnham, now living in Salisbury, Mass.; being a narrative of his long and useful life. Containing a recital of highly interesting incidents, relative to the revolutionary services and private life, of this distinguished soldier and friend of the departed and beloved George Washington.* Portsmouth, printed and sold at S. Whidden's printing office, 1814.

CHAMPNEYS, JOHN. *An account of the sufferings and persecution of John Champneys, a native of Charles-town, South Carolina; inflicted by order of Congress, for his refusal to take up arms in defence of the arbitrary proceedings carried on by the rulers of said place. Together with his protest, etc.* London, printed in the year 1778.

CONNOLLY, JOHN. *A narrative of the transactions, imprisonment, and sufferings of John Connolly, an American loyalist, and lieutenant-colonel in His Majesty's service. In which are shown, the unjustifiable proceedings of Congress, in his treatment and detention.* London, printed in the year 1783.

DAVIS, JOSHUA. *A narrative of Joshua Davis, an American citizen, who was pressed and served on board six ships of the British navy. The whole being an interesting and faithful narrative of the discipline, various practices and treatment of pressed seamen in the British navy, and containing information that never was before presented to the American people.* Boston, printed by B. True, no. 78 State Street, 1811.

DODGE, JOHN. *An entertaining narrative of the cruel and barbarous treatment and extreme sufferings of Mr. John Dodge during his captivity of many months among the British, at Detroit. In which is also contained, a particular detail of the sufferings of a Virginian, who died in their hands. Written by himself; and now published to satisfy the curiosity of everyone throughout the United States.* The 2d ed., Danvers, near Salem: printed and sold by E. Russell, 1780.

DRING, THOMAS. *Recollections of the Jersey prison-ship; taken, and prepared for publication, from the original manuscript of the late Captain Thomas Dring, of Providence, R.I., one of the prisoners.* By Albert G. Greene. Providence: H. H. Brown, 1829.

FANNING, NATHANIEL. *A narrative of the adventures of an American navy officer, who served during part of the American Revolution under Paul Jones.* New York, 1806.

FLETCHER, EBENEZER. *A narrative of the captivity and sufferings of Ebenezer Fletcher, of New-Ipswich: who was severely wounded in the battle of Hubbardston, at the retreat from Ticonderoga, in the year 1777, and taken prisoner by the British, at the age of 16 years; and who, after recovering in part from his wound, made his escape, and returned home. Written by himself, and published at the request of his friends.* Windsor, (Vt), printed by Charles Kendall, 1813.

FOX, EBENEZER. *The revolutionary adventures of Ebenezer Fox, of Roxbury, Massachusetts.* Boston: Munroe & Francis, 1838.

GRAYDON, ALEXANDER. *Memoirs of a life, chiefly passed in Pennsylvania, within the last sixty years. With occasional remarks upon the general occurrences, character and spirit of that eventful period.* Harrisburgh: printed by John Wyeth, 1811.

HANNA, JOHN SMITH. *A history of the life and services of Captain Samuel Dewees, a native of Pennsylvania, and soldier of the revolutionary and last wars. Also reminiscences of the revolutionary struggle (Indian war, western expedition, liberty insurrection in Northampton county, Pa.) and late war with Great Britain. In all of which he was patriotically engaged. The whole written (in part from manuscript in the hand writing of Captain Dewees,) and compiled by John Smith Hanna.* Baltimore, printed by R. Neilson, 1844.

HAWKINS, CHRISTOPHER. *The life and adventures of Christopher Hawkins, a prisoner on board the 'Old Jersey' prison ship during the revolution.* New York: printed for the Holland Club, 1858.

HENRY, JOHN JOSEPH. *An accurate and interesting account of the hardships and sufferings of that band of heroes, who traversed the wilderness in the campaign against Quebec in 1775.* Lancaster: printed by William Greer, 1812.

HERBERT, CHARLES. *A relic of the revolution, containing a full and particular account of the sufferings and privations of all the American prisoners captured on the high seas, and carried into Plymouth, England, during the revolution of 1776; with the names of the vessels taken—the names and residence of the several crews, and time of their commitment—the names of such as died in prison, and such as made their escape, or entered on board English men-of-war; until the exchange of prisoners, March 15, 1779. Also an account of the several cruises of the squadron under the command of Commodore John Paul Jones, prizes taken, etc. By Charles Herbert, of Newburyport, Mass., who was taken prisoner in the brigantine Dolton, Dec., 1776, and served in the U.S. frigate Alliance, 1779-80.* Boston, published for the proprietors, by C. H. Pierce, 1847.

HOWE, JOHN. *A journal kept by Mr. John Howe, while he was employed as a British spy, during the revolutionary war; also, while he was engaged in the smuggling business, during the late war.* Concord, N.H., L. Roby, printer, 1827.

MARTIN, JOSEPH PLUMB (?). *A narrative of some of the adventures, dangers and sufferings of a revolutionary soldier; interspersed with anecdotes of incidents that occurred within his own observation. Written by himself.* Hallowell, Me. (?), printed by Glazier, Masters & Company, 1830.

MOODY, JAMES. *Lieut. James Moody's narrative of his exertions and sufferings in the cause of government, since the year 1776; authenticated by proper certificates.* The 2d ed., London, printed by Richardson and Urquhart, 1783.

PERRY, DAVID. *Recollections of an old soldier. The life of Captain David Perry, a soldier of the French and revolutionary wars, containing many extraordinary occurrences relating to his own private history, and an account of some interesting events in the history of the times in which he lived, no-where else recorded. Written by himself.* Windsor, Vt., printed at the Republican & Yeoman printing office, 1822.

POTTER, ISRAEL RALPH. *Life and remarkable adventures of Israel R. Potter, (a native of Cranston, Rhode Island), who was a soldier in the American revolution and took a distinguished part in the battle of Bunker Hill (in which he received three wounds), after which he was taken prisoner by the British, conveyed to England, where for 30 years he obtained a livelihood for himself and family, by crying "Old Chairs to Mend," through the streets of London. In May last, by the assistance of the American consul, he succeeded (in the 79th year of his age) in obtaining a passage to his native country, after an absence of 48 years.* Providence: printed by J. Howard, for I. R. Potter, 1824.

PRIEST, JOSIAH. *A true story of the extraordinary feats, adventures and sufferings of Matthew Calkins, Chenango Co.; N.Y., in the war of the revolution—never before published. Also, the deeply interesting story of the captivity of General Patchin, of Schoharie, Co., N.Y., when a lad: by Brant and his Indians. In the same war: written from the lips of the respective heroes above-named.* Lansingburgh, printed by W. Harkness, 1840.

PRIEST, JOSIAH. *The Fort Stanwix captive, or New England volunteer, being the extraordinary life and adventures of Isaac Hubbell among the Indians of Canada and the West, in the war of the revolution, and the story of his marriage with the Indian princess, now first published from the lips of the hero himself.* Albany, printed by J. Munsell, 1841.

RATHBUN, JONATHAN. *Narrative of Jonathan Rathbun, with accurate accounts of the capture of Groton Fort, the massacre that followed, and the sacking and burning of New London, September 6, 1781, by the British forces, under the command of the traitor Benedict Arnold. By Rufus Avery and Stephen Hempstead, eye witnesses of the same.* New London (?), Conn., 1840.

ROBERTS, LEMUEL. *Memoirs of Captain Lemuel Roberts. Containing adventures in youth, vicissitudes experienced as a Continental soldier, his sufferings as a prisoner, and escapes from captivity. With suitable reflections on the changes of life. Written by himself.* Bennington, Vermont, printed by Anthony Haswell, for the author, 1809.

SEGAR, NATHANIEL. *A brief narrative of the captivity and sufferings of Lt. Nathan'l Segar, who was taken prisoner by the Indians and carried to Canada, during the revolutionary war. Written by himself.* Paris (Me.), printed at the Observer office, and published at the Oxford bookstore, 1825.

SHAW, JOHN ROBERT. *A narrative of the life and travels of John Robert Shaw, the well-digger, now resident in Lexington, Kentucky. Written by himself.* Lexington: printed by D. Bradford, 1807.

SHERBURNE, ANDREW. *Memoirs of Andrew Sherburne: a pensioner of the navy of the revolution. Written by himself.* William Williams, Utica; 1828.

SLOCUM, JOHN. *An authentic narrative of the life of Joshua Slocum: containing a succinct account of his revolutionary services, together with other interesting reminisences [sic] and thrilling incidents in his eventful life. Carefully compiled by his eldest son, John Slocum.* Hartford, printed for the author, 1844.

STOCKING, ABNER. *An interesting journal of Abner Stocking of Chatham, Connecticut, detailing the distressing events of the expedition against Quebec, under the command of Col. Arnold in the year 1775. Published by the relatives of Abner Stocking, now deceased.* Catskill, N.Y., Eagle office, 1810.

TALLMADGE, BENJAMIN. *Memoir of Col. Benjamin Tallmadge, prepared by himself, at the request of his children.* New York, T. Holman, book and job printer, 1858.

THACHER, JAMES. *A military journal during the American revolutionary war, from 1775 to 1783, describing interesting events and transactions of this period, with numerous historical facts and anecdotes, from the original manuscript. To which is added an appendix, containing biographical sketches of several general officers.* Boston, Richardson & Lord, 1823.

WALLACE, WILLIAM B. *To the honorable, the members of both houses of Congress, this condensed sketch of the service, and some of the privations and sufferings of William B. Wallace, a lieutenant of artillery of the U. States in the revolutionary war, chiefly relating to his captivity, is humbly submitted.* Frankfort, J. H. Holeman, printer, 1826.

WHITE, JOSEPH. *A narrative of events, as they occurred from time to time, in the revolutionary war; with an account of the battles, of Trenton, Trenton-bridge, and Princeton. By J. White, who was an orderly sergeant, in the regiment of artillery. Published at the earnest request of many young men.* Sold at No. 206, Main Street, Charlestown, 1833 (?).

Index

About the Editor

RICHARD M. DORSON is the best known and most respected authority in America in the field of folklore. Currently Distinguished Professor of History and Folklore at Indiana University and Director of their Folklore Institute, Dr. Dorson previously has taught at Harvard University, Michigan State University, and the University of Tokyo.

The author of numerous books on folklore, Professor Dorson's most recent Pantheon book is *America in Legend: Folklore from the Colonial Period to the Present*. The original hardcover edition of *America Rebels* received wide critical acclaim and was winner of the American History Publication Society Award.